The Essentials *of*
Finance *and*
Accounting *for*
Nonfinancial
Managers

THIRD EDITION

The Essentials *of*
Finance *and*
Accounting *for*
Nonfinancial
Managers

THIRD EDITION

Edward Fields

ᴬMACOM

American Management Association

New York • Atlanta • Brussels • Chicago • Mexico City • San Francisco
Shanghai • Tokyo • Toronto • Washington, D.C.

Bulk discounts available. For details visit:
www.amacombooks.org/go/specialsales
Or contact special sales:
Phone: 800-250-5308
Email: specialsls@amanet.org
View all the AMACOM titles at: www.amacombooks.org
American Management Association: www.amanet.org

This publication is designed to provide accurate and authoritative information in regard to the subject matter covered. It is sold with the understanding that the publisher is not engaged in rendering legal, accounting, or other professional service. If legal advice or other expert assistance is required, the services of a competent professional person should be sought.

Library of Congress Cataloging-in-Publication Data
  Fields, Edward (Financial consultant), author.
    The essentials of finance and accounting for nonfinancial managers / Edward Fields.—Third edition.
      pages   cm
    Includes bibliographical references and index.
    ISBN 978-0-8144-3694-3 (pbk.)
    ISBN 0-8144-3694-3 (pbk.)
    ISBN 978-0-8144-3695-0 (ebook)
  1. Accounting.   2. Finance.   I. Title.
  HF5636.F526   2016
  l658.15—dc23
                              2015028693

About AMA

American Management Association (www.amanet.org) is a world leader in talent development, advancing the skills of individuals to drive business success. Our mission is to support the goals of individuals and organizations through a complete range of products and services, including classroom and virtual seminars, webcasts, webinars, podcasts, conferences, corporate and government solutions, business books and research. AMA's approach to improving performance combines experiential learning—learning through doing—with opportunities for ongoing professional growth at every step of one's career journey.

Printing number
10   9   8   7   6   5   4   3   2   1

Contents

Introduction

This is a book for businesspeople. All decisions in a business organization are made in accordance with how they will affect the organization's financial performance and future financial health. Whether your background is in marketing, manufacturing, distribution, research and development, or the current technologies, you need financial knowledge and skills if you are to really understand your company's decision-making, financial, and overall management processes. The budget is essentially a financial process of prioritizing the benefits resulting from business opportunities and the investments required to implement those opportunities. An improved knowledge of these financial processes and the financial executives who are responsible for them will improve your ability to be an intelligent and effective participant.

The American economy has experienced incredible turmoil in the years since this book was first published. Before U.S. government intervention in 2008/2009, we were on the verge of our second "great depression." We witnessed the demise of three great financial firms, Bear Stearns, Lehman Brothers, and AIG. Corporate bankruptcies were rampant, with General Motors, Chrysler, and most of the major airlines filing. The U.S. government lent the banks hundreds of billions of dollars to save the financial system, while approximately seven million Americans lost their jobs (and most of these jobs will never exist again; see Chapter 6, "Key Financial Ratios," for a discussion of employee productivity trends).

The cumulative value of real estate in this country declined by 40 percent; combining this with the 50 percent drop in the stock market, millions of Americans lost at least half of their net worth. Accounting scandals caused the downfall of many companies, the demise of some major CPA firms, and jail time for some of the principals involved. (Enron would not have happened had its CPA firm done the audit job properly. Bernard Madoff's Ponzi scheme could not have been maintained had his CPA firm not been complicit.) More than ever, business and organization managers require a knowledge of finance and accounting as a prerequisite to professional advancement. It is for this reason that the second edition included additional accounting and regulatory compliance information and introduced the stronger analytical skills that are necessary to navigate the global economic turmoil.

The depth of the 2008 recession intensified competitive pressures as companies struggled to survive and regain their financial health and profitability. As important and valuable as financial knowledge was prior to the crisis (and the writing of the second edition of this book), it is even more so now.

This book distinguishes itself from similar finance and accounting books in many ways:

1. It teaches what accountants do; it does *not* teach how to do accounting. Businesspeople do not need to learn, nor are they interested in learning, how to do debits and credits. They do need to understand what accountants do and why, so that they can use the resulting information—the financial statements—intelligently.

2. It is written by a businessperson for other businesspeople. Throughout a lifetime of business, consulting, and training experience, I have provided my audiences with down-to-earth, practical, useful information. I am not an accountant, but I do have the knowledge of an intelligent user of financial information and tools. I understand your problems, and I seek to share my knowledge with you.

3. It emphasizes the business issues. Many financial books focus on the mathematics. This book employs mathe-

matical information only when it is needed to support the business decision-making process.

4. It includes a chapter on how to read an annual report. This helps you to use the information that is available there, including the information required by Sarbanes-Oxley, to better understand your own company. Sarbanes-Oxley is legislation passed by Congress and enforced by the Securities and Exchange Commission. The governance information required by this act is highlighted and explained, and its impact is analyzed. This chapter also identifies a number of sources of information about your competition that are in the public domain and that may be of great strategic value.

5. It includes a great deal of information on how the finance department contributes to the profitability and performance of the company. The financial staff should be part of the business profitability team. This book describes what you should expect from them.

6. It contains many practical examples of how the information can be used, based upon extensive practical experience. It also provides a number of exercises, including several case studies, as appendices.

Organization of the Book

This book is organized in four parts, which are followed by Appendices A through F and the Glossary.

Part 1: "Understanding Financial Information," Chapters 1 through 5

In Part 1, the reader is given both an overview and detailed information about each of the financial statements and its components. A complete understanding of this information and how it is developed is essential for intelligent use of the financial statements.

Each statement is described, item by item. The discussion explains where the numbers belong and what they mean. The entire structure of each financial statement is described, so that you will be able to understand how the financial statements interrelate with each other and what information each of them conveys.

The financial statements that are discussed in Part 1 are:

> The balance sheet
> The income statement
> The statement of cash flows

Part 1 also contains a chapter on how to read and understand an annual report. The benefits of doing so are numerous. They include:

> Understanding the reporting responsibilities of a public company
> Further understanding the accounting process
> Identifying and using information about competitors that is in the public domain

Managers are always asking for more information about what they should look for as they read the financial statements. In response to this need, the second edition of this book included greatly expanded Chapters 1, 2, and 3, along with a line-by-line explanation of each component of the financial statement; these chapters also include a preliminary analysis of the story that the numbers are telling. For most of the numbers, the book answers the questions: "What business conclusions can I reach by reading these financial statements?" and "What are the key 'red flags' that should jump out at me?"

Each of these red flags is identified. Questions that you should ask the financial staff are included, and the key issues and action items that need to be addressed are discussed.

Chapters 4 and 5 introduce the reader to generally accepted accounting principles (GAAP) and invaluable corporate documents, such as the annual report.

Part 2: "Analysis of Financial Statements," Chapters 6 through 8

Part 2 focuses on the many valuable analyses that can be performed using the information that was learned in Part 1. Business management activities can essentially be divided into two basic categories:

> ➢ Measuring performance
> ➢ Making decisions

Chapters 6 through 8 explain how to measure and evaluate the performance of the company, its strategic business units, and even its individual products.

Financial ratios and statistical metrics are very dynamic tools. This section includes analyses that will help the businessperson survive in our more complex economic environment. Technology has changed the way we do business. This section includes discussions of the customer interface, supply-chain management, global sourcing, and financial measurement and controls.

Now that we have learned how to read and understand financial statements, we also understand how they are prepared and what they mean. Part 2 identifies management tools that help us use the information in financial statements to analyze the company's performance. The ratios that will be covered describe the company's:

> ➢ Liquidity
> ➢ Working capital management
> ➢ Financial leverage (debt)
> ➢ Profitability and performance

Financial turmoil from 2007 to 2010 has resulted in the loss of millions of jobs in the United States. Since 2010, millions of jobs have been added as our economy recovered. Most of these jobs, however, did not return in their previous form. Companies are focusing on measuring how much business revenue they can achieve with a minimal increase in the number of employees. Technology, the ease of global sourcing and trade, and the pressures on improving financial performance have made intelligent financial analysis of the business an absolute necessity—and one capable of bringing great rewards.

In this regard, with the support of technology and improving business models, revenue per employee, discussed in Chapter 6, has become a key metric of a company's effectiveness and its ability to compete and achieve. At the end of Chapter 6, we have included a brief analysis which we call a "quick and dirty" financial review. This imitates a not-so-hypothetical situation—you have 10 minutes to review a set of financials (the buzz phrase that the in-group refers to when referring to the three financial statements) prior to a meeting, perhaps when time is limited or you just want a summary story of the information. The question is—What can you look at in the financials to get a quick sense of the company?

Chapter 7 amplifies the formulas and processes specific to return on assets, and Chapter 8 includes a discussion of overhead allocation, which also impacts financial analysis.

Part 3, "Decision Making for Improved Profitability," Chapters 9 and 10

Part 3 discusses the key financial analysis techniques that managers can use to make decisions about every aspect of their business. Financial analysis provides valuable tools for decision making. Financial analysis of a proposed business decision requires disciplined forecasting. It requires that management quantify all of the impacts that a proposed decision will have on the profitability and financial health of their company. A careful, thoughtful, and thorough financial analysis/forecast provides assurance that all of the issues have been considered. Managers can then make their decisions based upon their forecast.

Part 3 also explores and analyzes fixed-cost versus variable-cost issues within the context of strategic planning. These include:

➢ Supply-chain management
➢ New product strategy
➢ Marketing strategy
➢ Product mix and growth strategies
➢ Outsourcing options

Measuring the performance of profit centers is no longer a growing trend. It is now a necessary business practice. This is also true of investment decision making based upon cash flow forecasting techniques. The financial benefits of success are too valuable and the financial penalties for failure too severe for companies to make decisions without first extensively examining the cash flow issues involved in each proposal. Part 3 explains the technique called *discounted cash flow*. To determine the cash flow impact of proposed investment decisions, there are several measures using this technique:

➢ Internal rate of return
➢ Net present value
➢ Profitability index

The types of investments that are covered in this discussion are:

➢ Capital expenditures
➢ Research and development
➢ Acquiring other companies
➢ Marketing programs
➢ Strategic alliances

Part 4: "Additional Financial Information," Chapters 11 through 13

Part 4 describes in considerable detail some additional financial information that will benefit the businessperson. It includes discussions of the planning process and the budget, and why they are so important. It also covers the many ways in which the company may obtain financing. While this is not a direct responsibility of most members of the management team, knowledge of debt and equity markets and sources of corporate financing will be very useful for the business manager.

Appendices A Through F

In order to ensure that you have understood the information provided in this book, we have included six practice exercises in the appendices. One of the goals of this book is to make the information it provides really useful in your business management efforts. An effective way to achieve this is to practice the lessons and analyses.

Appendix A provides practice in constructing the three financial statements. This "fill in the blanks" exercise will reinforce the knowledge gained in Part 1.

Appendix B is a glossary "matching" test. Seventy-nine financial terms are given, along with their definitions, but not in the same sequence. This will reinforce understanding of the many terms and "buzzwords" that businesspeople must understand when they communicate with accounting people and use the information that they produce.

Appendix C is a comprehensive case study of a company that is (in a financial sense) severely underachieving. The company's past performance must be analyzed using the knowledge gained in Chapter 6, "Key Financial Ratios." The case study also includes the budget plan and forecasting techniques discussed in Chapters 10 and 12.

The format and content of financial information is seriously affected by the business the company is in. Thus, Appendix D provides a list of 10 companies and 10 sets of financial information. The goal is to figure out which set of financial information belongs to which of the 10 companies. Providing actual, recognizable companies provides the opportunity to understand how ratios behave and is another step forward in making the financial information really useful.

Appendix E is a case study that demonstrates a return on investment analysis using the concept of *discounted cash flow*, which is described fully in Chapter 10. The financial forecasting technique is very valuable and is applicable to many business situations, especially when they have strategic implications and/or involve significant financial risk.

Appendix F is a case study that provides practice in analyzing the opportunity to outsource production rather than accomplish it internally. The fixed cost/variable cost supply-chain issue is described in Chapter 9.

Answers are provided for all of the appendices, but please give the exercises a try before you peek.

Additional Background

We study financial management because doing so helps us to manage our business more intelligently.

As mentioned earlier, business management activities may be divided into two major categories:

➤ Measuring performance
➤ Making decisions

We measure the performance of products and markets in order to understand the profitability of the business. Financial knowledge concerning our company's products, markets, and customers enables us to make decisions that will improve its profitability.

The *income statement* measures the performance of the business for a period of time, whether it be a year, a quarter, or a month. It enables us to determine trends and identify strengths and weaknesses in the company's performance.

The *balance sheet* measures the financial health of the business at a point in time, usually at the end of a month, a quarter, or a year. Can the company afford to finance its future growth and pay off its debts?

Breakeven analysis helps us to understand the profitability of individual products. We use it to evaluate pricing strategies and costs. The company uses the results of this analysis in decisions concerning such things as outsourcing options, vertical integration, and strategic alliances.

This book surveys these financial tools. We will provide descriptions and definitions of their components so that you can gain an understanding of how they can help you and why you should understand them.

Accounting Defined

Accounting is the process of recording past business transactions in dollars (or any other currency). Training to become a certified public accountant (CPA) involves learning the rules and regulations of the following organizations:

> ➤ *The Securities and Exchange Commission.* This is an agency of the federal government that, among other responsibilities, prescribes the methodology for reporting accounting results for companies whose stock is publicly traded. Most private companies adhere to most of these rules, except for the requirement that they publish the information.

> ➤ *The Internal Revenue Service.* This agency oversees the filing of all corporate tax returns consistent with the tax legislation passed by the U.S. Congress.

> ➤ *The Board of Governors of the Federal Reserve System.* This executive branch federal agency prescribes the reporting and accounting systems used by commercial banks.

Two private accounting organizations are integral to the accounting profession:

> ➤ *The Financial Accounting Standards Board (FASB).* This is a research organization that evaluates, develops, and recom-

mends the rules that accountants should follow when they audit the books of a company and report the results to shareholders. The products of its efforts are reports known as FASB Bulletins.

➤ *The American Institute of Certified Public Accountants.* This is the accountants' professional organization (trade association). It is an active participant in the accounting dialogue.

The work of all of these organizations and the dialogue among them, along with the work of the tax-writing committees of the U.S. Congress, results in what are known as *generally accepted accounting principles.*

Generally Accepted Accounting Principles

The concept of 'generally accepted accounting principles' (GAAP) makes an invaluable contribution to the way in which business is conducted. When a CPA firm certifies a company's financial statements, it is assuring the users of those statements that the company adhered to these rules and prepared its financial statements accordingly.

Why Is GAAP Important?

The use and certification of GAAP provides comfort and credibility. The reader of the reported financial statements is typically not familiar with the inner workings of the company. GAAP gives a company's stockholders, bankers, regulators, potential business partners, customers, and vendors some assurance that the information provided in the company's annual report is accurate and reliable. It facilitates almost all business dealings.

Why Is GAAP an Issue for the Business Manager?

While accounting principles and practices are critical for the presentation of past history, their mechanics, requirements, and philosophies are not necessarily appropriate for the business manager who is seeking to analyze the business going forward. To understand this issue, we need to define financial analysis.

Financial Analysis

Financial analysis is an analytical process. It is an effort to examine past events and to understand the business circumstances, both internal and external, that caused those events to occur. Knowing and understanding the accounting information is certainly a critical part of this process. But to fully understand the company's past performance, it is important to also have information concerning units sold, market share, orders on the books, utilization of productive capacity, the efficiency of the supply chain, and much more. Every month, we compare the actual performance with the budget. This is *not* an accounting process. It is an analytical process that uses accounting information.

Accounting is the reporting of the past. The budget reflects management's expectations for future events and offers a standard of performance for revenues, expenses, and profits.

Financial analysis as a high-priority management process also requires forecasting. A *forecast* is an educated perception of how a decision that is being contemplated will affect the future of the business. It requires a financial forecast—a financial quantification of the anticipated effect of the decision on marketing and operational events, and therefore on cash flow.

Accounting/Forecasting/Budget Perspective

The end result of all the planning efforts in which a company engages, including forecasting, must finally be the making of decisions. These many decisions about people, spending allocations, products, and markets are included in a report called a *budget*. Therefore, the budget is really a documentation of all the decisions that management has already made.

The Issues

There are frequently cultural clashes between the accounting department and the rest of the company. This results from the false assumption that the philosophies and attitudes that are required for accounting are also appropriate in business analysis and decision making. The budget is not an accounting effort. It is a management process that may be coordinated by people with accounting backgrounds. A forecast need not adhere to accounting rules. There is nothing in accounting training that teaches accountants to deal with marketing and operational forecasting and decision-making issues. In addition, to the extent that the future may not be an extension of the past, it is conceivable that past (accounting) events may not be very relevant.

Accounting is somewhat precise. Forecasting, by its very nature, is very imprecise. When the preparation of the budget becomes "accounting-driven," those preparing it focus on nonexistent precision and lose sight of the real benefits of the budget and its impact on the bigger picture.

Accounting is conservative. It requires that the least favorable interpretation of events be presented. Business forecasting needs to be somewhat optimistic. Using a conservative sales forecast usually means that the budget will be finalized at the lower end of expectations. If the forecast is actually exceeded, as it is likely to be, the company will not be totally prepared to produce the product or deliver the services. In short, conservatism in accounting is required. Conservatism in business decision making can be very damaging.

Business is risky and filled with uncertainty. Accounting is risk-averse.

Resolution

To alleviate some of these cultural pressures, accountants need to learn more about the business—its markets, customers, competitive pressures, and operational issues—and all other business managers need to learn more about the financial aspects of business. This includes the language of accounting and finance, the financial pressures with which the company must deal, and the financial strategies that may improve the company's competitive position, operational effectiveness, and ultimate profitability.

Some Additional Perspectives on the Planning Process

The planning process is a comprehensive management effort that attempts to ensure that the company has considered all of the issues and challenges facing it. The management team will focus on the company's strengths and weaknesses as well as on the resources necessary to grow the business properly compared with the resources available.

The financial team is a critical contributor to this process. The following are some of the issues that require management focus.

The Customers

Why do our customers buy our products and services? Why do we deserve their money? These are critical questions that must be answered if we are to focus the company's energies and resources on those efforts that will sustain growth. We need to expand our definition of "the highest quality" and devote corporate cash and people to distinguishing the company from and staying ahead of the competition.

Do we really know our customers' needs, present and future? Are we prepared to support them in their goal of succeeding in their marketplace? Do they view us as a key strategic partner? After all, we are in business to help our customers make money. If we define our company's strategic mission accordingly, our customers' success will be ours. What we do is only a means to that end.

The Markets

Products and services are provided in numerous markets. These may be defined by:

➤ Geography
➤ Product application
➤ Quality and perception of quality
➤ Means of distribution
➤ Selling channel (direct, distributor, Internet)

The process of thinking through the company's future is an integral part of budget development. It requires that the management team be in touch with trends and developments that will enhance or detract from the company's marketplace position. Periodic "outside-the-box" reexamination of each of these issues provides opportunities for considerable marketplace and profit improvement.

Resources

People and money must be dedicated to the most profitable, fastest-growing segments of the business. These business segments represent the future of the company and should be properly supported. Are our strategies and practices designed to hang on to the more comfortable past rather than focusing on the future? Intelligent planning and management controls do not inhibit creativity and aggressive risk taking. In fact, they ensure that the most important opportunities receive the resources that they require if they are to succeed.

The Planning Process

The planning process involves the following elements:

1. Thinking through the future of the business
2. Enhancing communication among members of the management team so that plans and resources are consistently focused
3. Researching markets, competitors, and technologies to ensure currency of knowledge

4. Deciding among the identified opportunities and programs

5. Implementing those programs that contribute to the company's strategic position and profitability

6. Developing a budget that documents the plan, each of the decisions made, and each department's contribution to achieving company goals

7. Developing intelligent management controls to ensure that the company gets its money's worth

8. Identifying and dealing with disruptive forces

What can happen to us from pressures we don't know about? Borders Book Stores was destroyed by Amazon, not by Barnes & Noble. Tower Records by Apple Music. Camera film by smartphones.

Properly focusing the planning process on the company's strengths and weaknesses will help the company to achieve its strategic and financial goals. If the company truly understands its customers' needs and helps them to achieve their goals, its progress will continue.

When all of these factors are put on the table, management must decide what actions should be taken. The financial team helps management to determine:

➤ How much the programs will cost

➤ The forecast profitability benefits of the programs

➤ Whether these forecast achievements are considered excellent

➤ How much the company can afford

These questions are answered through the financial analysis of each proposal. The company will evaluate the plans using return on investment analysis, which is described in Chapter 10 of this book. Once the decisions have been made, they are documented in the budget. The budget identifies who will achieve what and how much will be spent.

The financial team will then determine whether the budget is guiding the company toward the achievement of its goals. It will do so through an analysis of the company's ratios. Ratio analysis is described in Chapter 6.

Accountants will then record the actual events as they occur each month. As described in Chapter 9, they will then compare the actual revenues and spending with what was budgeted. This is called variance analysis. This same chapter also describes some of the operating decisions that will be made in order to enhance performance and ensure budget success.

Since the business environment is constantly changing, financial analysis is an ongoing process. Assumptions must be reviewed frequently, and action plans must be developed and revised to respond to changes in those assumptions. Cash must be constantly monitored.

With this perspective on the issues involved, context has been developed. Turn to Chapter 1 to begin the discussion of financial statements.

PART 1

Understanding Financial Information

CHAPTER ONE

The Balance Sheet

The balance sheet is a representation of the company's financial health. It is presented at a specific point in time, usually the end of the fiscal (accounting) period, which could be a year, a quarter, or a month. It lists the assets that the company owns and the liabilities that the company owes to others; the difference between the two represents the ownership position (stockholders' equity).

More specifically, the balance sheet tells us about the company's:

- *Liquidity.* The company's ability to meet its current obligations.
- *Financial health.* The company's ability to meet its obligations over the longer term; this concept is similar to liquidity, except that it takes a long-term perspective and also incorporates strategic issues.

Financial strength reflects the company's ability to:

- Secure adequate resources to finance its future.
- Maintain and expand efficient operations.

> ➤ Properly support marketing efforts.
> ➤ Use technology for profitable advantage.
> ➤ Compete successfully.

The balance sheet also helps us to measure the company's operating performance. This includes the amount of profits and cash flow generated relative to:

> ➤ Owners' investment (stockholders' equity)
> ➤ Total resources available (assets)
> ➤ Amount of business generated (revenue)

Analyzing the data in the balance sheet helps us to evaluate the company's asset management performance. This includes the management of:

> ➤ Inventory, measured with an inventory turnover ratio
> ➤ Customer credit, measured using an accounts receivable measure known as *days' sales outstanding* or *collection period*
> ➤ Total asset turnover, which reflects capital intensity
> ➤ Degree of vertical integration, which reflects management efficiency and management of the supply chain

Mathematical formulas called *ratios* are very valuable in the analytical process. They should be used to compare the company's performance against:

> ➤ Its standards of performance (budget)
> ➤ Its past history (trends)
> ➤ The performance of other companies in a similar business (benchmarking)

Look at the balance sheet of the Metropolitan Manufacturing Company, shown in Exhibit 1-1, dated December 31, 2016. Notice that it also gives comparable figures for December 31, 2015. Providing the same information for the prior year is called a *reference point*. This is essential for understanding and analyzing the information and should always be provided. The third column describes the differences in the dollar amounts between the two years. This information summarizes cash flow changes that have occurred between December 31, 2015, and December 31, 2016. This very critical information is presented more explicitly in a report called the *sources and uses of funds statement* or the *statement of cash flows,* which is described more fully in Chapter 3. (The numbers in parentheses in the fourth column refer to the line items in Exhibit 3-1, The Sources and Uses of Funds Statement, which we discuss in Chapter 3.)

Expenses and Expenditures

Before we look at the balance sheet in detail, we need to understand the difference between the concepts of expenses and expenditures. Understanding this difference will provide valuable insights into accounting practices.

An *expenditure* is the disbursement of cash or a commitment to disburse cash—hence the phrase *capital expenditure.* An *expense* is the recognition of the expenditure and its recording for accounting purposes in the time period(s) that benefited from it (i.e., the period in which it helped the company achieve revenue).

The GAAP concept that governs this is called the *matching principle.* Expenses should be matched to benefits, which means that they should be recorded in the period of time that benefited from the expenditure rather than the period of time in which the expenditure occurred.

The accounting concepts that reflect this principle include the following:

➤ Depreciation
➤ Amortization
➤ Accruals

Exhibit 1-1. Metropolitan Manufacturing Company, Inc.
Comparative Balance Sheets
December 31, 2016 and 2015 ($000)

		2016	2015	Changes	See Line
1.	Cash	$ 133	$ 107	+26	(47)
2.	Marketable Securities	10	10		
3.	Accounts Receivable	637	597	+40	(43)
4.	Inventory	1,229	931	+298	(42)
5.	Current Assets	$2,009	$1,645		
6.	Investments	59	62	−3	(39)
7.	Fixed Assets				
8.	Gross Book Value	$1,683	$1,649	+34	(41)
9.	Accumulated Depreciation	(549)	(493)	−56	(35)
10.	Net Book Value	$1,134	$1,156		
11.	Total Assets	$3,202	$2,863		
12.	Accounts Payable	$ 540	$ 430	+110	(37)
13.	Bank Notes	300	170	+130	(36)
14.	Other Current Liabilities	58	19	+39	(38)
15.	Current Portion of Long-Term Debt	0	0		
16.	Total Current Liabilities	$ 898	$ 619		
17.	Long-Term Debt	$ 300	$ 350	−50	(44)
18.	Total Liabilities	$1,198	$ 969		
19.	Preferred Stock	150	150		
20.	Common Stock	497	497		
21.	Retained Earnings	1,357	1,247	+110	(34) (45)
22.	Stockholders' Equity	$2,004	$1,894		
23.	Total Liabilities and Stockholders' Equity	$3,202	$2,863		

> ➤ Reserves
> ➤ Prepaid Expenses

Let's review one example. Suppose a company buys equipment (makes a capital expenditure) for $100,000. The company expects the equipment to last (provide benefits) for five years. This is called the equipment's *estimated useful life*. Using the basic concept called straight-line depreciation (to be discussed later in this chapter), the depreciation expense recorded each year will be:

$$\frac{\$100,000}{5} = \$20,000$$

Each year there will be an expense of $20,000 on the company's income statement. Clearly, no such cash expenditures of $20,000 were made during any of those years, only the initial $100,000.

Assets

The assets section of the balance sheet is a financial representation of what the company owns. The items are presented at the lower of their purchase price or their market value at the time of the financial statement presentation (see the discussion of GAAP in Chapter 4).

Assets are listed in the sequence of their liquidity, that is, the sequence in which they are expected to be converted to cash.

1. Cash, $133,000

Cash is the ultimate measure of an organization's short-term purchasing power, its ability to pay its debts and to expand and modernize its operations. It represents immediately available purchasing power. This balance sheet category primarily consists of funds in checking accounts in commercial banks. This money may or may not earn interest for the company. Its primary characteristic is that it is immediately liquid; it is available to the firm now. This account may also be called Cash and Cash Equivalents or

Cash and Marketable Securities. Cash equivalents are securities with very short maturities, perhaps up to three months, that can earn some interest income for the company.

2. Marketable Securities, $10,000

This category includes the short-term investments that companies make when they have cash that will not be needed within the next few weeks or months. As a result of intelligent cash planning, the company has the opportunity to earn extra profit in the form of interest income from these securities. Some companies earn sizable returns from these investments, particularly when interest rates are high.

The securities that can be placed in this category include certificates of deposit (CDs), Treasury bills, and commercial paper. All have very short maturities, usually 90 to 180 days. CDs are issued by commercial banks. Treasury bills are issued by the U.S. government, and commercial paper is issued by very large, high-quality industrial corporations.

Purchasing these high-quality securities, which generally have little or no risk (with the exception of recent history, when regulatory oversight was deficient), gives a company the opportunity to earn interest on money that it does not need immediately.

3. Accounts Receivable, $637,000

When a company sells products to customers, it may receive immediate payment. This may be done through a bank draft, a check, a credit card, a letter of credit, a wire transfer, or, in the case of a supermarket or retail store, cash. On the other hand, as part of the selling process, the customer may be given the opportunity to postpone paying for the products or services until a specified future date. This is referred to as giving the customer credit. *Accounts receivable* is the accounting term that describes the value of products delivered or services provided to customers for which the customers have not yet paid. The typical time period that companies wait to receive these funds is 30 to 60 days.

In order to have accounts receivable, the company needs to have earned revenue. *Revenue* is the amount of money that the company has earned by providing products and services to its customers. Sometimes cash is received before revenue is earned, as when a customer makes a down payment. Retail stores usually receive their cash when they earn the revenue. For credit card sales, including PayPal and Apple iPay, this is usually the next day. Most other corporations receive their cash after they earn their revenue, resulting in accounts receivable.

A further word about revenue. It is not uncommon in certain businesses for the company to receive some advanced payment. As we just mentioned, there might be a down payment when an order is placed. And there are even circumstances when the company receives all of the cash before it actually earns the revenue.

When a company designs customized products for sale to one specific customer, for example, it may require payment in full before production actually begins. It may be hiring people specific to the job, buying materials not useful anywhere else, and making a product not sellable to any other customer, especially if the design is owned by the customer placing the order. The financial risk of the customer paying slowly or maybe not at all might be too great.

When a company licenses software for a three-year period, it may be required to pay for the three-year license in advance. Technically we do not buy software; we buy the privilege of using it for a specified period of time in the form of a license.The practice of paying in advance is quite common when hiring consulting firms for major long-term projects. Payments might be made monthly, in advance of the project's progress.

When a company receives funds in advance of the work done, this cash appears on the balance sheet as an asset called "deferred revenue." There will be a commensurate liability on the balance sheet to represent the work that the company "owes" to the customer. On day one of the project, these asset and liability amounts will be the same. If Metropolitan Manufacturing Company had received advanced customer payments (which it has not), the deferred revenue would appear as a current asset on the balance sheet, and as a long-term asset if the arrangement is expected to last more than one year.

4. Inventory, $1,229,000

This represents the financial investment that the company has made in the manufacture or production (or, in the case of a retail store, the purchase) of products that will be sold to customers. For manufactured goods, this amount is presented in three categories: finished goods, work in process, and raw materials.

Finished Goods. These are fully completed products that are ready for shipment to customers. The amounts shown on the balance sheet include the cost of purchased raw materials and components used in the products, the labor that assembled the products at each stage of their value-adding manufacture (called *direct labor*), and all of the support expenditures (called *manufacturing overhead*) that also helped to add value to the products. Products in this category are owned by the company, and thus are presented as assets. They will remain so until they are delivered to a customer's premises or the customer's distribution network (vehicles or warehouse) and the customer has agreed to take financial responsibility for them (the customer buys them).

Work in Process. Inventory in this category has had some value added by the company—it is more than raw materials and components, but it is not yet something that can be delivered to the customer. If the item has been the subject of any activity by the production line, but is not yet ready for final customer acceptance, it is considered work in process.

Raw Materials. Raw materials are products or components that have been received from vendors or suppliers and to which the company has done nothing except receive them and store them in a warehouse. Since the company has not yet put the raw materials into production, no value has yet been added. The amount presented in this category may include the cost of bringing the product from the vendor to the company's warehouse, whether this freight cost is paid separately, itemized in the vendor's invoice, or just included in the purchase price.

5. Current Assets, $2,009,000

This is the sum of the asset classifications previously identified: cash, marketable securities, accounts receivable, and inventory, plus a few more minor categories. It represents the assets owned by the company that are expected to become cash (liquid assets) within a one-year period from the date of the balance sheet.

Presentation of Current Assets. Accounts receivable is usually presented net of an amount called *allowance for bad debts.* Sometimes it is called "accounts receivable (net)." This is a statistically derived estimate of the portion of those accounts receivable that will not be collected. It is based on an analysis of the company's past experience in the collection of funds. This estimate is made and the possibility of uncollected funds recognized, even though the company fully expects to receive all of the funds in each account in its accounts receivable list. All of the amounts included in the accounts receivable balance were originally extended to creditworthy customers who were expected to pay their bills in a timely manner—otherwise credit would not have been extended to the customers. However, sometimes the unexpected does occur and some funds will not be collected.

This reserve or allowance for bad debts is statistically derived based on past collection experiences. It is usually in the range of 1 to 2 percent of accounts receivable. (There are exceptions to this, particularly for pharmaceuticals and medical products.) The amount is established by the company's internal accounting staff and is reviewed and revised annually based on the company's actual collections experience.

For Metropolitan Manufacturing Company, the calculation of net accounts receivable is as follows:

Accounts Receivable	$647,000
Allowance for Bad Debts	(10,000)
Accounts Receivable (net)	$637,000

Accounting for inventory also has some specific characteristics of which the reader should be aware.

The figure given for inventory is the amount it cost the company to buy raw materials and components and to produce the product. The amounts presented are based on the accounting principle *lower of cost or market*. If the economic value of the inventory improves because of selling price increases or improvement in other market conditions, or because the cost of replacing it has increased, the inventory amounts on the balance sheet do not change. This is true even if the raw material is a commodity, like oil, whose price in the marketplace increased considerably until late 2014. Inventory is presented at cost, which is lower than market value at that point in time. However, if the value of the inventory decreases because selling prices are soft or because the prospects for its sale have significantly diminished, then the balance sheet must reflect this deteriorated value. This could also occur if the cost to replace the commodity has decreased below the price originally paid. In this case, where market value is below cost, the inventory amounts will be presented at market. This cost deterioration in the oil business was dramatic between late 2014 and 2015.

The accounting process necessary to reflect this latter condition is called a *writedown*. The company would be required to write down the value of the inventory to reflect the reduced value. Oil companies that own inventory have been required to write down this inventory on their books. Some airlines bought enough gasoline to cover their needs for a year or so. The value of these *hedges*, which are treated as an asset, were also written down in early 2015.

6. Investments (and Intangible Assets), $59,000

There are a number of possible components of these two categories. These include:

> ➤ Ownership of other companies
> ➤ Partial equity stakes in other companies, including joint ventures
> ➤ Patents
> ➤ Trademarks
> ➤ Copyrights
> ➤ Goodwill

This information is also presented at the lower of cost or market. If the market value of a patent increases by millions of dollars above what the company paid for the right to use it or develop it, this very positive business development will *not* be reflected on the balance sheet. However, if the asset proves to be disappointing or without value, this must be reflected by a writedown or write-off. Accounting does not reflect the improved economic value of the assets, regardless of the business certainty of that improvement.

7. Fixed Assets

Fixed assets are assets owned by the company that are used in the operation of the business and are expected to last more than one year. They are sometimes called *tangible assets* and often represent a substantial investment for the company. Included in this category are:

> ➤ *Land.* This can be the site of an office, factory, or warehouse, or it might be vacant and available for future use.
> ➤ *Buildings.* This includes any structures owned by the company, such as factories or other production facilities, offices, warehouses, distribution centers, and vehicle parking and repair facilities.
> ➤ *Machinery and equipment.* This category includes all production machinery, office equipment, computers, and any other tangible assets that support the operations of the company.

➤ *Vehicles.* Trucks (tractors and trailers), company cars used by salespeople or managers, and rail cars owned by the company are included in this category.

➤ *Furniture and fixtures.* This also includes leasehold improvements to real estate on a long-term lease.

Again, fixed assets are tangible assets owned by the company that are used in the operation of its business and are expected to last more than one year. One of the generally accepted accounting principles identified in Chapter 4 is materiality. This relates to the significance or importance of an accounting event relative to the overall financial statement presentation. As a result, companies are permitted to identify a threshold dollar amount below which a purchased item will be recorded as an expense on the company's income statement and will not appear on the balance sheet at all, even though the item is expected to provide benefit for more than one year and therefore would otherwise be considered a tangible asset.

This threshold amount can be as much as several thousand dollars. Thus if the company buys a single desk for $1,000, it may be treated as an expense on the income statement and charged to the budget accordingly. However, if the company buys 20 of these desks (and the accompanying chairs), the desks will be presented as furniture and fixtures, recorded as a capital expenditure, and treated as a fixed asset on the balance sheet.

Thus, the amended definition of a fixed asset is a tangible item that the company buys, will use in the business, and expects to last more than one year, and that costs more than the predetermined threshold dollar amount when purchased.

8. Gross Book Value, $1,683,000

This records the original amount paid, at the time of purchase, for the tangible assets that the company currently owns, subject to the lower of cost or market accounting rule. This amount never reflects improved economic value, even if, for example, a piece of real estate was purchased 30 years earlier and has greatly increased in market value.

9. Accumulated Depreciation, ($549,000)

This is sometimes called the Reserve or Allowance for Depreciation. It is the total amount of depreciation expense that the company has recorded against the assets included in the gross book value.

When tangible assets are purchased and recorded on the balance sheet as fixed assets, their value must be allocated over the course of their useful life in the form of a noncash expense on the income statement called *depreciation*. The useful or functional life is estimated at the time the asset is purchased. Using one of several accounting methodologies, the gross book value is then apportioned over that time period. The accumulated depreciation amount on the balance sheet tells us how much has been recorded so far. The concept of a noncash expense is explored further later in this chapter.

10. Net Book Value, $1,134,000

This is the difference between the gross book value and the accumulated depreciation amounts. It has little, if any, analytical significance.

11. Total Assets, $3,202,000

This is the sum total of current assets, the net book value of fixed assets and investments, and any other assets that the company may own.

Important Accounting Concepts Affecting the Balance Sheet

Accounting for Fixed Assets

Suppose a company makes a capital expenditure of $100,000 for a fixed asset that is expected to last five years. The presentation of this in the financial statements would be as follows:

	Balance Sheet		Income Statement (annual expense)
Year 1			
Gross Book Value	$100,000	Depreciation Expense	$20,000
Accumulated Depreciation	(20,000)		
Net Book Value	$ 80,000		
Year 2			
Gross Book Value	$100,000	Depreciation Expense	$20,000
Accumulated Depreciation	(40,000)		
Net Book Value	$ 60,000		

The gross book value on the balance sheet will be $100,000. This is a record of what the company paid for the asset when it was purchased. During the first year, the annual depreciation expense on the income statement will be $20,000.

The accumulated depreciation on the balance sheet is the total amount of depreciation expense included on the income statement from the time the fixed asset(s) were purchased. The net book value is the difference between the two.

Notice that the gross book value remains the same in Year 2. This amount may increase if significant enhancements are made to the asset, or it may decrease if the asset deteriorates in value, resulting in a writedown. Generally, however, the amount will remain the same over the entire life of the asset.

The accumulated depreciation in Year 2 is the sum total of the depreciation expenses recorded in Years 1 and 2. It is cumulative.

In Year 5, and for as long as the asset is useful, it will remain on the balance sheet as:

Gross Book Value	$100,000
Accumulated Depreciation	(100,000)
Net Book Value	0

At this point, the asset has no "book" value. It is said to be fully depreciated. Its value to the business, however, may still be substantial. When the asset is ultimately retired, its gross book value, accumulated depreciation, and net book value are removed from the balance sheet.

Depreciation Methods. The most common method of depreciation, and the one used in this example, is called *straight-line*. It basically involves dividing the gross book value by the number of years in the useful life of the asset. Thus, in the example, the annual depreciation expense will be:

$$\frac{\$100,000}{5 \text{ yrs}} = \$20,000$$

There are three other methods that are often used. They are:

➤ Double-declining balance
➤ Sum of the years' digits
➤ Per-unit calculation

Double-Declining-Balance. Notice that in straight-line depreciation, depreciation expense for an asset with a five-year life is 20 percent (100 percent divided by 5 years) times the gross book value. (If the depreciable life were different from five years, the calculation would change.) In the double-declining-balance method, the percentage is doubled, in this case to 40 percent, but the percentage is multiplied by the net book value. The calculation of the depreciation expense based upon a gross book value of $100,000 is as follows:

Depreciation

Year	Expense Net Book Value × 40%	Remaining Balance
1	$100,000 × 40% = $ 40,000	$100,000 − $40,000 = $60,000
2	$ 60,000 × 40% = $ 24,000	$ 60,000 − $24,000 = $36,000
3	$ 36,000 × 40% = $ 14,400	$ 36,000 − $14,400 = $21,600
4	$ 21,600 ÷ 2 = $ 10,800	$ 21,600 − $10,800 = $10,800
5	$ 10,800	$ 10,800 − $10,800 = 0
	$100,000	

Notice that the first year's depreciation expense is double the amount that it would have been using the straight-line method. Also, when the annual expense becomes less than what it would have been under the straight-line method, the depreciation expense reverts to straight-line for the remaining years. Some companies use this method for tax purposes. The first and second years' expense is higher than what straight-line would have yielded, so the tax savings for those years will be higher. Tax rules for depreciation are changing all the time. The threshold amount used to determine what is a fixed asset and what is an expense also changes frequently.

Sum-of-the-Years'-Digits. In this method, numbers representing the years are totaled, then the order of the numbers is inverted and the results are used to calculate the annual depreciation expense. The calculations are:

$$1 + 2 + 3 + 4 + 5 = 15$$

Year	Annual Expense
1	$100,000 \times 5/15 = \$ 33,333$
2	$100,000 \times 4/15 = \$ 26,666$
3	$100,000 \times 3/15 = \$ 20,000$
4	$100,000 \times 2/15 = \$ 13,334$
5	$100,000 \times 1/15 = \$ \ \ 6,667$
	$100,000$

This method results in a depreciation expense for the first two years that is higher than that produced by straight-line but lower than that produced by the double-declining-balance method.

Per-Unit. The third depreciation method identified is often built into the cost accounting system of manufacturing companies. It involves dividing the cost of the fixed asset by the total number of units it is expected to manufacture during its useful life. If a machine is expected to produce 200,000 units of product over its useful life, the per-unit depreciation expense will be calculated as follows:

$$\frac{\$100,000}{200,000} = \$0.50 \text{ per unit}$$

If production during the first year is 60,000 units, the annual expense that first year will be 60,000 x $0.50 = $30,000.

In most manufacturing standard cost systems, the depreciation expense per unit is built into the manufacturing overhead rate or burden.

In all methods of calculating depreciation, accounting principles are not compromised. To summarize:

➤ Useful life determines the number of years of depreciation.
➤ Consistency is required.
➤ The total of the depreciation expense is usually equal to the original investment.

Accounting for Inventory: LIFO Versus FIFO

Accountants in a company that manufactures or sells products are required to adopt a procedure to reflect the value of the inventory. This is an accounting procedure and has no bearing on the physical management of the product. The accounting procedures are commonly known as *LIFO* and *FIFO*, which mean last-in, first-out and first-in, first-out. An example will best illustrate this.

A company purchases 600 of product at the following prices:

Units	Price		Expenditure
100 units @ $1.00 each			$ 100.00
200 units @ $2.00 each			$ 400.00
300 units @ $3.00 each			$ 900.00
600 units			$1,400.00

Now suppose that 400 units are sold and 200 units remain in inventory. The accounting questions are: What was the *cost* of the goods that were *sold?* And what is the value of the inventory that *remains?*

Under LIFO, the goods that were purchased last are assumed to have been sold first. Therefore, the cost of goods sold (COGS) would be $1,100 and inventory would be $300, calculated as follows:

Cost of Goods Sold:

$$
\begin{array}{lll}
& 300 \text{ units} \times \$3.00 = \$\ \ 900 \\
& \underline{100} \text{ units} \times \$2.00 = \$\ \ \underline{200} \\
\text{COGS} & 400 \text{ units} \qquad = \qquad \$1,100 \\
\end{array}
$$

Inventory:

$$
\begin{array}{lll}
& 100 \text{ units} \times \$2.00 = \$200 \\
& \underline{100} \text{ units} \times \$1.00 = \underline{\$100} \\
\text{Inventory} & 200 \text{ units} \qquad\qquad\ \$300 \\
\end{array}
$$

Under FIFO, the goods that were purchased first are assumed to have been sold first. Therefore, the cost of goods sold would be $800 and inventory would be $600, calculated as follows:

Cost of Goods Sold:

$$
\begin{array}{lll}
& 100 \text{ units} \times \$1.00 = \$100 \\
& 200 \text{ units} \times \$2.00 = \$400 \\
& \underline{100} \text{ units} \times \$3.00 = \underline{\$300} \\
\text{COGS} & 400 \text{ units} \qquad\qquad \$800 \\
\end{array}
$$

Inventory:

$$
200 \text{ units} \times \$3.00 = \$600
$$

Companies may also identify the actual cost of each unit if this can be readily done or calculate a running average. In this example, the per-unit value of cost of goods sold and inventory would be:

$$\$2.33 \times \$1,400/600 \text{ units}$$

This gives a value of $933 for cost of goods sold and $467 for inventory.

Liabilities (line 18)

Liabilities are the amounts that the company owes to others for products and services it has purchased and amounts that it has borrowed and therefore must repay.

Current liabilities include all money that the company owes that must be paid within one year from the date of the balance sheet. *Long-term liabilities* are those that are due more than one year from the date of the balance sheet. Included in current liabilities are accounts payable, short-term bank loans, and accrued expenses (which we have included in other current liabilities). There are no issues of quality in these classifications, only time. The current liabilities and current assets classifications are time-referenced.

12. Accounts Payable, $540,000

Accounts payable are amounts owed to vendors or suppliers for products delivered and services provided for which payment has not yet been made. The company has purchased these products and services on credit. The suppliers have agreed to postpone the receipt of their cash for a specified period as part of their sales process. Normally this money must be paid within a 30-to 60-day time period.

13. Bank Notes, $300,000

This amount has been borrowed from a commercial bank or some other lender and has not yet been repaid. Because the amount must be repaid within one year, it is classified as a current liability. This amount includes only the principal owed. It does not include interest that will be due in the future because that money is not yet due.

14. Other Current Liabilities, $58,000

This category includes all the short-term liabilities not included in any other current liability category. They are primarily the result of accruals. At any given point in time, the company owes salaries and wages to employees, interest on loans to banks, taxes, and fees to outsiders for professional services. For example, if the balance sheet date falls on a Wednesday, employees who are paid each Friday have worked for three days up to the balance sheet date. Thus, the company owes these employees three days' pay as of the balance sheet date, and that liability is recorded as an accrual on the balance sheet and an accrued expense on the income statement.

15. Current Portion of Long-Term Debt

This category includes liabilities that had a maturity of more than one year when the funds were originally borrowed, but that now, because of the passage of time, are due in less than one year as of the date of the balance sheet.

16. Total Current Liabilities, $898,000

This is the total of all of the funds owed to others that are due within one year from the date of the balance sheet. It includes accounts payable, short-term loans, other current liabilities, and the current portion of long-term debt.

17. Long-Term Debt, $300,000

Long-term debt is amounts that were borrowed from commercial banks or other financial institutions and are not due until sometime beyond one year from the date of the balance sheet. Their maturity ranges from just over one year to perhaps twenty or thirty years. This category may include a variety of long-term debt securities, including debentures, mortgage bonds, and convertible bonds. If the category is titled Long-Term Liabilities, it may also include liabilities to tax authorities, including the IRS, states, and foreign governments.

Stockholders' Equity, $2,004,000 (line 22)

Stockholders' equity represents the cumulative amount of money that all of the owners of the business have invested in the business since the date the corporation began. They accomplished this in a number of ways. Some of the investors purchased preferred shares from the company. For Metropolitan Manufacturing Company, the cumulative amount that these investors put in is $150,000. Other investors (or perhaps the same people) purchased common shares from the company. The cumulative amount that they put in is $497,000. The third form of investment takes place when the owners of the company (the owners of common stock) leave the profits of the company in the business rather than taking the money out of the company in the form of dividends. The cumulative amount of this reinvestment is represented on the balance sheet by the retained earnings of $1,357,000.

Remember that the amounts shown for preferred stock, common stock, and retained earnings are the historical amounts that the company received when it sold those securities and retained the profits. There is no relation between these amounts and the current value of the business or its shares, should they be bought and sold on a market.

19. Preferred Stock, $150,000

Holders of this class of stock receive priority in the payment of returns on their investment, called *dividends*. Preferred stock carries less risk than common stock (to be discussed next) because the dividend payment is fixed and must be made before any profit is distributed (dividends are paid) to the holders of common stock. Holders of preferred shares will also have priority over common shareholders in getting their funds returned if the firm is liquidated in a bankruptcy. The holders of preferred shares are not considered owners of the business. Hence, they generally do not vote for the company's board of directors. However, a corporate charter might provide that they do get to vote for the board of directors if the preferred dividend is not paid for a certain period of time.

Although preferred shares are sometimes perceived as a "debt" of the company without a due date, they are not actually a debt of the company, but rather are part of equity. Because the preferred dividend is not an obligation of the company, unlike interest payments on long-term debt, these securities are considered to have a higher "risk" than long-term debt. Because of this higher risk, the dividend yield on preferred stock will usually be higher than the interest rate that the company pays on long-term debt.

20. Common Stock, $497,000

The owners of common stock are the owners of the business. This balance sheet line amount represents the total amount of money that people have invested in the business since the company began. It includes only those stock purchases that were made directly from the company. The amount presented is the historical amount invested, not the current market value of those shares. In most cases, for each share owned, the holder is entitled to one vote for members of the board of directors. There are some companies that have different classes of common stock with different numbers of votes per share. This explains why some families or individuals can control very large corporations even though they actually own a small minority of the shares.

21. Retained Earnings, $1,357,000

When the company achieves a profit in a given year, the owners are entitled to remove those funds from the company for their personal use. It is their money. However, the decision to distribute profits to the shareholders in the form of dividends is made by the board of directors (representing the owners), usually on a quarterly basis. The board of directors evaluates the company's cash position, the net income that the company is achieving, and it considers the desire of the shareholders to receive dividends. When it believes that this is warranted, the board will "declare" a dividend payment and, soon thereafter, distribute the funds.

However, if the business is in need of funds to finance expansion, pay down debt, or take advantage of other profitable opportunities, the owners may leave all or part of their profit in the company. The portion of the total profits of the company that the owners have reinvested in the business during its entire history is called retained earnings. The retained earnings on the company's balance sheet is the cumulative net income that the company has achieved throughout its entire history minus the cash dividends that the company has paid to its shareholders throughout its entire history. The difference between these is the cumulative amount retained.

Collectively, preferred stock, common stock, and retained earnings are known as *stockholders' equity* or the *net worth* of the business.

Total Liabilities and Stockholders' Equity, $3,202,000 (line 23)

On most balance sheets, the accountants will total the liabilities and stockholders' equity. Notice that this amount is equal to the total amount of the assets. While this is something of a format consideration, it does have some significance that we can review here.

The balance sheet equation (Assets = Liabilities + Stockholders' Equity) is always maintained throughout the entire accounting process. The equation is never out of balance. If a company stopped recording transactions at any point in time and added up the numbers, assets minus liabilities would be equal to stockholders' equity.

The balance sheet equation also holds for any business or personal transaction. You cannot buy a house (asset) for $400,000 unless the combination of the amount you can borrow (liabilities) and the amount you have in your own funds (equity) is equal to that $400,000 amount. The asset is what you buy; the liability and the equity are how the purchase is financed.

Assets = Liabilities + Equity: $400,000 = $300,000 + $100,000

If you can borrow only $300,000 and you don't have $100,000 in cash, you cannot buy the house for $400,000. This analogy is exactly applicable for business transactions and the corporate balance sheet.

Additional Balance Sheet Information

Description of Marketable Securities

Short-term marketable securities are investments that the company makes because it has extra cash available that it will not need for at least a few months. The company buys these securities in order to earn interest; for a large company, the amount involved can be substantial. Apple has billions of dollars. These securities may have some risk, but they usually do not involve a high degree of risk. They can have maturities of between one month and one year.

Certificates of Deposit. Certificates of deposit, or CDs, are issued by commercial banks. They are very similar to the CDs that consumers can buy in their local bank, except that the amounts are larger.

Treasury Bills. These are essentially the same as CDs, except that they are issued by the U.S. government.

Commercial Paper. Commercial paper behaves very much like CDs and Treasury bills, but it is issued by very large industrial corporations that need to borrow funds for a very short period of time. It is purchased by banks and by other corporations that have excess money to invest.

Types of Short-Term Debt

Here is a brief summary of the various sources of financing available to support the business.

Revolving Credit. This is a short-term loan, usually from a commercial bank. While it is often *callable* by the bank at any time, which means that the bank can demand repayment with minimal notice, it often remains open for extended periods of time. It is usually secured by the company's accounts receivable and inventory. Some banks require the company to pay off this loan for at least one month during the year, probably during its most "cash rich" month. Such a loan may also be called a working capital loan.

Zero-Balance Account. This type of short-term working capital loan has a very specific feature: Customer payments go directly to the bank, which uses the funds to reduce the outstanding loan. This benefits the company by reducing its interest expense. When the company writes checks, the bank deposits enough funds in the company's account to cover the payments, increasing the outstanding loan. Hence the checking account always has a zero balance.

Factoring. This is a short-term working capital financing technique in which the company actually sells its accounts receivable to a bank or to a firm called a factoring company. Customer payments are made directly to the bank that owns the receivable. This is a fairly expensive form of financing, often costing 2 to 4 percent per month. Sometimes the sale of the accounts receivable is *without recourse.* This means that the bank assumes the credit risk of collecting the funds from the company's customers.

Types of Long-Term Debt

There are several kinds of securities that a company can issue in order to acquire debt financing for extended periods of time. The maturity of these securities is always more than one year and could be as much as thirty or forty years, or even longer. The interest on these securities is known as the coupon rate.

Debentures. Debentures are corporate bonds whose only collateral is the "full faith and credit" of the corporation. They usually pay interest to their holders on a quarterly or semiannual basis. In a bankruptcy, the holders of these bonds would be general creditors.

Mortgage Bonds. Mortgage bonds are similar to debentures, except that the collateral on the loan is specific assets, usually real estate. The holders of these securities are said to be "secured lenders" because of the specified collateral. In a bankruptcy, the owners of mortgage bonds will generally have the right to all of the specified assets until their claims are satisfied.

Subordinated Debentures. These are exactly the same as debentures, except that, in the event of bankruptcy, holders of these securities must wait until all holders of mortgage bonds and debentures have been financially satisfied before they can claim any of the assets of the company. Hence their lien on the company's assets is "subordinated." Because of this riskier position, the interest rate on subordinated debentures will be higher than that on mortgage bonds and senior debentures. Bonds that are really subordinated may be labeled "high-yield" or "junk bonds."

Convertible Bonds. These bonds are the same as debentures except that their holders have the option of turning them in to the company in exchange for a specified number of shares of common stock (converting them). There is an "upside" growth opportunity for holders of these securities, because if the company does very well, the price of the common shares for which the bond can be exchanged increases. As a result of this additional financial benefit, the interest rate on a convertible bond will usually be much lower than the rate on a regular debenture. The common stock price at which conversion is worthwhile is often called the *strike price*. It is much higher than the stock price at the time of original issue.

Zero-Coupon Bonds. These are bonds with a long-term maturity, probably 10 to 20 years. They are very different from other bonds in that the company pays no annual interest. Instead, it sells the bond at a significant discount from its face value. Since the buyer receives the face value of the bond at maturity, the buyer is effectively earning "interest" each year as the value of the bond increases. For example, a 10-year, $1,000 bond with a 9 percent interest rate will be sold for $422.40, which is its present value, or the amount that, if invested at 9 percent, would equal $1,000 in 10 years. If the buyer holds this bond for 10 years, the company will pay the buyer the full $1,000. The investor will achieve an effective annual yield of 9 percent. The interest rate will be slightly higher than that on a regular debenture. Pension funds that don't need the annual cash income find this attractive. The seller enjoys the fact that no annual interest payments need be made, giving the company the cash for many years to grow its business. Of course, the company must repay the full $1,000 at maturity.

Analysis of the Balance Sheet

An extensive, detailed description of how to analyze the financial statements is given in Chapter 6 of this book, "Key Financial Ratios." However, you have an opportunity to draw some preliminary conclusions as you read these financial statements. Keep in mind that these are observations, not conclusions. They provide a direction for the analyst to focus and sharpen inquiry.

Cash

At the risk of stating the obvious, every company needs to have some cash on hand in order to pay its bills, meet its payroll, handle contingencies, and take advantage of opportunities. The issues are: How much cash should the company have, and what should we be looking for?

1. A company can be OK with no cash (really zero) if it has a zero-balance line of credit with a bank. We described this earlier in this chapter.

2. If the cash balance is growing from period to period (month to month or year to year), it may be because the company is "saving up" for a major expenditure.

3. If the cash balance is growing from period to period and the company's accounts payable are also increasing, the company may be accumulating cash at the expense of its suppliers.

4. As the cash balance grows, if more of these funds are invested in short-term marketable securities, this demonstrates that the company has no immediate need for these funds.

5. As the amounts of marketable securities continue to grow, it may be possible to conclude that the company has more than adequate funds to finance its future. This may also suggest that the company has adequate funds to finance its future, *and/or* that its growth prospects are limited and it has not yet decided what to do with the extra funds.

6. If the company has large amounts of cash and marketable securities (as in item 5), it may be that the major stockholders are already very wealthy and do not want the personal tax liability resulting from a dividend distribution.

Examples of companies that fit the description of items 4, 5, and 6 include Apple Computer, Microsoft, Cisco Systems, Oracle, and Intel. They are all cash-rich beyond imagination, have more money than they can ever use, and have major shareholders who are multibillionaires. Their growth has slowed, in part because of their massive size (success). With the exception of Oracle's relatively "small" transactions, they cannot make major acquisitions because of antitrust issues. Pfizer Pharmaceuticals was in this cash-rich situation, but it used the funds to make an acquisition of a major pharmaceutical company that passed antitrust review. Disney has also recently acquired a major source of content, Marvel Entertainment, in a largely cash transaction. As recently as 2008, Microsoft reported interest income of approximately $1 billion, earned from investing in short-term marketable securities.

This experience would have been far exceeded in the 2013–2015 time period by quite a few companies except for the fact that interest rates and income are at historical lows.

Accounts Receivable

Providing credit to customers is inherently neither good nor bad, despite the negative prejudices held by some in the accounting community. Companies provide credit to their customers because doing so facilitates the sale, because it helps them to sell more product per selling event, and because they will not make the sale if credit is not provided. Sometimes companies foolishly provide credit because "we have always done business this way," without giving much thought to how it affects the firm and its financial health. Do your own objective evaluations, develop a positive strategy, and consider the following:

1. Accounts receivable should increase as revenue increases. However, they will not necessarily decrease as sales decline. Diminishing sales, either because of tough economic times or because of the company's inability to respond to competitive pressure, will cause the company to become timid in its collection processes.
2. Providing credit is a sales tool. It is a competitive advantage versus companies that cannot afford to provide credit to customers.
3. The more product is sold per selling event, the more profitable the sale and the company will be.
4. Economies of scale and marketplace penetration each contribute to improved profitability.
5. Providing extended credit terms enhances a strategy of gaining economies of scale. If this is the strategy, the gross profit margin on the income statement should be improving.
6. Accounts receivable will increase as a result of an increase in the company's selling process. This is to be expected and enjoyed.

7. It is in fact true that 20 percent of a company's customers account for 80 percent of the company's overdue accounts receivable (80/20 rule). If the customers are small, buy little per selling event, or buy only the less profitable products in the company's offerings, they are probably not worth the effort and should be asked to use a credit card to pay for purchases.

Inventory

Companies are not required to provide the details of their inventory on their balance sheets, although some do. Knowing the component amounts of raw materials, work in process, and finished products is certainly helpful. These details are often not given on the company's summary balance sheet. For public companies, however, there is a good chance that these amounts are provided in the footnotes to the financials, which appear in the 10-K and the annual report. Digging deep and learning the facts is a very valuable pursuit.

Raw Materials and Purchased Components. An increasing trend may result from:

- ▷ Higher purchase prices. This may result in the company's gross profit margins being squeezed.
- ▷ Buying more product in anticipation of projected higher production and sales volume.
- ▷ Purchasing more product per purchase event. This should result in a lower purchase cost per unit and improved company gross profit margins.
- ▷ Trends toward outsourcing more of the value-adding process. This is essentially adding more value-added purchased components with the benefit of reducing in-company work in process inventory.
- ▷ Unjustified optimism. The company is buying too much or selling too little.

With the use of technology and the improved sophistication of supply-chain management practices, sales growth should be faster than the growth of raw material and components inventory.

Work in Process. Technology, supply-chain process improvement, economies of scale, and outsourcing should cause work in process inventory to grow more slowly than either sales or the other two classes of inventory.

If work in process inventory is growing faster than sales and also faster than the sales forecast, the result will be diminishing profitability and cash flow. The company is still going to finish the product, spending money to produce products that it will have difficulty selling. Selling prices will have to be cut, diminishing gross profit margins. Unused raw materials and components can be readily sold back to suppliers, although at a penalty; thus, raw materials is a somewhat liquid asset. Excess work in process inventory, however, has almost no market value and can only be a cash flow drain.

Finished Product. In general, if the company is performing well, the growth of finished product inventory should be slower than sales growth. This is the result of intelligent sales forecasting and technological advances in supply-chain management, and also because sales growth should precede production growth.

Inventory growth may precede sales growth when seasonal sales are a factor, such as before Christmas, Easter, the summer, or back to school. Because of the narrow time window, companies must have product available.

If suppliers are domestic, product can often be ordered as needed. Because so much outsourcing is global, however, purchasing is often done once or twice a year. This can cause severe seasonal swings in finished product that need to be considered when analyzing the financial statements.

Retail chains have particularly unusual inventory cycles. Toys for Christmas are ordered in the preceding January. Spring fashions are viewed the previous summer.

Many retail chains have created inventory "middleman" companies. These are independently owned, often one-or two-customer businesses. They buy product at the customers' direction and then hold the inventory until it is needed, in a "just in time" delivery service. This minimizes inventory on the books of the retail chain and offers the appearance of "lean" inventory management.

There are companies that provide only custom-designed products. In such cases, finished goods inventory should be minimal, with the company accumulating only enough product to allow efficient shipment and customer scheduling.

Remember, inventory on a company's books is what the company owns, not necessarily what it has in its possession. A company may buy product on consignment, which means that it is in the company's possession but it is owned by the supplier. Or a company may sell product on consignment, which means that the company owns it but the customer possesses it.

One more thought on working capital, inventory, and accounts receivable: Technology has and will continue to redefine how business gets done. This will cause some of the trends, and the resulting ratios that will be used, to change radically, as described in Chapter 6. Consider the sale of software. More and more software is downloaded via the Internet. The buyer selects the "product," pays with a credit card, and downloads the software. There is no inventory, no accounts receivable, and, in a tangible sense, no product in any traditional sense. Be conscious of these dynamics as you read the financial statements.

Fixed Assets

Remember that the gross book value amount on the balance sheet represents only those items that cost more than the threshold amount when purchased. The gross book value, therefore, may not include assets that cost less than $1,000 or $5,000 or $50,000, depending on what the company established as the threshold.

Depreciation and net book value are essentially accounting

conventions. The only business number that has real value as an analytical tool is the gross book value, which is a historical record of the amounts paid for the assets when they were purchased. Given that, the relationship between gross book value and accumulated depreciation provides a hint of how old the assets are. Here are some examples:

Gross Book Value	$100
Accumulated Depreciation	0
Net Book Value	$100

These assets are new. The company has not yet begun depreciating them.

Gross Book Value	$100
Accumulated Depreciation	50
Net Book Value	$ 50

These assets are 50 percent depreciated. In an average mix of assets, they are probably five to seven years old.

Gross Book Value	$100
Accumulated Depreciation	100
Net Book Value	$ 0

These assets are fully depreciated. They are probably 10 years old or more.

Reading this information in a company's financials will provide some insights into how modern its production capability is. If the company is not replacing its assets, either it cannot afford to (cash flow issues), it has considerable excess capacity, or there has not been much technological change in the equipment. Excess capacity will encourage the company to cut selling prices and pursue marginal, less profitable business. Where there have been technological improvements, use of older equipment will result in inefficiencies in operations. Margins will be less than competitive benchmarks. The company with the older equipment will probably be slower to respond to customer orders and its service will not be as good.

Compare the increase in the gross book value with the capital expenditure amount on the statement of cash flows (this will be discussed further in Chapter 3). Then consider the following three possibilities:

1. If the amount of capital expenditures and the increase in the gross book value are the same or similar, then the company's capital budget effort is pure expansion and/or diversification.

2. If the amount of capital expenditures is much larger than the increase in gross book value on the balance sheet, then the capital budget effort is largely replacement and modernization.

3. If there is a significant amount of capital expenditures but no change or a decline in the gross book value, then the company is probably replacing assets with much more technologically advanced equipment. An example of this is replacing a server that originally cost $25,000 five years ago with one that cost $10,000 but has three times the power.

Projects that require significant capital expenditures usually achieve a positive cash flow in two to four years (a nuclear power plant is certainly one exception to this). If the company has significant capital expenditures, check the increase in short-term bank debt and long-term debt (either bank or bonds). If a major project is being financed with short-term debt, the company will be required to refinance or renegotiate the loan every few months. (Because the cash flow from the project will be negative for a while, the company will have no choice.) This may cause a cash flow squeeze if financing conditions become too difficult (as in 2008–2009) or if interest rates rise significantly (as they probably will in 2017). The desired strategy is to finance projects with borrowings with long-term maturities and/or with cash. The goal is to achieve the benefits of the project (positive cash flow) before the debt comes due. This becomes a "self- financing project."

Short-Term Debt

There are a few areas of focus here that may prove critical in any analysis:

1. As previously discussed, there can be problems if this debt is used to finance projects that will not achieve a positive cash flow for a few years.

2. Compare the amount owed with the total line of credit from banks that the company has available. This information is found in the footnotes. If the line of credit is nearly or fully used, the company will have few attractive options if it needs more funds. It may end up having to pledge all of the company's assets as collateral on the loan. (This is less of a concern if the company is in a seasonal business and is at the peak of its buying season.)

3. Companies in the retail business should have high debt in September to November and almost no debt in January, after Christmas.

4. If a company's short-term debt keeps expanding, but its inventory and accounts receivable grow even faster, it is using banks to compensate for poor working capital management. Eventually, the banks will stop management from continuing this practice by threatening to call or actually calling the loan (demanding repayment), which they can do on very short or no notice.

Long-Term Debt

This could be due for repayment in 20 years or 366 days from the date of the financials. As a potential cash flow issue, find out the details from the footnotes.

If a company's debt is ever "rescheduled," it means that the company did not expect to have the funds available for a scheduled repayment to the debt holders, so the due date was "rescheduled," meaning postponed. This both gives the company more time and makes the banks' balance sheets look better because they do not show overdue loans.

Convertible debt may be a very positive form of long-term financing. It provides the company with a bargain interest rate and provides more equity when the company is more successful and the bondholders convert their debt to equity. Refer to the appropriate footnote to make sure that the interest rate on this debt is truly a bargain, i.e., that it is below interest rates paid by similar companies. If the interest rate is not a bargain, issuing the convertible security may have been a means of gaining financing as an alternative to bankruptcy. In that situation, investors would not put equity funds into the business. They would "invest" by buying convertible bonds, thereby being creditors if the company fails, but sharing in its success if it succeeds.

Preferred Stock

This is an attractive form of financing if the company is a utility. Because it is part of stockholders' equity, the value of this stock is part of the basis and increases what the utility can charge its customers.

Because preferred dividends are not tax deductible to the company, for most companies, this is a very expensive, undesirable means of obtaining financing. Companies will issue preferred stock when debt is not an available choice and debt holders want more equity in the company. In a bankruptcy, debt holders will have access to any remaining assets before the owners of the preferred or common shares do. Selling preferred stock is almost never viewed as a good strategy. A good amount of the funds that the U.S. government invested in banks and the auto companies as part of the TARP program in 2008/2009 was in the form of high-dividend-yielding preferred stock.

A company will issue cumulative preferred shares only if it is in a very high-risk financial condition. *Cumulative* means that if the company misses one or more scheduled dividend payments, it must make them up before it can pay dividends to common shareholders. Of course, if the company does not survive, preferred shareholders will probably lose their entire investment.

Common Equity

Check the change in the number of common shares outstanding between financial statements. If it is increasing, the company is selling stock, possibly to employees who have stock options. If the number of shares outstanding is decreasing, the company is buying back its own stock on the open market. This helps it to improve the earnings per share (EPS) number.

Recently many companies have enjoyed impressive profits and have generated an excellent cash flow. Activist investors are demanding a "return of capital." This means that any funds in excess of what is needed to run the business and finance future expansion should be returned to shareholders. It is, after all, their money. In 2015 companies had trillions of dollars in cash, far beyond what they could ever use. They would like to increase dividends and buy back shares but are subject to a serious impediment, U.S. corporate tax liabilities.

Most of these funds were earned and are deposited outside the United States. Companies have already paid taxes to the non–U.S. countries in which they earned these funds. They are not obligated to pay U.S. corporate taxes (often over 30 percent) until the funds are repatriated back home. To pay a dividend of $100 million, the company would have to bring these funds back to the United States and pay $30 million in taxes, something they are very reluctant to do.

Slightly off topic but important nonetheless, in their quest to avoid paying taxes cash-rich companies are borrowing billions of dollars in the United States and using the funds to pay dividends. Apple, with over $150 billion in cash just borrowed $15 billion to increase its dividend and expand its share buyback program.

Recalculate the earnings per share by dividing this year's net income by last year's number of shares outstanding. This will tell you how much of the year-to-year improvement in EPS is the result of true improved net income performance and how much is attributable to the reduced number of shares outstanding. Here is an example:

	2016	2015
Net Income	$900	$1,000
Shares	875	1,000
EPS	$1.03	$1.00

It appears that EPS "improved" from $1.00 to $1.03 between 2016 and 2017. By standard measures, there is improvement. However, the improvement clearly came about because the company used its cash to buy back stock, not because it improved net income. If you recalculate as mentioned above (divide this year's net income by last year's shares outstanding), the resulting EPS would be $.90 ($900/1000 shares), a more revealing number. While buying back shares with excess cash is a good strategy, a financial analyst should not be fooled if the improving EPS results only from share buybacks and not from improved operation.

There are many takeaways in this first chapter:

We have made a good start in learning the definitions and the accounting rules that govern the presentation of accounting information.

As you will see in the first three chapters, the financial statements (the balance sheet that we've just reviewed here in Chapter 1, the income statement and the statement of cash flows that we'll learn about in Chapters 2 and 3) are very intertwined. Focus on the line references that appear in all three chapters to see how this works.

When using this financial information to analyze a business, we need to be sure that we are interpreting the numbers correctly. As you saw in our final discussion of EPS above, things are not always what they seem. The choice of measure can sharply affect outcome.

A Point to Ponder

An asset is something that the company owns that helps in operating the business. What are the employees worth? Big companies spend billions of dollars hiring them, paying them, and also often make a sizable "investment" in their training and development, but this investment is not recognized in accounting because it does not create a tangible or sellable asset like inventory. In a consulting firm, law firm, CPA firm, software development company, and other service businesses, the employees are usually the only valuable asset. Yet their value appears nowhere on the traditional financial statements.

CHAPTER TWO

The Income Statement

The income statement, often called a *statement of operations* or a *profit and loss statement* (P&L), describes the performance of the company over a period of time, usually a month, a quarter, or a year. This information measures the company's achievement (revenue) and the resources (expenses) that were expended in order to produce that achievement. The income statement is summarized as follows:

$$Revenue - Expenses = Profit$$

The difference between revenues achieved and expenses incurred is called *profit* or *net income*.

The following paragraphs describe the details of the income statement. As a reference, we have provided a five-year history of the Metropolitan Manufacturing Company in Exhibit 2-1. This is part of the same set of financials as the balance sheet in Chapter 1.

The numbers in the section titles refer to the line items on the income statement, shown as Exhibit 2-1.

Exhibit 2-1. Metropolitan Manufacturing Company, Inc.
Statements of Profit and Loss for the Years Ending December 31 ($000)

		2016	2015	2014	2013	2012
24.	Revenue	$4,160	$3,900	$3,800	$3,700	$3,400
25.	Cost of Goods Sold	−2,759	−2,593	−2,500	−2,420	−2,200
26.	Gross Margin	$1,401	$1,307	$1,300	$1,280	$1,200
		34%	34%	34%	35%	35%
27.	General and Administrative Expenses	−1,033	−877	−1,025	−950	−1,000
28.	Depreciation Expense	−56	−50	−50	−50	−45
29.	Net Income Before Tax	$ 312	$ 380	$ 225	$ 280	$ 155
30.	Federal Income Tax	−156	−190	−112	−140	−78
31.	Net Income	$ 156	$ 190	$ 113	$ 140	$ 77
32.	Cash Dividends	−46	−46	−73	−95	−40
33.	Change in Retained Earnings	+$110	+$144	+$40	+$45	+$37

24. Revenue, $4,160,000

This is the dollar amount of products and services that the company provided to its customers during the year. This is often called *sales*; in Great Britain, it is called *turnover* or *income*. A sale is achieved when the customer takes ownership of and/or responsibility for the products.

Achieving revenue is quite distinct from "making a sale." You might use the latter phrase when you and the customer agree to terms. You might say that the sale is recognized when the purchase order is received. However, revenue is not recorded until the customer has received and approved of the products or services that were purchased.

Revenue is the value of products or services that is delivered to a satisfied customer. The customer either pays cash or promises to pay in the future; in the latter case, the amount is recorded as an accounts receivable.

Be clear that earning revenue is *not* the same as receiving the cash for products and services. Cash can be received prior to the recording of revenue. For example, a customer may make a down payment or deposit or may pay in advance for a magazine subscription. More commonly, however, businesses receive cash after the revenue is earned, resulting in accounts receivable. One type of business in which the receipt of cash and the recording of revenue might occur at the same time is the checkout counter at a supermarket.

The amount of revenue achieved by Metropolitan Manufacturing Company is $4,160,000. This is after reductions for price discounts and allowances for possible returns and warranties. For example:

Gross Amount at List Price	$4,310,881	
− Price Discounts	− 86,218	(2.0%)
− Allowances for Returns and Warranties	− 64,663	(1.5%)
= Revenue	$4,160,000	

Many companies record their revenues in this much detail in order to monitor their price discounting practices and other reductions from revenue.

25. Cost of Goods Sold, $2,759,000

Cost of goods sold is the cost of producing or purchasing the goods that are delivered to customers. This amount is subtracted from revenue in order to determine *gross profit* or *gross margin*. Cost of goods sold includes the following elements:

➤   Raw materials

➤   Purchased components

➤   Direct labor (this includes the wages and other payments made to those who actually manufacture the product and possibly their direct supervisors)

➤ Operating and repairing the equipment used to manu-facture the products

➤ Other manufacturing expenses, including utilities and maintenance of the production facility

The amount recorded as cost of goods sold is part of the difference between expenses and expenditures, discussed in Chapter 1. Cost of goods sold is an expense, and cost of production is an expenditure. Cost of goods sold will be different from cost of production because of changes in inventory. If inventory levels decrease during the period, then the cost of goods sold will be higher than the cost of production by the amount of the change in inventory.

If this were a service business, the equivalent of cost of goods sold would be called direct cost. Direct cost is the sum total of all of the spending necessary to provide the company's customers with a valuable experience. It includes the wages paid to all the people who interface with the customers, plus all of the support spending necessary to help those people perform their jobs.

26. Gross Margin, $1,401,000

This measures the profitability achieved as a result of producing and selling products and services. It measures manufacturing efficiency and the desirability of the company's products in the marketplace. Gross margin percentage is another measure of that performance.

27. General and Administrative Expenses, $1,033,000

This amount represents the cost of operating the entire infrastructure of the company. Included in this category are staff expenses (accounting, computer operations, senior management), selling expenses (salaries, travel), promotional expenses (advertising, trade shows), and research and development (technological research).

28. Depreciation Expense, $56,000

This is the portion of prior capital expenditures that has been allocated to the current year and is recorded as an expense in that year. It is not a cash expenditure.

29. Net Income Before Tax, $312,000

This amount is equal to revenue minus all operating and nonoperating expenses incurred by the company. This may also be called "Pre-Tax Income." For Metropolitan Manufacturing Company, Inc., it is:

Revenue	$4,160,000	
− Cost of Goods Sold		2,759,000
− General and Administrative Expenses		1,033,000
− Depreciation Expense		56,000
	− $3,848,000	
= Net Income Before Tax	$ 312,000	

30. Federal Income Tax, $156,000

In the United States, corporations pay approximately 34 percent of their profit to the federal government in the form of income taxes. For the Metropolitan Manufacturing Company example, however, we used a rate of 50 percent to keep the calculations simple. This 34 percent corporate tax rate is usually much higher than the rate big companies actually pay. Many companies do not pay U.S. corporate taxes on profits earned elsewhere in the world. They actually pay those taxes only after the funds are repatriated back to the United States.

31. Net Income, $156,000

This is the amount of profit that the corporation has achieved during the year. All expenses related to purchases from vendors and all other operating expenses have been taken into account. The owners of the business may keep this profit for their personal use (dividends) or reinvest all or part of it in the corporation to finance expansion and modernization (retained earnings). This is the number used by public companies to calculate earnings per share. It is also the number used in many of the financial ratio calculations discussed in Chapter 6.

32. Cash Dividends, $46,000

This is the portion of the year's profits that were distributed to the owners of the business. The remainder (the portion of net income that was not paid to the owners) was retained in the business each year. Therefore:

Net Income	$156,000
− Cash Dividends	46,000
= Increase in Retained Earnings	$110,000

33. Change in Retained Earnings, $110,000

This represents the portion of the profits that the owners reinvested in the business in the year 2016. The cumulative amount that the owners have reinvested in the business since its inception is $1,357,000. This is the cumulative retained earnings; it appears on the balance sheet on line 21. Notice on the balance sheet that line 21 increased by $110,000 in 2016, which represents that year's reinvestment.

Analysis of the Income Statement

A decline in revenue is not necessarily bad. There are times when revenue is flat but gross profit is improving. This is often a sign that the company is "cleansing" its product mix, or eliminating those products whose profitability is much less than the company average. It may be doing this for a number of possible reasons:

➢ The products are just not very profitable.

➢ Available productive capacity is limited, and the company will use these newly available facilities to produce faster-growing, higher-margin products.

➢ The products being eliminated are not of high enough quality, impairing the company's reputation as a provider of high-quality products.

➢ The eliminated products were consuming large amounts of cash, as they required high levels of inventory and accounts receivable to support the business.

➢ The company decided to outsource the production of these products to third parties. It continues to provide the products to its customers, but it now earns a sales commission rather than the full revenue.

➢ The company now leases some equipment to customers rather than selling it outright. Revenue will decline for a while. This happens when software providers convert to a software licensing strategy rather than sell the software outright. More IT companies will experience this phenomenon as they increasingly provide cloud computing rather than selling or licensing the software at all.

➢ The company unilaterally eliminates a line of products because it seeks to redefine its image and position in the marketplace. A terrific example of this is CVS, which used to be a drugstore chain. CVS rebranded itself as a health company in 2014. It accomplished this in part by eliminating sales of all tobacco products, thereby forgoing tens of millions of dollars in revenue and profits. There was no public or legal pressure to do this. By adding pharmacy benefit management and other medical services to its retail stores, CVS now has more revenue and profitability than it did before the strategy change.

If revenue is increasing but the gross profit percentage is decreasing, the company is probably gaining more business by reducing its selling prices. If revenue is increasing and gross profit percentage is decreasing, but the gross profit dollars are increasing, the company is reducing its price to sell more product and the strategy has been tremendously successful. An increase in gross profit dollars improves the company's cash flow. There is no negative connotation to reducing prices if the strategy is necessary and successful. This is especially true if the company has excess capacity. Selling lower-margin but profitable high-quality products will improve cash flow and profitability.

General and administrative expenses should generally increase more slowly than revenue. Economies of scale, efficiency, and the fact that general and administrative expenses are essentially fixed costs support this financial relationship. However, there are exceptions to this. In some companies that are driven by research and development (R&D) investments (think biotech and information technology), R&D expense may be included in the general and administrative expenses line. Certainly an R&D-driven company should be increasing the amount of this investment, consistent with the available funding and the success of its ongoing efforts.

Provision for Federal Income Tax

This is the corporate tax rate, which is usually in the 34 percent range, times the income before tax. It is not necessarily the amount of taxes that the company actually paid. This is because the accounting methodology used for a company's financial reports to shareholders is different from the methodology that the company uses in preparing its tax return. The average corporate tax rate actually paid by corporations in the United States is approximately 20 percent. There are many explanations for this. Here are two:

Profits earned overseas by American companies are not subject to U.S. corporate income tax until the cash flow from the profits is repatriated to the United States. This is always subject to change under varying versions of what Congress calls "reform" and "tax holiday."

Most companies that make capital expenditures will capitalize the expenditures on the shareholders' reports (place the item on the balance sheet as a fixed asset), yet expense the same expenditures on the company's tax return. This is perfectly legitimate and common. This will lower the company's profit on the tax return, resulting in a lower payment. The difference between the accounting provision of 34 percent and the amount actually paid will appear on the company's balance sheet as a liability, usually called *deferred taxes* or *income taxes payable.*

Net Income

Remember that this is not the amount of cash that has actually been generated by the business. Cash from revenue generated may not yet have been collected, and many expenses, particularly depreciation, are not expenditures.

If the company is performing well, net income should increase much faster than revenue. Growth enhances efficiency and provides financing for technological investment. Companies with a high proportion of fixed costs should show considerable profit improvement relative to revenue growth. (This is called "operating leverage.") Of course, the reverse is also true. Declining revenues can decimate a high-fixed-cost business. Think back to the steel, aluminum, and auto businesses in the 2008–2010 time period.

Net income can improve during a period of severe revenue decline. This can be the result of a drastic reduction in headcount and other areas of overhead. The massive cost cutting in 2008–2009 led to the loss of more than five million jobs.

More than half of these jobs were classified as general and administrative. As a result, many companies returned to profitability in 2009 despite serious revenue contractions. This is OK for a while (it's much better than not returning to profitability and going bankrupt). However, if the headcount reductions were of "unnecessary" people, why did it take a revenue contraction to precipitate the decision? If the headcount reductions included people who were working on R&D and other development projects necessary for future prosperity, how long will it take for the company to reemploy those resources and achieve the benefits of their efforts?

Oil and natural gas companies experienced severe revenue declines in the 2014–2015 time period, not because of volume declines but as a result of price declines in the 50 percent range. Oil sold in 2015 for as little as $45 per barrel although it had been averaging $100 per barrel in 2013. In fact, because of speculation and political turmoil in some oil-producing parts of the world, it spiked to as high as $140 per barrel in the period before 2014.

CHAPTER THREE

The Statement
of Cash Flows

The third critical financial statement, along with the balance sheet and the income statement, is called the *statement of cash flows*. In the past, it was called the *sources and uses of funds statement*, which is a more accurate description of the information it contains. It describes in summary form how the company generated the cash flows it needed (sources) to finance its various financial opportunities and responsibilities (uses) over the past year. The sources and uses of funds statement for Metropolitan Manufacturing Company is shown in Exhibit 3-1. As you go through it, notice that the line items appear on the balance sheet in the column labeled "Changes." In fact, the sources and uses of funds statement describes the changes in the balance sheets between two successive years, in this case 2016 and 2015. What we will do in this section is:

- ➤ Present a sources and uses of funds statement.
- ➤ Discuss the meaning and analysis of each number.

Exhibit 3-1. Metropolitan Manufacturing Company, Inc.
Sources and Uses of Funds for the Year Ending December 31, 2016

Sources of Funds

34. Net Income	$156,000
35. Depreciation	56,000
36. Increase in Bank Notes	130,000
37. Increase in Accounts Payable	110,000
38. Increase in Other Current Liabilities	39,000
39. Decrease in Investments	3,000
40. Total Sources of Funds	$494,000

Uses of Funds

41. Capital Expenditures	$ 34,000
42. Increase in Inventory	298,000
43. Increase in Accounts Receivable	40,000
44. Decrease in Long-Term Debt	50,000
45. Payment of Cash Dividends	46,000
46. Total Uses of Funds	$468,000
47. Net Increase in Cash Balance in 2016	26,000
48. 2015 Ending Cash Balance	107,000
49. 2016 Ending Cash Balance	$133,000

> ➤ Describe how each number was developed, relating it back to its source on the balance sheet.

> ➤ Restate the numbers in the statement of cash flows.

> ➤ Analyze the statement of cash flows and the information that it does and does not provide.

The paragraph numbers beginning below refer to the line items in Exhibit 3-1.

Sources of Funds

34. Net Income, $156,000

The company's profits are a major source of funds. Therefore, net income is traditionally listed first. This number is also the "bottom-line" number in the income statement that we saw in Exhibit 2-1 as line 31. In addition, it strongly affects the retained earnings amount on the balance sheet (line 21). Net income causes retained earnings to increase. Payment of cash dividends causes retained earnings to decrease. Therefore, the $110,000 change in retained earnings (income statement, line 33) is the net of:

Net Income	$156,000	(31 and 34)
− Dividends	− 46,000	(32)
= Change in Retained Earnings	$110,000	(33)

35. Depreciation Expense, $56,000

In a more formal version of this statement, this item would be preceded by the heading: "Add Back Items Not Requiring the Disbursement of Cash." The explanation of this is related to the discussion of expenses and expenditures in Chapter 1. When net income was calculated, an expense item was subtracted (line 28) that did not require a cash expenditure during this period and will never require one in the future. The item is depreciation expense. The expenditures related to this expense—i.e., capital expenditures—have already been made.

The depreciation expense was subtracted on line 28 for two reasons. First, generally accepted accounting principles (GAAP) require this. Second, depreciation expense is deductible as an expense for corporate income tax purposes, and so including it provides tax benefits. However, for the sources and uses of funds statement, it is added back because in terms of cash flow, it was not a "real"(expenditure) subtraction during this period.

36. Increase in Bank Notes, $130,000

During the year, Metropolitan Manufacturing Company raised $130,000 in additional short-term bank financing. This was added to its previously existing short-term bank debt of $170,000. Notice that Metropolitan Manufacturing Company added to its short-term debt while also paying off some long-term debt. By its very definition, the long-term amount that was paid off was not due. If it had been due, it would have been classified as "current portion of long-term debt," which is a *current* liability. There could be several explanations for this financing strategy, but it probably was related to the difference between short-term and long-term interest rates. Metropolitan probably borrowed short-term funds at a lower interest rate and used some of the funds to reduce its long-term loan, which had a higher interest rate.

37. Increase in Accounts Payable, $110,000

When a company buys products and services on credit, the purchases are being financed by the supplier, who provides the product or service but does not receive payment for it at that time. Overall, an increase in accounts payable shows that the company is being financed by its vendors to a greater degree. This is not an analysis of the strategy of buying on credit, which involves having vendors finance purchases or extend payment periods to lengthy terms to provide a cheap source of cash. In an accounting report, like this one, it is merely a statement that the amount of accounts payable is larger than it was in the past. An increase in accounts payable can result from the following actions:

➤ Taking more time to pay bills
➤ Buying more product on credit
➤ Paying higher prices for credit purchases

38. Increase in Other Current Liabilities, $39,000

Any increase in a liability is a source of funds. Since this category is made up primarily of accruals and similar items, it naturally increases each year as the company gets larger.

39. Decrease in Investments, $3,000

The company sold some investments that were on the books for $3,000. These investments could have been bonds, long-term certificates of deposit, or possibly the common stock of another company.

40. Total Sources of Funds, $494,000

This is the sum of:

Net Income	$156,000
Depreciation	56,000
Increase in Bank Notes	130,000
Increase in Accounts Payable	110,000
Increase in Other Current Liabilities	39,000
Decrease in Investments	3,000
	$494,000

Uses of Funds

41. Capital Expenditures, $34,000

The company used $34,000 to add to its fixed assets. This is evidenced by the increase in the gross book value of fixed assets. Since assets are presented at the lower of cost or market, the only explanation for an increase in gross book value is the purchase of new fixed assets. Even if the older fixed assets here increased in economic value, like real estate, remember that the financial statements never reflect improved economic value.

42. Increase in Inventory, $298,000

While inventory is sold and replenished many times during the course of the year (this is discussed more fully in Chapter 6), on a net basis, Metropolitan has invested an additional $298,000 in inventory. The increase in the level of inventory could be the result of any combination of the following:

> ➤ Replacement costs were greater than the cost of what was sold.

- Costs per unit purchased have remained the same, but the number of units in inventory has increased.
- The mix of products on hand has changed in the direction of the more expensive products.

It cannot be determined simply from these inventory numbers whether inventory increased because sales forecasts were overly optimistic or because actual sales were disappointing. We do not know if this inventory increase was in raw materials, work in process, or finished goods. Analysis of these issues will be necessary. The only thing that is certain is that the financial investment in inventory has increased.

The reverse can be true as well. In 2014 oil companies showed drastic reductions in the inventory numbers on their balance sheets. In fact the inventory quantity of oil in barrels increased because of excess supplies in the market. The dollar decrease on the balance sheets resulted from the 50 percent price reductions that were endured.

43. Increase in Accounts Receivable, $40,000

The company has "invested" this additional amount in financing its customers. This may be the result of any of the following:

- Higher sales levels, either because prices are higher or volume is greater
- Extending credit terms to give customers more time to pay
- A deterioration in collection performance

Providing customers with credit terms is a marketing investment that, the company hopes, will produce more and happier customers who purchase more product. However, not enforcing those credit agreements is a sign of either accounting sloppiness or marketplace weakness (fear that customers are buying only because they can take their time in paying and would not buy if they could not have the extended time).

44. Decrease in Long-Term Debt, $50,000

Metropolitan Manufacturing Company used $50,000 to reduce its long-term debt. The rules of accounting provide strong evidence that this was a voluntary act. Long-term debt, by definition, is not due within the current year. As mentioned in the discussion of the increase in short-term bank debt, if this amount were due, it would have been classified as a current liability, most likely current portion of long-term debt. This payment could have been made because of any combination of the following:

- ➤ The interest rate on the long-term debt was high.
- ➤ The company had extra cash.
- ➤ The company used the proceeds from lower-cost short-term bank debt.
- ➤ The long-term debt was selling at a discount from par value on a public market. The difference between par and the amount paid to buy it back at a discount is recorded as other income on the profit and loss statement.

45. Payment of Cash Dividends, $46,000

The board of directors of Metropolitan Manufacturing Company voted to pay the holders of preferred and common shares cash dividends amounting to $46,000. Such dividends are traditionally but not necessarily voted on and disbursed on a quarterly basis.

Notice that retained earnings on the balance sheet (line 21) was affected by two activities, net income and cash dividends, as follows:

Retained Earnings 12/31/15		$1,247,000
Plus: Net Income, 2016	$156,000	
Minus: Cash Dividends, 2016	− 46,000	
Equals: Change in Retained Earnings, 2016		$ 110,000
Retained Earnings 12/31/2016		$1,347,000

46. Total Uses of Funds, $468,000

This is the sum of:

Capital Expenditures	$ 34,000
Increase in Inventory	298,000
Increase in Accounts Receivable	40,000
Decrease in Long-Term Debt	50,000
Payment of Cash Dividends	46,000
	$468,000

47. Cash Reconciliation

Here is a review of the cash reconciliation between the two years.

Beginning Cash Balance (1/1/16)		$107,000
Plus: Sources of Funds	$494,000	
Minus: Uses of Funds	− 468,000	
Equals: Increase in Cash		$ 26,000
Ending Cash Balance (12/31/16)		$133,000

Statement of Cash Flows

Generally accepted accounting principles requires a specific format for this information that is different from the more analytical
format that we presented here. This format, called the *statement
of cash flows*, is found in all published annual reports of public
companies and also in the financial reports of almost every other
company whose financials are prepared and produced by certified
public accountants. The information is presented in three sections:

➤ Cash flows provided by/used for operations
➤ Cash flows provided by/used for investments
➤ Cash flows provided by/used for financing

It is important to be familiar with and understand this format
because most financial information that is available is presented
in this manner. Note that uses of funds are shown in parentheses,
indicating outflow, and that sources of funds are shown without

parentheses, indicating inflow. The statement of cash flows for Metropolitan Manufacturing Company is shown in Exhibit 3-2.

Before you begin the process of analyzing the data provided in Exhibit 3-2, it would be very useful for you to review the content and structure of the financial statements. To accomplish this, complete the financial statements exercise in Appendix A.

Analyzing the Statement of Cash Flows

Data becomes high-quality information if it helps the analyst to better understand the business, including its issues and problems and its strengths and weaknesses. When evaluating whether or not to provide funding to implement a proposed decision, having high-quality data means that the best information is available, supporting the decision that is best for the future of the company.

Exhibit 3-2. Metropolitan Manufacturing Company Inc.
Statement of Cash Flows for the Year Ending December 31, 2016

Net Income	$156,000	
Depreciation	56,000	
Increase in Inventory	(298,000)	
Increase in Accounts Receivables	(40,000)	
Increase in Accounts Payable	110,000	
Increase in Other Current Liabilities	39,000	
Cash Flow Provided by (Used for) Operations		**$ 23,000**
Capital Expenditures	$(34,000)	
Sale of Investments	3,000	
Cash Flow Provided by (Used for) Investments		**$(31,000)**
Increase in Bank Debt	$130,000	
Decrease in Long-Term Debt	(50,000)	
Payment of Dividends	(46,000)	
Cash Flow Provided by (Used for) Financing		**$ 34,000**
Net Cash Increase		**$ 26,000**
Add: Beginning Cash Balance		107,000
Cash at End of Year		$133,000

The following are some thoughts about evaluating the statement of cash flows in this context. Does it really provide high-quality decision and analytical support? As a key metric, is it consistent with the actions that we want managers to take?

Cash Flow Provided by (Used for) Operations

Cash flow can be improved by slowing down payments to suppliers. An increase in accounts payable is a cash inflow. However, if the company postpones paying its suppliers until a point far beyond its agreed-upon payment terms, is this really a positive performance achievement? We think not. The company is forgoing profitable cash discounts and impairing relationships with suppliers, and it risks not receiving product in a timely manner, all to "improve" cash flow from operations.

Interest income from short-term investments appears in the net income amount. This is really not a cash flow from operations. Operations means making and selling products, the company's business. The company can give the appearance of improving its operating cash flow by keeping cash idle rather than reinvesting it in the needs of the business, like buying machinery and hiring additional salespeople.

Gains from the disposal of assets (one-time events) are also included in net income in the category "other income and expenses." Selling underachieving assets and businesses is certainly a positive strategy, and doing so certainly may generate valuable cash flow. But this is hardly a cash flow from an operating activity.

Interest expense on loans is also included in the net income amount. This cash outflow should really be characterized as a financing activity, rather than being included as part of operations.

Traditionally, the concept of free cash flow is defined as:

Cash Flow Provided by Operations
Minus: Capital Expenditures
Equals: Free Cash Flow

This has the connotation of "discretionary" cash flow and is often used by analysts to identify the amount of funds that the company has available to implement profitable, market-penetrating opportunities. This is far from valid and should be viewed critically.

> ➤ This definition implies that capital expenditures carry a higher priority than debt service (paying principal and interest to creditors). Paying required debt service certainly is more critical than capital expenditures (think default or bankruptcy). It's like remodeling your kitchen and then not having the funds to pay the mortgage.

> ➤ In order to "improve" free cash flow and "look better," this metric motivates the company to fail to make necessary improvements, thereby reducing capital expenditures, in order to make free cash flow appear more favorable.

For Metropolitan Manufacturing Company, here is a more valuable, reconstructed statement of cash flows. Sadly, it is not consistent with generally accepted accounting principles—the almighty GAAP—and would probably not be acceptable in audited financial statements. However, remember that we are not doing accounting here. We are analyzing the business and are not bound by "accounting rules."

We propose some changes in the free cash flow formula:

Step 1: From net income in "Cash Flows Provided by Operations":

> ➤ Remove interest income. It becomes part of cash flows from investing activities. Buying interest-bearing securities, such as CDs or Treasury securities, is an investment. While doing so is worthwhile, it is not a "regular" part of operations and therefore not an "operating activity."

> ➤ Remove interest expense. Borrowing is a financing activity. Paying interest expense on those borrowed funds is also a financing expense. It becomes part of cash flows from financing activities.

> ➤ Remove gains or losses from sale of assets. This is an investing activity. Although often not, it is supposed to be a one-time event.

Step 2: From Cash Flows Provided by Operations itself, remove changes in accounts payable. Accounts Payable is financing from vendors for products and services purchased and should be part of cash flows from financing activities.

Free cash flow would then become:

Cash Flows Provided by Operations (minus the items just
    listed)
Minus: Cash Flows for Debt Service
Equals: A Better Version of Free Cash Flow

Be clear that we are not telling the accounting profession that their prescribed format is wrong. We never want to enter that debate. We seek to analyze our business and develop information that is useful in doing so. The goal of a metric, like the statement of cash flows, is to measure the financial health of a company so we can make intelligent management decisions. The revised format described here better accomplishes that.

CHAPTER FOUR

Generally Accepted Accounting Principles: A Review and Update

The role of the Financial Accounting Standards Board (FASB) was briefly described in the introduction. This is a research organization, made up primarily of accountants. The FASB, along with the entire accounting profession, has, over time, developed a series of rules called *generally accepted accounting principles* (GAAP). In addition, the FASB publishes what are called *FASB Bulletins.* These are a series of more than one hundred publications that describe what corporate reporting methodologies should be. Most of these methodologies have been adopted and are now incorporated into accounting practice. A broad analogy is that the GAAP rules are the basic constitution and the bulletins are proposed amendments. Here are some of the fundamental GAAP rules.

The Fiscal Period

All reporting is done for predetermined periods of time. Reports may be issued for months or quarters, and certain reports are issued covering annual periods. Accounting fiscal periods usually coincide with calendar periods, although not necessarily with the calendar year. A few companies define their fiscal month as 28 days and their calendar year as 13 of those months. Other companies adopt a *fiscal year* of, say, July 1 to June 30 (possibly to make the year-end tax season easier) or February 1 to January 31 (to include the Christmas selling season). Municipal governments time their fiscal years to begin three months after the beginning of the fiscal years of their respective state governments. This gives the municipality three months to determine how much state aid they will receive from the state prior to the deadline of the municipal government. State governments in turn time their fiscal year to begin three months after the federal fiscal year. Similarly, this provides the state with three months to learn what federal aid will be available prior to the deadline for the state budget.

The Going Concern Concept

When accountants are keeping the books and preparing the financial statements, they presume that the company will continue to exist for the foreseeable future. If there is serious doubt about this, or if the company's ceasing operations is a certainty, the financial statements (essentially the balance sheet) will be presented at estimated liquidation value. If the company is in serious financial trouble and its future existence is in doubt, the outside CPA firm, as part of its audit process, is required to comment on this financial condition in its certification letter to shareholders. It must make a concrete statement in which this concern is explicitly expressed.

Historical Monetary Unit

Accounting is the recording of *past* business events in dollars (or in the currency of the country in which it is domiciled). In the

United States, financial statements, and in fact all financial accounting, report only in dollars. While units of inventory, market share, and employee efficiency (such as revenue per employee) are critical business issues, reporting on them is not within the realm of financial accounting responsibility.

Financial statements depicting past years are presented as they occurred. The selling prices of the products and the value of assets may very well be different today, but reports of past periods are not adjusted to reflect current economic conditions.

Conservatism

The principle of conservatism requires that "bad news" be recognized when the condition becomes possible and the amount can be estimated, whereas "good news" is recognized only when the event (transaction) has actually occurred.

One example of this is the *allowance for bad debts* on the balance sheet, which is recorded before the losses are actually incurred. It is recognized that some of the company's accounts receivable may not be collected. The total amount of uncollectible accounts receivable is estimated and the allowance is recorded before the company finds out which customers (if any) actually will not pay their bills. Another example is reserves for inventory writedowns, which are recorded before the dated or out-of-style products are actually put up for sale at distress prices. It is clear on December 26 that any remaining Christmas items will have to be sold at deeply discounted prices. The writedown is recorded on December 26, not when the items are actually put on sale. Revenue, however, is not recorded, no matter how certain its receipt may seem from a business point of view, until the product is actually delivered or the service is actually provided to the customer. Payment in advance, while increasing the certainty of the sale in a business sense, does not change the accounting rule. Revenue is recorded only when it is earned.

Quantifiable Items or Transactions

In a business sense, the value of the company's workforce and the knowledge that the employees possess may be the company's critical competitive advantage. However, because that value cannot be quantified and expressed in dollar amounts, accounting does not recognize it as an asset. The value of trademarks and franchise names is also generally not included. Coke, Windows, and Disney are certainly franchise names with worldwide recognition. While the business value of a franchise name can be almost infinite if it is maintained, the name is not an asset on the balance sheet because its value cannot be quantified.

Consistency

Accountants make many decisions when preparing a company's financial statements. These include, but are not limited to, the choice of depreciation method for fixed assets and the choice of LIFO or FIFO accounting for inventory. Once these decisions have been made, however, each successive set of financial statements must employ the same methodology. When a major change in accounting methodology is made, the accountants must highlight that change and redo past financial statements (the reference points) to reflect it. Only then can comparative analysis and trends be valid. We don't want an analysis of two successive sets of financials to be distorted because of changes in accounting methodology. Also if the accounting methodology of the prior year (the reference point) has been changed, right on the top of those numbers it will say "restated." If the changes are significant (material), there will probably also be a footnote with a fuller explanation of the changes.

Full Disclosure

When a major change in accounting methodology occurs, accountants must take steps to be certain that the readers of the financial statements are fully aware of that change and how it affected the financial results.

Materiality

An event that is material, or significant, is one that may affect the judgment, analysis, or perception of the reader of the information. Events that are perceived as *material* must be disclosed separately and highlighted accordingly. This is a relative concept. Something that is significant in a company with annual revenues of $20 million might be largely irrelevant in a multibillion-dollar enterprise.

Significant Accounting Issues

There are some major accounting issues that all businesspeople should know about.

The Sarbanes-Oxley Act

This legislation was passed by the U.S. Congress in 2002. A number of accounting scandals, most notably that involving the infamous Enron, caused government officials and the accounting profession to reexamine how accounting is done, the concept of the audit process, and corporate governance. The act was named after its sponsors, Senator Paul Sarbanes of Maryland and Congressman Michael Oxley of Ohio. Many improvements in corporate governance have occurred since 2002. Some were specifically required by Sarbanes-Oxley; others reflected the purpose of the legislation. Among these improvements are:

> ➤ The chief executive officer and chief financial officer of the company must sign a letter certifying that the contents of the annual report are true and that they take full responsibility for those contents. This letter is included in the annual report. They also must certify that the company's internal controls are effective in ensuring that the contents of the annual report are true and the financial statements

are accurate. Ignorance of deception is no longer an option for those responsible. "I didn't know" is no longer an acceptable defense in any legal or regulatory matter.

➤ The concept of transparency has become increasingly important. The company must tell the readers of the annual report more of what they need to know about the company and its financial condition. In particular, the existence of *off-balance sheet financing* must be revealed and discussed.

➤ The management of the board of directors has been improved. The audit committee of the board is responsible for overseeing the efforts of the outside accounting firm. At least one member of that committee (and hopefully more than one) must have a background as a certified public accountant (CPA). This seems so obvious now. How can a committee provide intelligent oversight of a CPA firm when no one on the committee has any background in that business?

➤ It has long been a practice that the audit firm is selected by the shareholders, not the board of directors and not senior management. If you own stock in a company, you receive a notice of the annual meeting as well as the opportunity to vote for the election or reelection of members of the board of directors. Also included in this package, which is called a "proxy statement," is the opportunity to vote for or against the outside audit firm. While there is no choice among possible alternatives, there is at least the opportunity to vote against the incumbent firm if enough shareholders are not happy with their performance. Understand that switching CPA firms is very expensive and disruptive. But in the past few years, firms have been replaced.

➤ The compensation committee of the board of directors must consist of only outside, independent directors. No employees may serve on this committee. Previously, there had been situations where subordinates would approve the compensation and bonus packages of their boss or two coworkers would mutually agree to each other's compensation.

➤ One of the major criticisms of boards of directors was, and to some extent still is, that the members did not really pay close enough attention to the management of the company. They were friends of the chairman and didn't want to be critical, or they were too busy with their main jobs or with their work on many other boards. Some businesspeople are career board members and serve on seven or more boards. It has become clear, based upon many boards that were not doing their jobs, that some board members cannot possibly provide adequate attention to all of their responsibilities. As a result of some provisions of Sarbanes-Oxley and also shareholder activism, many board members are being forced to resign or are not being nominated for reelection and thus are allowed to disappear from the scene gracefully.

"Safe Harbor" Provision

This is officially called the *Private Securities Litigation Reform Act of 1995*. What this legislation does is protect the CEO and the company from legal liability resulting from statements made to the public that turn out to be incorrect if the statements were made in good faith, based upon what was known at the time.

Many public companies conduct or participate in public forums with security analysts and shareholders. Every three months, there is one of these forums, usually in the form of a conference call, which may be "attended" by thousands of telephone participants and listeners. Every owner of the company's shares may listen in (schedules can be found on the company's website). During this meeting, the CEO will make pronouncements about the company's future, which includes "guidance," or a forecast of the company's expected revenue and net income growth. Under this act, if the CEO projects 15 percent profit growth and the amount actually achieved is 10 percent or 20 percent, the CEO cannot be accused of hiding the truth if the forecast was made in good faith, based upon what was known at the time the forecast was presented. This does not preclude the fact that many shareholders will sell their shares if the CEO's forecasts do not prove credible.

The following statement, or something similar, appears in many annual reports. This particular statement is a direct quote on the subject from the 2014 annual report of the Walt Disney Company (page 54):

> . . . We may from time to time make written or oral statements that are "forward-looking" including statements made in this report and other filings with the SEC and in reports to our shareholders. Such statements, for example, express expectations or projections about future action that we may take, including restructuring or strategic initiatives, or about developments beyond our control including changes in domestic or global economic conditions. These statements are made on the basis of management's views and assumptions as of the time the statements are made and we undertake no obligation to update these statements. There can be no assurance, however, that our expectations will necessarily come to pass.

Disney goes on to list and explain all of the possible risks that conceivably could adversely affect their company and its performance. Basically it is saying, "We do the best we can but cannot predict the future or any extraneous events with total accuracy and take no responsibility to do so."

Fair Value Accounting

The economic and financial turmoil and crisis during the 2008–2012 period has been beyond the imagination and anticipation of most businesspeople, government regulators, and the general public. The uncertainty, business dislocation, and financial loss have caused damage that is estimated to be in the trillions of dollars. One of these areas of financial uncertainty involved the actual value of the assets on a company's books. The focus was on assets owned by banks, particularly marketable securities. The solvency of many banks, and maybe the entire financial system, depended on a rational determination of these values.

Realizing this problem at the very beginning of the financial crisis, the FASB created SFAS No. 157, *Fair Value Measurements*. This provides a more standardized methodology that banks (and others) are to use to value marketable securities on their balance sheets. The rules establish the definition of market value as "an exit price, representing the amount that would be received to sell an asset . . . in an orderly transaction between market participants."

The rules also provide for three classifications of assets. This methodology allows the reader to have a strong sense of the logic that the company used to value its assets. These classifications are:

> *Level 1.* Quoted prices in active markets for identical assets are available. Think of a quote for a New York Stock Exchange–listed public company.

> *Level 2.* There is available information about prices for identical assets. However, there may not be an actual quote.

> *Level 3.* No direct quotes or information is available to value these assets.

CHAPTER FIVE

The Annual Report and Other Sources of Incredibly Valuable Information

E very analyst and business professional should be intimately acquainted with the information available in the public do-main that he can access and use for a variety of purposes. The sources discussed here will include:

> The annual report
> The 10K report to the Securities and Exchange Commission
> The *Wall Street Journal*
> *Forbes* and *Fortune* magazines and their websites
> The Public Register Annual Report Service (PRARS)

There is an enormous amount of valuable information available that everyone should be aware of. Much of it is free and readily accessible on the Internet.

The Annual Report

The annual report should be read for the many valuable insights that it provides:

> - It is a wonderful review of the accounting process and the concept of generally accepted accounting principles (GAAP).
> - You can learn a great deal about your own company from its annual report. This includes how it perceives itself strategically and ethically and how it presents itself to the rest of the world.
> - The information contained in your competitors' annual reports provides valuable insights into their financial condition, performance, and strategies.

Every company whose stock is traded freely by shareholders is called a *public company.* According to the various securities laws passed by Congress in the 1930s and amended many times since, any company with at least 500 shareholders who can vote their own shares independently is considered public and is subject to the rules and regulations of the Securities and Exchange Commission. There are many private companies that provide shares to their employees through a 401(k) or similar plan. However, because the company, not the employee "owners" of the shares, votes those shares in trust, the company maintains its private status.

Not all companies are subject to SEC regulation—only those whose shares are registered and publicly traded. Company size is not an issue here. Some very large (multibillion-dollar) companies are private, and some very small companies have publicly traded shares.

There are three essential themes in the annual report. It is a combination of a regulatory requirement, a public relations vehicle, and what we'll call the middle ground: strong tradition. Many companies include information in their annual report that is not specifically required. However, because that information has historically been presented every year, it becomes expected, and its omission would raise question.

The pure public relations aspect of the annual report includes all photographs and presentations that convey the company's public image, its reputation as a good corporate citizen, and product promotion. The corporate self-promotion effort begins on the outside cover. Here are some sample statements from recent annual reports:

Global Growth and Industry Leadership	(Halliburton)
Growing from Within	(United Technologies)
Improving Health for Life	(BioSante)
Lasting Solutions	(Artes Medical)
Accelerating Our Growth	(Endo Pharmaceuticals)
Building on the Elements of Success	(Sepracor)
Investing in People and Product Success	(Sciele Pharma Inc.)
Forces for Life	(Sanofi Aventis)

All of these reports (which are only a minute sample of those available) have photographs of people whose health has been improved or whose lives were saved, of beautiful construction projects that the company has completed, or of the technologically advanced products that the company has provided.

These are announcements to:

1. *The public.* Science, engineering, and helping people provide a positive image.
2. *The company's employees.* Their company is in the forefront as a "knowledge" company. This emphasizes their value to the company (despite the millions who were laid off over the years).
3. *Security analysts.* Science companies are very attractive to investors. Companies that used to do R&D and then manufacture their products are now outsourcing much of their production. Fast-growth, high-margin scientific research

and development is much more attractive to the investment world than manufacturing. The stock of a company that was previously a manufacturer will perform better if the security analysts and investors know of and believe in its repositioning strategy. Science and engineering will improve the company's image in the investment community, which will assign a higher price/earnings ratio to its stock. Security analysts like a high-margin, fast-growth company with recession-resistant special products. If the company is relatively small, it becomes a takeover candidate. Biotech companies that outsource "mundane" manufacturing sell at much higher price/earnings ratios than companies known as "old pharma."

The inside cover provides a highlights section. Many companies merely repeat such themes as science, fast growth, helping people, and similar cliches. Other companies get more serious and include summary financial information from the income statement and balance sheet, and also stock market data—earnings per share and stock prices. For example, DuPont spends over $1 billion per year in research and development and averages more than $5 billion per year in capital expenditures and acquisitions of other companies. It is (and wants us to know that it is) dedicated to knowledge and is a modern and efficient business.

The CEO's Letter to Shareholders

The chief executive officer (CEO) is required to write a letter to shareholders. This letter includes a description and analysis of all business events of the past year that have had a significant (read "material") impact on the performance and condition of the company. It also includes considerable commentary on how the company sees its future.

This letter is reviewed as part of the audit process. It must present all issues in an even-handed manner. Negative as well as positive events must be presented in a logical, cohesive way so that the reader will learn useful information. Bad news is often presented early in this letter so that the positive corrective actions that are already in process can be described. The company wants to convey the idea that management is on top of things and knows what has to be done. Management's credibility is at stake.

In a classic letter written a few years ago by GE's CEO, Jeffrey Immelt, he was very blunt, honest, and even intimate. It begins, "Dear Fellow Owners," not the then-standard "Dear Stockholder." Immelt's personal net worth declined by many millions of dollars as a result of the stock market crash of 2008–2009. So did the wealth of all GE shareholders. When the stock had declined by 50 percent during this period, Immelt bought more shares as a show of confidence. That particular investment cost him vast sums until the market turned positive in March 2009. In his letter, Immelt added, "In the past, I believed that our diversified portfolio would protect us in all kinds of economic cycles. But we never anticipated a global financial system failure and its continuing economic fall-out." The stock of GE is up over 400 percent since that time. GE drastically reduced its exposure to financial investments by se-verely downsizing the operations of GE Capital, which was one of the largest financial entities in the country at its peak. Unfortu-nately, GE has replaced some of that investment in energy-related products, which as of 2015 are struggling because of the price of oil and the European recession.

Despite these cycles, GE is one of the most successful compa-nies of the past 30 years. Its stated strategy is classic:

> ➢ Be global.
> ➢ Drive innovation.
> ➢ Build relationships.
> ➢ Leverage strengths.

GE is among the last of the true conglomerates; its portfolio includes aircraft engines, energy products, and appliances. It has sold its TV stations. Its strategy is to operate as the number one or number two company in each industry or to exit the business. GE

Capital has been greatly downsized and will ultimately be only a very small part of the overall business.

These letters to the shareholders are generally written by a team whose profession is described as "financial public relations" or "investor relations." This internal team, supported by outside consultants, is responsible for all phases of GE's relationship with its investors and others who are interested in its financial performance, including the annual report presentation, shareholders' meetings, security analysts' meetings, and general communications. The letter is audited by the company's outside CPA firm to assure its compliance with GAAP, its accuracy, and its fairness.

Public Relations

Large companies like GE, Verizon, and Johnson & Johnson have a multitude of interlocking constituencies. The stockholders, who often include employees and their pension funds, are the voters who elect the board of directors, which in turn appoints the officials responsible for regulatory issues, including taxes, corporate governance, and relationships with government agencies such as the Food and Drug Administration (FDA) and the Environmental Protection Agency (EPA). The annual report is also a presentation to the company's customers, some of whom may also be stockholders. Some of these customers may also be government agencies. GE and other companies want to influence the way they are viewed by the world. To accomplish this, they devote a considerable portion of their annual report to a description of each of their businesses. The Johnson & Johnson annual report, for example, contains a very effective presentation of its businesses, including financials, easy-to-understand charts, and photographs of happy people, including patients whose health is improving, happy employees, and so on. (You get the picture.) The photographs want to convey to the world that the employees are "just people," building shareholder value by helping "other people." The choice of photographs (and the decision to include them at all) is motivated by public relations considerations and supports the image and message that the company is presenting.

Going back in history to a letter that was composed with great skill, we look at the CEO letter in Disney's 1999 annual report. This letter provides some interesting perspectives. It is addressed to "Disney Owners and Fellow Cast Members." Employees of all Disney theme parks are known as cast members. This letter indicates that this company holds those cast members in very high esteem. It presents, in a very direct manner, some very pointed themes.

1. *Revitalize underperforming areas (home video and consumer products).* Right up front, the letter describes an issue in cliché terms, then identifies the focus of the comment. Disney is focusing on some specific issues that need to be addressed and wants us to know that it knows what these priorities are. Notice, also, that bad news is presented first, followed by a lengthy discussion of remedial actions that are currently in progress.

2. *Achieve greater profitability from existing assets (control costs).* The letter describes the need for greater efficiency and indicates that the company does not need to remain in all its current businesses forever. The company's strategic sourcing program means more pricing and service cooperation from vendors who seek to continue in that capacity.

3. *Capital efficiency initiatives to drive long-term growth (how best to invest).* Disney has included outside partners in many of its ventures and to some extent is becoming a theme park management company. This provides more focus on and cash from its core competencies. This is particularly true in its Paris Disneyland and the even newer theme park in China. Disney partners with local companies to help it cross political and cultural barriers.

4. *Continued product development (being Disney).* Disney is an entertainment company that is quite successful in its cross-branding strategy. Its parks, cruises, movies, TV and cable, and consumer products mostly carry the Disney brand and cross-sell each other.

A review of Disney's annual reports over the past 10 years suggests that the company continues to emphasize the same themes.

During the 2009–2010 time period, it purchased Marvel Entertainment, which owns approximately five thousand trademarked cartoon characters. This added the content of these characters to the Disney distribution network. Prior to that it purchased Pixar Studios from Steve Jobs. Jobs, at the time of his death, was the largest shareholder of Disney beyond the Walt Disney family. It has also purchased the Star Wars franchise (Lucas Films) and will begin to market the "package" in 2015. The "package" will probably include movies, products, and theme park events.

Management Discussion and Analysis

Traditionally, this section of the annual report provides an extensive, somewhat detailed review of the past year. In paragraph form, the company discusses its financial results in considerable detail. For example, DuPont presents considerable information about the results of each of its business units. This is referred to as *segment reporting*. The Warren Buffett letter in the Berkshire Hathaway annual report is a classic in his analysis of the economy and the performance of almost every individual company in its portfolio. He goes into great detail on the performance of individual executives. Know that BH owns Heinz, Geico, and many other well-known companies.

Many years ago, when companies diversified into somewhat unrelated businesses, it became difficult for analysts to benchmark these companies against their competitors because their business identity was difficult to determine. The result was a requirement that a company include in its annual report financial information for each of its business segments. The accounting document that specifically required this information is called *Statement of Financial Accounting Standards (SFAS) No. 131, Disclosures About Segments of an Enterprise and Related Information.* Companies' resistance to providing this information resulted from their desire to avoid providing competitors with valuable information. Companies are very careful in defining each of their segments because of the information about each segment that they must provide. While segment reporting provides only summary information, that information is competitively valuable.

Disney is one of the most successful companies in the 2012–2016 time period. Its revenues are growing in excess of 8 percent annually and its stock price has almost tripled (thank you, Walt). It reports revenue and operating income for each of its segments. These include:

> Media Networks *(including ESPN, ABC, and the Disney channels)*

> Parks and Resorts *(at full capacity in 2014)*

> Studio Entertainment *(Marvel, Pixar, Lucas, Disney)*

> Consumer Products *(retail stores, products in their theme parks)*

> Interactive *(websites, streaming TV)*

DuPont has drastically redefined its identity and its segments over the years. It used to be "DuPont Chemical Company." It has become crisp, brisk, in-your-face-modern "Dupont." By following the reporting of its segments, we can see that DuPont has divested itself of commodity business, sold off its less important sectors, such as pharmaceuticals, in which it was a minor player. All of its current businesses are high-value-added, science-oriented products.

Segment reporting information may appear either in the Management Discussion and Analysis section of the annual report or buried deep in the report's footnotes. Wherever in the annual report it is located, it will usually provide information on revenues, operating income, assets, and capital expenditures for each segment. Much of this information is broken down by geography. Many companies will provide an assessment of the future strategies for each business and possibly include a financial forecast. Some, but very few, will reveal the risk-adjusted hurdle rate that they use to evaluate capital expenditures. The significance of this is discussed in Chapter 10 of this book, "Return on Investment."

There are a few very effective ways to use this information. Acquire the annual reports of:

- ➤ *Your competitors.* In their annual reports, these companies will reveal some of their future expectations and (surprisingly) identify and describe specific ongoing projects and strategic alliances. Their segment financials are a wonderful source of benchmark information. Observation of any year-to-year redefinitions of the segments may reveal changing strategic directions.

- ➤ *Your suppliers.* In their reports, these companies may reveal their managements' perceptions of future sales. Your company is one of their customers. So they are in fact identifying what they think you will buy, in terms of quantities, technologies, and perhaps geography. The airline industry's forecast of new planes needed becomes a guideline to GE for the number of engines it may sell, to Alcoa for how much aluminum it may sell, and to Honeywell for the sales of cockpit electronics that it may enjoy.

- ➤ *Your customers.* Their forecasts and strategic direction may translate to your forecasts and strategic direction, as well. Technological advances may define new generations of products. Consider Dell Computer with "Intel (computer chips) Inside," or the advances in the Internet driving sales of cell phones.

"Safe Harbor" Provision

For the company as a whole and for each segment, the annual report provides a considerable amount of information about the company's expectations for the future. This part of the report is called an "outlook." Management must be very careful about this presentation. It might cause existing and potential stock market investors to make decisions about their investments in the company that could have an undesirable outcome. If this discussion is handled correctly, the company cannot be blamed for this because it is not giving advice; it is merely presenting management's assessment of the future.

As discussed in Chapter 4, many companies provide a disclaimer statement for this outlook, carefully stating that they cannot be held responsible for the outlook's accuracy. They can thus protect themselves from liability resulting from statements made by senior management. We saw this in Disney's statement in Chapter 4.

One of the most honest and revealing statements was provided by GE in its annual report a few years back. It viewed its past performance and its expectations for the future in a very explicit manner. It was able to do this legally because of the protection of the safe harbor provision. The company was very even-handed in discussing its weaknesses as well as its strengths. Without this provision, the annual report would become a totally compliance-focused document with much less valuable information and would have provided no sense of the company's future. Imagine the politics and legal issues that would arise if the company had to publish its budget. The lawsuits would be unwieldy if the company didn't make its numbers. The legal situation might even be worse if actual performance exceeded budgeted projections. Therefore, management simply discusses the company's future in general terms and is protected from litigation when it does so. No forecast numbers are provided, and rightly so. Only strategies and issues are included in the discussion.

GE provides the following in its 2008 annual report:

	Goal	Performance	Change From Prior Year
Revenues (in $ billions)	$190–$195	$183	+6%
Earnings (in $ billions)	$24.2	$18.1	(19%)
EPS	$2.42	$1.78	(19%)

Report of Independent Accountants

This is a letter written by the company's outside accounting firm. It is addressed to the stockholders of the company, to whom the accounting firm reports, and sometimes also to the board of directors. When the company sends out the notice of the annual meeting, it will include a proxy statement that identifies the major issues that will be decided by shareholder vote at the annual meeting. If a shareholder does not attend the meeting, that shareholder's vote is not sacrificed. Rather, the shareholder may vote by "proxy." (This essentially means that the shareholder may vote over the Internet or by mail.) One issue that always appears on the proxy statement is whether the stockholders approve (or not) of the board of directors' recommendation to renew the contract of the outside CPA firm. The vote almost always confirms the board's recommendation. No alternative CPA firm is named. However, in circumstances where there have been extreme problems with the audit process or with accounting integrity, the stockholders, through this somewhat democratic process, do have the ability to discontinue the CPA firm's services.

The Audit Process. The company's internal accounting staff is responsible for keeping the books and producing the financial statements. Larger companies have an organization called internal audit that is separate from the accounting staff and, to some degree, reviews the accounting staff's work. In some cases, the audit staff may not be part of the controller's organization at all. The 2006 annual report of United Technologies is a classic. It describes the role of internal auditors and the internal control process very well:

> The management of UTC is responsible for establishing and maintaining adequate internal control over financial reporting. Internal control over financial reporting is a process designed to provide reasonable assurance regarding the reliability of financial reporting and the preparation of financial statements for external reporting purposes in accordance with accounting principles generally accepted in the United States. Because of its inherent limitations,

internal control over financial reporting may not prevent or detect misstatements.Management has assessed the effectiveness of UTC's internal control over financial reporting as of December 31, 2006. In making its assessment, management has utilized the criteria set forth by the Committee of Sponsoring Organizations (COSO) of the Treadway Commission in Internal Control. (p. 50)

This letter is signed by all of the key UTC executives: the CEO, COO, vice president of finance, and vice president of accounting and finance.

While these internal auditors are employees of United Technologies, they function as surrogates for the outside CPA firm and support the external auditing efforts. UTC's outside CPA firm is PricewaterhouseCoopers, LLP. With the demise of Arthur Andersen, PricewaterhouseCoopers and KPMG have become the dominant CPA firms. These are both multinational CPA firms with offices in most parts of the world and thousands of partners.

Auditors ensure that transactions were recorded correctly. They verify the accuracy of the financial statements and the many estimates that were made by management. All publicly traded companies in the United States are required to have their financial statements audited. Most large private companies have their financial statements audited, as well. This process is becoming global, as it facilitates international transactions and ventures.

The Letter. The CPA firm writes a letter to the stockholders. Most companies' letters are the same, but they reveal some very interesting information about the accounting process. Here is a standard letter:

We have audited the accompanying consolidated balance sheet of ABC Company . . . and related consolidated statements of income, retained earnings . . . and cash flows for each of the three years. . . . These financial statements are the responsibility of the Company's management. Our responsibility is to express an opinion on these financial statements based upon our audit. We conducted our audit in accordance with auditing standards generally accepted in the United States. Those standards require that we plan and perform the audit to obtain reasonable assurance about whether the financial statements are free of material misstatement. An audit includes examining, on a test basis, evidence supporting the amounts and disclosures in the financial statements. An audit also includes assessing the accounting principles used and significant estimates made by management.

This letter has some very interesting features that provide insights into the accounting and audit processes. The first sentence makes the CPA firm's role very clear: It audited. The next statement confirms that the ABC Company is responsible for the numbers. The CPA firm expresses an *opinion* on the financial statements. This is a very simple term that has been the subject of an incredible amount of controversy over the years. The letter does not refer to a warranty, fact, or guarantee. That is why this letter is often called "the opinion letter." The CPA firm uses the term *assurance* later in the letter, just to reinforce its role.

Notice that the CPA firm examines the numbers "on a test basis." The accounting firm does not verify every item in the company's books. Instead, it takes samples: it selects a certain number of customers to confirm accounts receivable, selects a certain number of vendors to confirm accounts payable, and uses similar measures to confirm payroll, inventory, and all other significant (read material) items. The burden is on the company to prove that assets are listed at the lower of cost or market and that all other accounting principles have been adhered to.

The last statement in the letter confirms that the financials reflect *estimates*. Depreciation expense is based upon the estimated number of years that the machinery will last. Reserve for bad debts is an estimate, or projection of the portion of the accounts receivable that will not be collected. The pension fund calculation is based upon projections of how much money employees will have earned when they retire and how many employees will be eligible. These numbers are based on the best available information, but they are all nonetheless estimates.

After all of the accounting and auditing work has been done, the CPA firm will provide one of three responses. An *unqualified opinion* really means an opinion without qualification or reservation. It indicates that the company being audited has done a very good job in keeping its books and preparing its financial statements in accordance with generally accepted accounting principles.

A *qualified opinion* means that everything is fine, with one exception. The company and the CPA are generally in agreement, but they have "agreed to disagree" on one aspect of the presentation. This is usually an interpretation of a GAAP issue or the accounting for a single business event, such as the purchase or sale of a business. The letter will describe the auditors' position on the issue in question. If the client company is in serious financial trouble, to the point that its continuance as an ongoing business is in question, the audit letter will also discuss this issue.

No opinion or an *adverse opinion* results when the accounting books are in such disarray that the auditors cannot confirm the numbers. Control procedures may be poor or absent. Accounting irregularities will certainly trigger this result, as will a pattern of not adhering to GAAP. A major company does not change CPA firms casually. The relationship between the company and the accounting firm has been built up over many years and involves a considerable degree of cooperation and trust. If the CPA firm resigns or is asked to do so, this is usually evidence of severe disagreements over the accounting process or the reporting of results. The sudden, unexpected resignation of the chief financial officer or chief accounting officer (the controller or, in government and certain regulated industries, the comptroller) is often an indicator that something is wrong. Not always, but be alerted. It's much easier for the CPA firm to reassign accountants than to lose a client if personality or culture is an issue.

Footnotes

The footnotes to the financial statements are a critical part of the annual report presentation and also contain some useful information:

1. We can learn more about the company's acquisition, divesture, and strategic alliance efforts. There may be possible clues to the company's strategic direction. Prices of transactions are sometimes included.

2. More and more companies are providing an analysis of how they manage the risk associated with being global. This includes currency exchange rates, commodity prices, and interest rates. Some companies actually include in the annual report documentation of every conceivable risk that they may experience.

3. We can learn what lines of credit a company has and what interest rates it is paying on debt securities and earning on investments in marketable securities.

4. Many companies describe the legal, environmental, and regulatory issues that they face. Very interesting information about the tobacco lawsuits of the 1990s appears in Philip Morris's annual reports of that era.

5. From the segment reporting section, we can determine the key ratios for each of a company's businesses. This is an excellent way for you to focus on those segments against which you compete.

6. Executive compensation and huge severance packages paid to failed executives have frequently been on the front pages of the media during the 2008-2012 era of government bailouts and massive corporate bankruptcies. TheStreet .com is a very well known investment research and media company founded by Jim Cramer, famous for his daily stock market show on CNBC. That company's 2008 annual report actually defines severance packages for key executives, as follows:

With "Cause"

Without "Cause" or for "Good Reason"

Change of Control

Termination after Change of Control

Death or Disability

Non-renewal of agreement

The severance compensation ranges from nothing to a full year's salary, prorated bonus, benefits, and exercise of stock options. The company actually asks the stockholders to vote on the employment contracts of key executives, something that most boards of directors are unwilling to do.

Other Important Information in the Annual Report

1. Financial and statistical information for five or ten years is often included. This provides a valuable overview of the company's performance and the consistency of that performance. It is interesting to compare the 10-year history with the behavior of the U.S. and global economies during the same period. This may provide some indication of how economic events have affected the company and how it has dealt with this environment. The Johnson & Johnson annual report provides a wonderful example of this.

2. A list of the members of the management team and the board of directors is provided. Which executives are invited to join the board may provide an indication of the company's succession plans. Outside directors who are or were CEOs of other companies may become candidates for the top job at this company if the management team does poorly and an outside perspective is required.

3. We learn which board members belong to the various board committees. This will enable us to be sure that there is at least one CPA on the audit committee and that there are no full-time employees on the compensation committee.

4. Somewhere in the back of the annual report there appears a section with what appears to be routine information. It includes:

   ➤ The place and time of the annual meeting

   ➤ How to get a 10-K report

   ➤ How to contact various departments in the company with questions

   ➤ Whether the company has dividend reinvestment and direct stock purchase programs

   ➤ How to get additional information

These may not seem like startling bits of information, but gaining the right to receive this information required many years of effort on the part of many people. Company management used to be a "closed club" in many ways. Shareholders had very few rights other than the right to sell their shares if they were not happy with their investment. Over time, however, a group of people known as *shareholder activists* came into being. It would be reasonable to assume that the management team used much less friendly terms to describe these people. The current group of these instigators are usually hedge fund managers. They are the folks who take large positions in companies, ask for board seats, demand increased dividends and share buybacks, and sometimes even a change in management. For a long-term perspective on this movement, every businessperson should know about the Gilbert brothers, John and Lewis (discussed below).

The Gilbert Brothers: The Original Shareholder Activists

Background

If you saw the movie *Wall Street,* you saw Michael Douglas as Gordon Gekko browbeat the board of directors of a multinational company because the directors were arrogant and detached from the needs of the stockholders and the company. They were making big salaries and bonuses even though the company was not performing well. There were too many senior executives who were not doing much except consuming time and space. This is not make-believe. In fact, the role was modeled on two real-life people, John and Lewis Gilbert. Everyone who is in business and everyone who is interested in the stock market should know what they did.

Their Contribution

The Gilbert brothers were born early in the twentieth century in very financially comfortable circumstances. They dedicated their lives to having fun, making money, and creating an environment in which companies' boards of directors and senior management were actually accountable to their bosses, the shareholders. They were the original shareholder activists. Among the improvements that they caused or contributed are the following principles:

> - Members of the board of directors should actually own shares of stock in the company.
> - Stockholders should receive adequate notice of scheduled annual meetings.
> - Stockholders should receive audited financial statements before the annual meeting. Previously, meetings had some times been postponed because the financial statements weren't yet "available."
> - Annual meetings should be held in a location that is geographically convenient, so that some shareholders can actually attend. An issue in the Transamerica lawsuit, described later, was that the insurance company held its annual meetings in Delaware rather than in California, where its operations and many of its shareholders were located. The tradition of remote locations for annual meetings has been changed.
> - Shareholders can present resolutions for shareholder vote. In 1942, the Securities and Exchange Commission ruled that not only can shareholders present resolutions for a

vote, but their proposals must be circulated to other shareholders at company expense. The current practice is to
include the resolutions in the proxy statement and include
management's recommendation of a vote *for* or *against*
them.

> Shareholders can ask questions at annual meetings and
  actually expect that these questions will be answered. It
  was common in the 1930s for annual meetings to be filled
  with company employees who would shout down any
  stockholder who made an unfavorable comment. It was
  Lewis Gilbert's eviction from an annual meeting that accelerated the brothers' efforts at reform. He asked a pointed
  question of the chairman and was arrested and charged
  with disorderly conduct.

> Senior managers' compensation should be related to the
  profitability of the company. Putting executive pay in the
  proxy statement had its effect as early as 1937. The
  chairman of Bethlehem Steel had to take a pay cut after
  receiving pressure from the Gilberts. The event received
  headline coverage from *Business Week* and the *New York
  Times*. This remains an unresolved issue, however. Million-
  dollar severance payments to failed CEOs and billions of
  dollars in bonuses to retain employees of bankrupt
  companies are still headline news.

> Auditors are elected by shareholders, not by management.
  Auditors should be present at annual meetings to answer
  shareholders' questions. The concept of internal auditors
  who would assure the integrity of the company's financial
  information was promoted by Lewis Gilbert as early as the
  1930s.

> Stockholder proposals are included in proxy statements, as
  mentioned earlier. In 1945, the Gilbert brothers sued Trans-
  america Insurance Company because management refused
  to include in its proxy statement proposals that the Gilberts
  had made. The judge ruled, "A corporation is run for the
  benefit of its stockholders and not only for that of its

managers." This was a fundamental change in attitude and practice.

These issues seem somewhat obvious in this modern day of shareholder activism and the availability of seemingly unlimited amounts of information through the Internet. When Lewis and John Gilbert hit their full stride in the 1940s, the opposite was true. They are known to have annoyed more than one board chairman with their questions, stockholder resolutions, and challenges.

The Effort Continues

Many years ago, the brothers created a foundation, appropriately called Corporate Democracy, Inc. A team of 10 was organized that travels to many dozens of annual meetings, wherever and whenever they may be held. Meetings that can be reached only after multiple plane rides and car rentals are very rare these days, because of the Gilberts. In addition, Securities and Exchange Commission regulations have increased accountability, and the Internet has vastly expanded the availability of information. However, the effort continues, building momentum for a process that began many years ago.

One of the most significant improvements in shareholder rights relates to a company's treatment of security analysts, as opposed to those who are "just shareholders." Companies traditionally invited a select few analysts to very comfortable corporate retreats, where management would share its thoughts about the company's past performance and its expectations for the future of the business. This would be followed up with conference calls and other forms of communication with these select few. In fact, these analysts were often given information before it was made available to the general public. They could then advise their clients of critical developments before the general public was aware of them. When a public announcement was finally made, the clients of many of these analysts had already traded the stock. To prevent the perception and the fact that the favored few were privy to valuable, otherwise private information, companies now must invite everyone to listen in on their conference calls. Major developments, including financial information, are now announced to everyone at the same time, either through a press release or through an SEC filing. All of these improvements in disclosure have come about because of the original shareholder activists.

In reading the list and description of these reforms, you may be thinking, "Are you kidding? These are so obvious." However, we accept these practices as obvious only because the hard work of many people over a long period of time.

Modern-Day Activists

There are many contemporary corporate activists who have some similarities to the Gilbert brothers, but in many respects are quite different. John and Lewis Gilbert were not motivated by personal financial gain. It is not certain that they ever gained financially from their efforts. Instead, their focus was on corporate governance, or the management of public companies in ways that would ensure shareholder rights, fairness, and management accountability. The modern group of activists has been motivated by financial gain (many have exceeded a billion dollars in personal worth), yet their efforts have resulted in improved management accountability, better disclosure, and also an enhanced focus on governance.

The current notables include Wilbur Ross, Eddie Lampert, Nelson Peltz, and Carl Icahn. Their approach is to take sizable positions in companies whose assets are worth a lot more than the company's market capitalization (stock price × number of shares outstanding). With a sizable voting block and sometimes board seats, they force improvements in strategy, sometimes changes in senior management, a general overhaul of how the business operates, and maybe sale of the company. Wilbur Ross gains control of target companies and hires new management teams. Eddie Lampert got control of Sears and Kmart, concluding that the real estate they owned was worth more than the cost of buying a controlling interest in both mammoth companies. Unfortunately, he did this just before the real estate bubble burst in 2006, and he is still trying to make his strategy work.

Carl Icahn gained fame with a different approach. He is known as a pioneer of the strategy known as "greenmail" (just like blackmail). He would take large positions in underperforming companies, ridicule management's performance, and promise to remove the current management after he took control. To get rid of him and protect their jobs, the management would have their company buy back only his shares at a substantial premium to their current value. This diluted the value of most stockholders' shares, depleted the free cash on the company's balance sheet, and made Icahn a richer man as he disappeared from the scene. Greenmail made Icahn money while his presence caused major improvements by fearful managers. Carl Icahn did actually manage a business, TWA, for seven years in the late 1980s, and ended up selling its pieces. These days, his interests include Time Warner and Motorola, among many others.

If an activist is someone who identifies bad, underachieving management and causes improvements, then one of the most subtle players is Jim Cramer of the cable network CNBC. His daily stock market show includes a "wall of shame." On it he highlights CEOs whose companies are performing so poorly that the top person needs to go or as he says, "They need to retire to spend more time with their family." On his television show, Cramer says that he cannot benefit from the ownership of stock so he is never promoting a strategy for his own benefit.

The 10-K Report

The 10-K is an annual report that goes directly to the Securities and Exchange Commission. It contains all of the reports required by regulatory agencies that are contained in the annual report, and more besides. There is no public relations information or photographs. Some 10-K reports contain considerable biographical information about the directors and executives, similar to what is provided in the proxy statement.

The 10-K report of an Internet company that had had a series of particularly disappointing years described the future risks that the company faced in continuing in business:

- Uncertainties associated with the company's limited operating history
- Operating losses and the potential need for additional funds
- Unproven acceptance of the company's products in a developing market
- Dependence on continuing use of the Internet
- Reliance on advertising revenues and uncertainty concerning the adoption of the Internet as an advertising medium
- Dependence on a limited number of advertisers
- Operating in a new and highly competitive market, with low barriers to entry
- Variations in quarterly results of operations; seasonality
- The need to develop and maintain brand recognition
- Dependence on key personnel and a shortage of qualified information technology (IT) people
- The strain on the company's resources as a result of continued growth
- Inability to identify potential acquisitions and to integrate operations
- Inability to expand and manage international operations
- Dependence on content providers
- Dependence on strategic alliances
- Risk of capacity constraints and systems failures
- Online security risks
- Inability to protect intellectual property
- Liability for informational services
- Government regulation
- Concentration of stock ownership

➤ Volatility of stock prices

➤ The antitakeover provisions of Delaware corporate law

The full disclosure provisions of GAAP certainly have caused this company to put its cards on the table. It would be helpful if every company were this honest and forthright in assessing its future. The company also described in considerable detail how it was coping with each of these risks. It would be valuable to learn what your company and its competitors identify as the risks that might prevent them from being successful in the future. With full disclosure, the company is also minimizing the risk of lawsuits because the reader has been "warned."

The Proxy Statement

The proxy statement is the package of information that each shareholder receives as part of the annual meeting announcement. Because most shareholders do not attend the annual meeting, they are invited to vote by "proxy." This is a mail-in or Internet ballot that is essentially the same as an absentee ballot in national elections. Shareholders get to vote for:

➤ The annual contract with the CPA firm

➤ Members of the board of directors

➤ Proposals to change the corporate bylaws

➤ Executive stock option and incentive plans

➤ Proposals submitted by shareholders

The votes are always yes or no options, and the proxy almost always indicates the vote that is recommended by the board of directors. The proxy package also includes other information that is of great interest:

1. Notification of the fact that a list of all shareholders is available at corporate headquarters and at the annual

meeting. This is of special interest to shareholder activists like the Gilberts, who seek to arouse interest in a particular issue. It is also valuable to potential acquirers of the company, who need to communicate with shareholders to seek support for their efforts.

2. A list of the members of the board of directors, their affiliations, and their compensation. Board members may receive an annual retainer, a fee for each board meeting, a fee for each committee meeting, stock options, and deferred compensation. For Fortune 500 companies, this could amount to $100,000 or more annually.

3. The compensation package for each corporate officer, including deferred compensation and stock options. It is a very positive situation if every director and corporate officer has a stake in the success of the company, and if their rewards are commensurate with that success, or the lack of it.

4. A description of executive pension and severance packages. There has been considerable negative press concerning departed executives who were paid more for leaving involuntarily than they received when they were employed. The rationale is that their staying with the company would have been more expensive.

Other Sources of Information

There are three ways of obtaining a hard copy of an annual report. The first is from the company itself. The second is through a service provided by a company called Public Register. The Public Register Annual Report Service is accessed through Public Register's website (www.prars.com). The service provides the annual reports of thousands of companies, for free. The companies in the Public Register database are organized by industry and geography and are alphabetized, so finding the reports you want is easy and convenient. The reports can also be downloaded. The *Wall Street Journal* has a similar service.

The most comprehensive of these services is Morningstar Reports. Morningstar is a Chicago-based organization that is a leading provider of investment information, research, and analysis. It can easily be accessed through the Internet. For most companies, Morningstar's website provides:

- A description of the company's businesses
- A listing of its officers
- Three years of financial statements, including the income statement, balance sheet, and statement of cash flows, in considerable detail
- Selected financial ratios segmented by category:
  - Financial strength
  - Management effectiveness
  - Profitability

The management effectiveness ratios include return on equity and return on assets. Profitability ratios include gross profit percentage, operating margin, and return on sales.

The most interesting and helpful section of the report compares the ratios of the subject company with the average ratios for its industry. It is very helpful to use the web pages that provide the ratios of the subject company, industry averages, and the Standard & Poor's 500 companies. The benchmarking value of this information is extraordinary. The ratios are classified into these categories:

- Stock market information including the price/earnings ratio (P/E) and price/cash flow
- Growth rates of revenues and earnings
- Financial strength
- Profitability
- Management effectiveness
- Efficiency

There are approximately 50 ratios. To make the information even more valuable, if that were possible, at the end of the ratios section are the stock symbols of the other companies in the industry database.

The Securities and Exchange Commission

The Securities and Exchange Commission (SEC) is a federal government, executive branch agency responsible to the public for assuring fairness in the securities markets. It was formed by the Securities Exchange Act of 1934, known as the "truth in securities" law. This law, together with the Securities Act of 1933 that preceded it, requires public companies to provide investors with financial and other significant information about securities that are being offered to the public. These laws also prohibit deceit, misrepresentation, and fraud in the sale of securities.

Companies with assets of at least $10 million whose securities are held by more than 500 independent shareholders are required to file with the SEC. Registration provides the shareholders the information they need if they are to make informed investment decisions. Investors who lose money on their shares can seek to recover damages if they can prove that they based their investment decision on information that was misleading, incomplete, or inaccurate. All SEC filings are available on the Internet at the SEC website, www.sec.gov.

SEC rules also govern the solicitation of shareholder votes. Proxy statements must be filed with the SEC before the solicitation actually occurs.

Anyone who wishes to make a tender offer for more than 5 percent of a company's stock must also file with the SEC. A tender offer is an offer to purchase shares in large quantities. Tender offers are often announced in the *Wall Street Journal* in an advertisement called a "tombstone." Many individuals or companies that anticipate making an unfriendly tender offer (one that the management of the target company is expected to resist) often purchase 4.99 percent of the stock before the event. Once their holdings exceed

5 percent and their intentions become public, the stock price will move up. Therefore, the buyer will keep its holdings below the threshold until as late in the process as possible in order to keep its intentions a secret.

The securities laws also govern the actions of insiders. Anyone who has critical information that is not available to the general public, far beyond just company management, can be perceived as an insider. Insiders may certainly buy and sell shares, but they must notify the SEC of their transactions. This includes accountants, lawyers, secretaries, and even the printer who prints the financial statements. Most stock market websites provide information about management purchases and sales of company stock.

PART

Analysis of
Financial
Statements

CHAPTER SIX

Key Financial Ratios

R atios are mathematical calculations that the company can use to evaluate its performance. They help the company to determine whether trends are improving or deteriorating. They are calculated by comparing two numbers with each other. The most valuable use of ratios is to compare this year's ratios with the same ratios for the previous year, and also with the ratios of other companies in a similar business. Ratios also serve as goals for future performance.

Statistical Indicators

Many of us use statistical indicators, many of which are ratios, to monitor the business. These key indicators include:

- ➤ Output per labor hour
- ➤ Capacity utilization
- ➤ Market share
- ➤ Sales orders
- ➤ Average length of a production run

- ➤ Passenger revenue miles (airlines)
- ➤ Responses to mailings (direct mail)

Some of these productivity measures are immediate in nature. They can be monitored on an hourly or daily basis, and management can make immediate adjustments in response to them. These are very much "real-time" indicators.

These statistical indicators are very much the domain of internal management. While internal statistical information would certainly be interesting to outsiders and might be valuable to them, they have little or no access to this information. Interestingly, in the automobile business, information concerning units produced, units sold, and available inventory is public information. But this is an exception.

First-level line managers in both sales and operations require detailed statistical information on a regular basis and also very frequently. Operations supervisors fine-tune machinery, redeploy labor resources, and manage the logistics of inventory. Sales managers direct daily or weekly sales calls, deploy resources at trade shows, and determine immediate customer satisfaction. Senior managers don't require this degree of detail to carry out their responsibilities, and certainly not on an hourly, daily, or perhaps even weekly basis. The higher a manager's level of responsibility, the more an overview is the necessary perspective. This explains why, as managers progress through the organization's ranks, their concerns and perspectives become more financial and strategic.

Financial Ratios

Financial ratios provide more of an overview. They help management to monitor the company's performance over a period of time, perhaps a week or a month. In order to fully appreciate and properly use the financial ratios, it is important that the analyst:

- ➤ Understand the business and its products.
- ➤ Analyze the company's performance within the context of the economic climate.

- ➤ Be aware of the legal and regulatory issues that the company faces.
- ➤ Look at the ratios within the context of the competitive environment.
- ➤ Be knowledgeable about industry averages and ratio behavior.

People with a wide variety of interests use financial ratios to analyze the business. These include:

External

- ➤ Security analysts
- ➤ Potential and existing stockholders
- ➤ Bankers and other lenders
- ➤ Suppliers and their credit managers
- ➤ Competitors
- ➤ Regulators

Internal

- ➤ Board of directors
- ➤ Senior management
- ➤ Operations, sales, finance, human resources, and marketing
- ➤ Strategic planners

Each of these groups has its own perspectives and needs. Developing a marketing strategy requires an understanding of the company's financial ability to support growth. Suppliers assess the company's ability (not its willingness) to pay its bills in accordance with the agreed-upon credit terms.

Ratios must be evaluated within their context. The value of statistical indicators has been discussed. Many business and environmental factors have been identified. As mentioned previously, ratios are extremely valuable when they can be observed as part of a trend and also when they are compared with the same ratios for competitors.

Financial ratios can be divided into four major groupings:

1. Liquidity ratios
2. Working capital management ratios
3. Measures of profitability
4. Financial leverage ratios

There are many different ratios, and, for each, the exact definition may vary.

What follows is an extensive description of the key ratios, presented with very workable definitions.

Liquidity Ratios

Liquidity ratios measure and help in evaluating a company's ability to pay its bills on a regular week-to-week or month-to-month basis. There are two commonly used ratios that help to evaluate this, the current ratio and the quick ratio.

Current Ratio

The current ratio compares *current assets* with *current liabilities*. The specific ratio is:

$$\text{Current Ratio} = \frac{\text{Cash} + \text{Marketable Securities} + \text{Accounts Receivable} + \text{Inventory} + \text{Other Current Assets}}{\text{Accounts Payable} + \text{Bank (Short-Term) Debt} + \text{Accrued Liabilities} + \text{Other Current Liabilities}}$$

A current ratio below 1.0 means that current assets are less than current liabilities. This is a clear indication that the company has liquidity problems. However, a ratio in excess of 1.0 is not necessarily an indication that the company is sufficiently liquid. Higher is not necessarily better. The ratio may be high because the company has too much inventory or does a poor job of collecting its accounts receivable in a timely manner. Conversely, the ratio may be low because the company does not have or cannot afford the levels of inventory necessary to serve its customers in a competitive manner. Too much working capital is poor asset management; it is very expensive, can restrict cash flow, and inhibits the company's ability to grow and prosper.

An appropriate ratio can be intelligently developed by evaluating each individual component. The questions to be answered include:

➢ How much cash and near cash does the company need in order to pay its bills and manage its very short-term liquidity?

➢ What credit terms should the company offer its customers as part of its strategy to satisfy those customers?

➢ What levels of finished goods inventory are needed to serve the marketplace?

➢ How much raw materials and components inventory is required to ensure efficient supply chain management and thereby efficient production operations?

These and other questions need to be answered in order to develop the current ratio that the company should try to achieve. Usually a "range of desirability" is created to adjust for seasonality and peak periods. So, an example of the target ratio to ensure intelligent asset management might be 1.8 to 2.2. Companies that manufacture winter clothing, for example, will have high finished goods inventory in the September–November time frame as they prepare to sell to retail chains and then very high accounts receivable in the November–January period after that winter clothing is sold and the manufacturer is waiting for its customers' money.

Metropolitan Manufacturing Company Current Ratio

	2016	2015
Current Assets	$2,009,000	$1,645,000
Current Liabilities	$898,000	$619,000
Current Ratio	2.23	2.65

Metropolitan's current ratio has declined somewhat, although all of the absolute amounts have increased significantly. Bank debt and accounts payable have increased, primarily to finance the much higher levels of inventory. There is no evidence of a problem as long as the interest on the bank debt and the conditions or restrictions imposed by the loan are not too burdensome. The ratio itself remains at a reasonable level, especially for a manufacturing company.

Quick Ratio ("Acid Test" Ratio)

The quick ratio has the same purpose as the current ratio, but its time frame is more immediate. It is calculated the same way as the current ratio, except that it does not include inventory. So the ratio is:

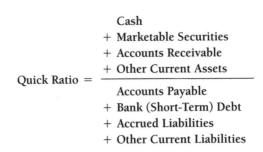

$$\text{Quick Ratio} = \frac{\begin{array}{l}\text{Cash} \\ +\ \text{Marketable Securities} \\ +\ \text{Accounts Receivable} \\ +\ \text{Other Current Assets}\end{array}}{\begin{array}{l}\text{Accounts Payable} \\ +\ \text{Bank (Short-Term) Debt} \\ +\ \text{Accrued Liabilities} \\ +\ \text{Other Current Liabilities}\end{array}}$$

In order to use the quick ratio as an analytical tool, it must be understood that there is a great difference in liquidity between accounts receivable and inventory. When a company is owed money by its customers (accounts receivable), it has already done its work; it has fulfilled its commitment to those customers by delivering fine products and services. Whatever money was necessary to accomplish this has already been spent. However—and it is a big however—in order to "liquefy" its inventory, the company must spend additional funds. Raw material and work in process inventory have not yet become finished product; there is still work to be done, and funds must be spent. While finished goods inventory has been completed, it has not yet been sold and delivered. Therefore, inventory is not a very liquid asset. It is classified as a current asset because it is expected to become cash in less than a year, possibly within six months or even two months. Thus, inventory is a liquid asset when compared to fixed assets and long-term investments, but it is not liquid in the way that marketable securities and accounts receivable are.

Given all this, a quick ratio in the vicinity of 0.8 is probably acceptable. Because a service business has no or little inventory, its current and quick ratios will be the same.

	2016	2015
"Quick" Assets	$780,000	$714,000
Liabilities	$898,000	$619,000
Quick Ratio	0.87	1.15

Metropolitan's quick ratio has declined from a level that was extremely comfortable to one that is merely comfortable. This presumes, of course, that the terms of the bank debt are not onerous and that the company's very heavy investment in inventory proves to be profitable. We will examine these issues further when we analyze working capital management.

Exceptions to Comfortable Levels

There are exceptions to our prior statement concerning comfortable levels for these liquidity ratios. If the current and quick ratios were in the comfortable range, but a substantial amount of the bank debt were due the next day, the future of the company would be in serious jeopardy. If the current ratio were in the comfortable range, but the finished goods inventory that it had on hand was not what the customers wanted at that time, then the company's ability to deliver product to its customers in a timely manner would be impaired, even though its current ratio was acceptable.

Ratios of Working Capital Management

These ratios and measures assist a company in evaluating its performance regarding the management of the credit function, as reflected in its accounts receivable, and also the management of inventory.

Days' Sales Outstanding

Days' sales outstanding (DSO) measures the average number of days that the company is taking to collect accounts receivable from its customers. The formula is:

$$\frac{\text{Annual Revenue}}{365} = \text{Average Revenue per Day}$$

$$\frac{\text{Accounts Receivable}}{\text{Average Revenue per Day}} = \text{Days' Sales Outstanding}$$

When a company extends credit terms, it gives its customers the opportunity to pay the company later rather than paying upon receipt of the company's products or services. So the customer has received excellent products and services, which it can now use for its own profitability, yet it did not have to pay at the time it received them. Credit terms are provided because giving credit helps to sell product. Extending credit gives the company a competitive advantage (and not doing so would probably put it at a competitive disadvantage).

If average days' sales outstanding is 43 days, that means that, on average, it is taking that many days to collect owed funds from the customer, from the date of the invoice to the date when the funds are collected. This should be measured against the credit terms of sale. If credit terms are 30 days, an average collection period of between 40 and 42 days should be perceived as acceptable. A collection period in excess of 50 days requires an examination of credit risk, the management of the credit process, and the future relationship with late-paying customers. Cash sales, if any, should be excluded from the calculation.

Metropolitan Manufacturing Company Days' Sales Outstanding

2016:

$$\frac{4,160,000}{365} = \$11,397 \qquad \frac{637,000}{11,397} = 56 \text{ days}$$

2015:

$$\frac{3,900,000}{365} = \$10,685 \qquad \frac{597,000}{10,685} = 56 \text{ days}$$

Assuming that Metropolitan's credit terms are 30 days, the company's accounts receivable are too high. The salespeople probably do not communicate these terms of sale clearly, if they communicate them at all, and collection procedures overall need to be improved. The company can add a "free" $11,397 to its bank account for each day that average days' sales outstanding is reduced. To analyze receivables management further, and to ensure that this conclusion is not distorted by statistical or seasonal aberration, the finance manager should also prepare an aging of accounts receivable.

Aging of Accounts Receivable

An aging of accounts receivable is a detailed listing of how long the company has been waiting for its customers to pay their bills. Generally, much of the accounts receivable balance may not yet be due, as the amounts will have been billed less than 30 days earlier. A considerable sum might be more than 45 days old, or more than 15 days overdue. The existence of bills that are more than 45 days old is a strong indicator of the customers' inability or unwillingness to pay, or of a feeling on the part of the customers that there is no particular pressure to do so.

The aging for Metropolitan Manufacturing Company as of December 31, 2016, is:

Less than 30 days	$280,000
30–45 days	196,000
45–60 days	135,000
Above 60 days	36,000
Total	$647,000

Metropolitan Manufacturing Company clearly has some problem receivables. The probability that the company will be able to collect those that are more than 60 days old is not great. The collections people in the accounting department clearly have challenges ahead if they are to get that money. The desirability of continuing to do business with those customers should be evaluated. Those customers whose receivables are in the 45- to 60-day range should receive some attention before they too become a worsening problem. Clearly, Metropolitan Manufacturing must change its attitude and those of its customers and begin to change some of its philosophies and practices.

Improving Management of Receivables

Reducing accounts receivable without jeopardizing sales volume is a most effective way for your company to improve cash flow. The following list gives some basic concepts of credit management that you should consider when you are negotiating with existing and potential customers. Not every idea will work in all situations, and some of these ideas may not be appropriate for your business at all. However, nothing will work if you don't try it.

1. *Credit is a sales tool.* Credit is granted to customers (permitting them to defer payment on merchandise that they already possess and are benefiting from) in order to motivate them to buy, and also in order to provide an additional competitive advantage. Put credit extension to the test. Will it affect whether or not the customer buys from

you? Will it lead the customer to buy more or to buy again? You are entitled to your money. You have earned it; you have spent money to make the sale, and you have provided the customer with the finest product or service of its kind.

2. *Never make the extension of credit automatic.* It is an integral part of the negotiating process. Train your sales, service, and delivery people to reinforce your credit strategies.

3. *Cheerfully extend credit if the customer asks for it and deserves it.* Ask the customer how much time he would like to have. Never extend credit for an automatic 30 or 60 days. Some customers will ask for less time than you would otherwise have granted. Customers will pay faster in order to maintain credibility with a very important supplier.

4. *Train your customers to pay fast.* Understanding that old habits die slowly, let the quality of your products and services, rather than your willingness to be a banker, be your customers' motive for buying from you.

5. *Get the clock ticking.* Agreed-upon credit terms should start the day the product is delivered, not the day when the invoice is mailed. Mail out invoices and statements more frequently. This is effective and is rarely noticed. Give the customer the invoice upon delivery, if possible. This reduces mailing expenses and makes the customer even more conscious of the responsibility to pay you fast.

6. *Never apologize for asking for your money.* You earned it by providing the finest products and services in your marketplace.

7. *Use technology to become more efficient and effective.* Invoices can be sent by e-mail. This alone saves a day or two compared to regular mail. Create a wire transfer mechanism whereby the customers' money is sent directly from their bank account to your company's bank account by wire. In their personal lives, many people are very comfortable paying their bills online. Your customers should pay this way, as well. These steps alone could save

two or three days of mail time. In addition, the time it takes to clear an out-of-state check will be reduced or eliminated.

8. *Save money by encouraging use of plastic.* Sending out an invoice for $50, $100, or even $200 is very expensive. The cost of invoicing and waiting for your money will shrink the profits on your sale. As an alternative, train the people who take phone orders to ask for a credit card on these and maybe even larger orders. This accelerates cash flow and the credit card fee is much less than the expense of an invoice. This clearly works on Internet orders.

9. *Search for opportunities to reduce your outstanding receivables.* Start slowly, with your new customers and your least desirable existing customers. Train them and those who work for you. Set yourself a six-month target and work toward it. Watch your bank account grow.

Inventory Turnover Ratio

The inventory turnover ratio provides a helpful overview of how effectively the company manages what may be its most valuable asset, its inventory. It describes the relationship between the cost of the product that was sold over the course of a year and the average inventory the company has maintained to support those sales. The formula for the inventory turnover ratio is:

$$\frac{\text{Cost of Goods Sold}}{\text{Average Inventory}} = \text{Inventory Turnover}$$

The resulting inventory turnover is expressed as follows:

> ➤ A turnover of 6 times translates to two months' inventory on hand, on average.
> ➤ A turnover of 12 times translates to one month's inventory on hand, on average.
> ➤ A turnover of 25 times translates to two week's inventory on hand, on average.

Of course, determining the appropriate amount of inventory for a company is much more complex than calculating this ratio, however valuable the ratio may be. The cost of inventory includes the following:

- Acquisition cost
- Transportation in and out
- Insurance
- Personal property taxes
- Warehouse overhead
- Labor expense
- Computer and related expenses
- Interest expense
- Physical deterioration
- Seasonal obsolescence

The cost of not having enough inventory or of having the wrong inventory includes:

- Unhappy customers
- Lost market share
- Higher production costs in the form of overtime or extra shifts
- Purchasing small quantities at short notice
- Paying extra for accelerated transportation

Finished Goods Inventory

Efficiency of production. The more efficient the production operations are, the less finished product a company must maintain. If operations are inefficient, the company will have to maintain a safety stock of finished product to ensure adequate customer service.

Made to Order/Made for Stock. A company that makes product without an order in hand will have to maintain extra inventory

because of the uncertainty associated with what products customers will require. A company that makes products in response to
specific orders, especially custom-designed products, will require
very little or no finished product on hand other than the inventory
that is being accumulated for shipment.

Forecasting Sales. The more effectively a company can predict
what its customers will want, the less finished product inventory it
will require. If there is great uncertainty concerning the customers'
needs and/or the directions that the markets will take, the company will have to keep more product on hand to assure customer
service.

Lead Times. The more notice the customers give the company concerning their product requirements, the less extra inventory the
company must maintain.

Low-value-added distributors must have on hand adequate
supplies of almost everything they sell in order to serve their customers competitively. In fact, their *value added* is precisely their
having everything on hand, ready for immediate delivery or
pickup. The ultimate low-value-added business is a supermarket.
It changes the nature or content of the product very little; all it
does is take crates of 12 or more items, open them, and put the
items on convenient shelves. Its value added is having 40,000 of
these products in one large, clean, comfortable room. And, a supermarket cannot run out of any essential items and hope to keep
its customers happy.

Number of Warehouses. Some companies serve their entire marketplace from a single warehouse. This is efficient if the marketplace
is geographically concentrated and can be properly served from
that one location. It can be effective even if the marketplace is national in scope if the product is very valuable or orders are very
large, making transportation a small part of the total cost. It can
also be effective if deliveries are not too time-sensitive, so that surface or ocean transportation can be used.

However, in the absence of any of these conditions, many businesses must use a network of warehouses, and perhaps even satellites of those warehouses, to serve their customers. If a company has warehouses at multiple locations, inventory levels relative to volumes sold will be higher than those of a business with a single warehouse. Safety stocks will also be higher to protect against transportation uncertainties. Minimum stocks of each product line must be stored in order to assure customer service. The offset to these higher costs and inventory levels should be more timely customer service and more efficient transportation, with products being transported in bulk over long distances from the factory to each warehouse rather than being transported individually from the central warehouse to each customer. A financial analysis of these alternatives should be provided to assure cost efficiency.

Raw Materials/Purchased Components

Product Diversity. The greater the variety of products that a company manufactures, the greater the amount of raw materials and components that it must keep on hand. For each type of product, the company must keep a minimum stock of materials and components on hand. This is especially true when the company's finished products have few, if any, components in common. Commonality of components contributes considerably to the minimization of inventory. An excellent example of this is the automobile industry. Many different models of cars actually have many components, including the frames, in common. In fact, there are many different models of cars that are actually the same car, despite their different appearances and perceptions of quality.

Supply-Chain Management. Technology has had a dramatic impact on inventory management and has resulted in drastic reductions in all forms of inventory. When a company goes online with its vendors, its product needs are automatically communicated to those vendors electronically. This shortens lead times, reduces mistakes, and accelerates the supply-chain process. Greater competitive intensity forces suppliers to provide faster delivery of high-quality products. Safety stock can be reduced when quality problems are reduced.

Concentration/Diversity of Vendors. Technology, especially the business-to-business capabilities of the Internet, has created both incredible supply-chain turmoil and incredible opportunity at the same time. Internet hookups between a vendor and its customers give that vendor a considerable competitive advantage, assuming that the vendor's performance remains at the highest quality levels. On the other hand, product websites and transportation logistics have created a nationwide supply market. Companies used to buy product from relatively local vendors. Now they can access the Internet and locate suppliers all over the country—some of which they did not know even existed. This reduces the difficulty of market entry. The intensity of the resulting competition, along with very dependable transportation support from companies like FedEx and UPS, leads to lower purchase costs, shorter lead times, and less inventory.

Metropolitan Manufacturing Company Inventory Turnover

	2016	2015	
Cost of Goods Sold	$2,759,000	$2,593,000	(line 25)
Ending Inventory*	$1,229,000	$931,000	(line 4)
Inventory Turnover	2.24 times	2.79 times	

*In general, the inventory figure used is the average of the beginning and ending inventories, or perhaps a running average. In this example, for simplicity, I have used ending inventory.

The inventory turnover ratio for Metropolitan Manufacturing Company is quite low. This could be because Metropolitan's business is very inventory intensive. Perhaps Metropolitan is a very vertically integrated manufacturing company. Or perhaps Metropolitan is a very service-intensive business with short lead times, resulting in a need for vast quantities of finished goods inventory. Or the company could be purchasing raw materials inventory in large quantities in order to take advantage of valuable quantity discounts. If this last explanation is true, Metropolitan's gross profit margins should be considerably above the average for its industry. Alternatively, the high levels of inventory could be the result of gross inefficiencies, ineffective purchasing, or overly optimistic sales forecasts that are not being achieved. Knowledge of Metropolitan's industry, its operations plan, and its competitors would be very valuable in reaching an accurate conclusion.

Measures of Profitability

These ratios assist management and others in the evaluation of the company's achievements. They focus on:

> Profitability achieved by the management team (net income)

> Assets invested in the business (gross assets)

> Revenue achieved by the business (top line sales)

> The funds that the owners have invested in the business (equity)

Some review of terms will be helpful. The line numbers used here and later in the chapter refer to the financial statements in Chapters 1 and 2 (Exhibits 1-1 and 2-1).

24. Revenue: The value of products and services sold.

25. Cost of goods sold: The cost of the labor, materials, and manufacturing overhead used to produce the products sold.

26. Gross profit: Revenue minus cost of goods sold.

27. General and administrative expenses: The cost of operating the company itself; this category includes all other support spending necessary to conduct the business.

28. Depreciation (and other noncash) expenses.

29. Net income before taxes.

30. Provision for income taxes.

31. Net income.

Another figure that does not appear in Exhibit 2-1, but that will be used in this analysis, is earnings before interest, taxes, and depreciation and amortization, known by its acronym, EBITDA. If it appeared in the exhibit, it would be line 27a, and it will be referred to that way here.

Our analysis of these numbers would be improved if we knew more about the Metropolitan Manufacturing Company. This we call "context." These items include:

- Its business and products
- The competitive environment
- Its degree of globalization
- Its budget for the year 2017 and its plans for subsequent years
- Legal and regulatory issues
- Whether it is a public or a private organization
- Its capacity utilization
- Its fixed cost/variable cost mix

The selection of the numbers to use in the analysis depends upon:

- What is being measured
- Who is doing the analysis
- Which managers are being measured
- Style and measurement attitude

Issues of Selecting Measurements

The board of directors of the company, as well as security analysts and credit analysts, is concerned with the performance of the company as a whole. Therefore, the measure that they use to evaluate companywide performance will probably be *net income*. Increasingly, however, security analysts, who are concerned with the company's performance within the context of the stock market, are using EBITDA.

Many analysts consider the provision for income taxes to be a passive expense. To begin with, the amount of federal income taxes shown on the company's income statement is not the actual amount of federal income taxes that the company paid. It is essentially the corporate tax rate, currently 34 percent, multiplied by the amount of net income before tax. As a result, many analysts use the pretax amount to measure profitability.

Many companies enjoy profitability in their international operations and also in their exporting from the United States. Of those, quite a few of these "American" companies are technically domiciled outside of the United States in what the IRS and others call "tax havens." Others actually invoice international customers through these low tax havens, thereby avoiding U.S. corporate taxes. All of these companies, regardless of their tax strategy, report a provision for income tax of 34 percent, the American corporate tax rate. This is one of the major reasons why analysts use EBITDA, believing that using a net income amount distorts a true analysis of the company's performance.

Analysts are often very concerned with and focus on the operating cash flow that was generated by the business. To look at this, they often use EBITDA. EBITDA is also used to evaluate the performance of those who manage individual businesses, strategic business units, and individual divisions and subsidiaries (in addition to the previous tax discussion). The rationale is that the managers of these entities are not responsible for, and therefore need not be concerned with, taxes and the income and expenses associated with corporate financings, i.e., interest income and interest expense. They are evaluated on those results for which they are responsible, and over which they have considerable control. Hence, operating cash flow is used as the metric, best defined as EBITDA.

To measure the performance of an individual product, gross

profit should be used. The resulting ratio is the gross profit percentage, calculated as follows:

$$\frac{\text{Gross Profit}}{\text{Revenue}} = \text{Gross Profit Percentage}$$

For Metropolitan Manufacturing Company in its entirety, this
is:

	2016	2015	
Gross Profit	$1,401	$1,307	(line 26)
Revenue	$4,160	$3,900	(line 24)
Gross Profit Percentage	34%	34%	

It should be noted that in this discussion, gross profit and gross
margin are considered to be synonymous terms and are used interchangeably. Some companies differentiate the two, which is an
issue that we will discuss later when we deal specifically with product profitability analysis.

A gross margin of 34 percent is a considerable achievement
for a manufacturing company. This suggests that the company is
providing some value added through its business. A warehouse
distributor might have gross margins in the 20 to 25 percent range,
while a manufacturer of high-end medical products, pharmaceuticals, or computer chips might enjoy margins of as much as 60 to
70 percent on some of its products. We should note, however, that
despite an additional investment in inventory of $298,000 in 2016,
Metropolitan's gross margin did not improve.

Return on assets (ROA) measures the profitability of the company relative to the total amount of assets the owners have invested in the business. These assets include working capital (cash,
marketable securities, accounts receivable, and inventory), tangible assets (capital equipment and land and buildings), and financial assets (long-term marketable securities, subsidiaries, and
intangible assets). The equation for return on assets is:

$$\frac{\text{Net Income}}{\text{Assets}} = \text{Return on Assets}$$

In addition to measuring the overall performance of the company, as return on assets does, return on equity (ROE) includes a measurement of the company's ability to use borrowed funds (financial leverage) effectively as well as the owners' money (stockholders' equity). This will also affect the company's ability to attract new investors. Without debt, a company's ROA and ROE will be the same. The more debt is successfully used to expand the business, the greater the improvement in return on equity compared with return on assets will be. However, excessive reliance on borrowed funds involves considerable risk, as we will see later when we discuss financial leverage. The formula for return on equity is:

$$\frac{\text{Net Income}}{\text{Stockholders' Equity}} = \text{Return on Equity}$$

Technological progress over the past ten years has drastically changed the perception of the concept "investing in the business." As we have stated elsewhere, an investment is the exposure of cash and other resources in the business to achieve stated profitability and other business goals. In accounting, an investment is the purchase of fixed assets. Most investments in the past 10 years have been in software and scientific research. These successful initiatives have dramatically improved productivity and profitability. For better or worse, the traditional ROA and ROE ratios do not measure these well.

Return on sales measures the overall operating efficiency of the company. Among the questions that it answers are: Is the production facility operating effectively? Are the administrative departments performing their responsibilities efficiently? As the company focuses its product mix towards more high-value-added, higher-margin products, the return on sales ratio should also improve. The equation for return on sales is:

$$\frac{\text{Net Income}}{\text{Revenue}} = \text{Return on Sales}$$

Metropolitan Manufacturing Company Operating Performance

Return on Assets:

		2016	2015
$\dfrac{\text{Net Income}}{\text{Assets}}$	=	$156,000 / $3,202,000*	$190,000 / $2,863,000*

*Year-end amounts are used.

Return on Assets	4.9%	6.6%

We can readily observe that not only has Metropolitan's net income actually declined in dollar amounts, but its ROA has declined even more severely as a result of the increase in the company's asset base.

Return on Equity:

		2016	2015
$\dfrac{\text{Net Income}}{\text{Stockholders' Equity}}$	=	$156,000 / $2,004,000	$190,000 / $1,894,000
ROE		7.8%	10.0%

Metropolitan's ROE has also declined. Notice that the company's ROE is greater than its ROA because of its use of financial leverage (borrowed funds). This calculation, for simplicity, uses end-of-year balances. We also used these for the ROA calculation. Either is correct and accurate as long as the numbers used are consistent from year to year.

Metropolitan is reinvesting a considerable portion of its profits in the business rather than distributing most of the profits to its owners in the form of cash, as can be seen from the substantial increase in the retained earnings number (line 21) on the balance sheet. This is a very positive sign. Also, line 33 on the income statement tells us exactly how much of the profits were reinvested in the business. In 2016, this amount was $110,000 out of a total net income of $156,000. The difference is explained by a cash dividend payment of $46,000.

Management/owners reinvesting a sizable portion of the company's net income in the business is a very positive sign because it demonstrates their confidence in the business. It also indicates that while the management recognizes the need to modernize and expand the business, it does not want to rely too heavily on debt to finance the company's growth. Instead the managers are willing to use reinvested profits as part of the financing. Unfortunately, one short-term result of this decision may be, as happened here, a decline in ROE, and this may be perceived as negative. Had the net income stayed flat at $190,000 rather than declining, ROE would still have gone down, but not by as much as what was reported.

Therefore, companies sometimes face the dilemma of having to choose between the long-term benefits of expansion and modernization and the appearance of more favorable short-term results. Metropolitan's owners were willing to take the longer-term view. If this were a public company, they would have to explain their decision to the Wall Street crowd.

Return on Sales:

		2016	2015	
Net Income		$156,000	$190,000	(line 31)
Revenue	=	$4,160,000	$3,900,000	(line 24)
ROS		3.75%	4.9%	

Metropolitan's financial ratios clearly indicate declining performance. There are several possible explanations:

➤ Intense competition causing pricing pressure and declining margins

➤ Operational inefficiency

➤ Spending to prepare for future strategic moves

➤ Too small and in too many businesses compared with stronger competitors

> Aging technology
> Secular decline of its products

If reduced prices and/or volume were the cause of the decline in the ratios, we would normally expect gross profit margins to have declined as well. However, the gross profit margin did not decline, but remained constant at 34 percent. This could still be the explanation if the company reduced its manufacturing costs commensurately, as evidenced by lower cost of goods sold. Quantity discounts stemming from larger-quantity purchases of raw materials and purchased components could have contributed to maintenance of the margins. This probably did happen, since inventory levels were much higher and inventory turnover was much lower. So perhaps, the company protected its 34 percent gross margins through inventory purchases. While we consider these issues, let's not lose sight of the fact that revenue did increase by more than 6 percent between 2015 and 2016 (line 24). It would be very helpful if we knew whether the increase in revenue was explained by price changes, volume changes, product mix changes, additions of new products, or a combination of these. This is critical information that typical financial reports may not provide, but should.

Notice that annual depreciation expense increased only slightly between 2015 and 2016 (line 28), even though the company made capital expenditures amounting to $34,000 (line 41). This suggests that the capital expenditures probably involved replacement of assets rather than expansion. If there had been an expansion, annual depreciation expenses would have increased.

General and administrative expenses increased appreciably between 2015 and 2016 (line 27). The backup detail would tell us whether this spending was an investment in the company's future, such as expanding the sales organization or increased spending on research, or whether it was additional spending on important, but not critical, added staff.

Financial Leverage Ratios

Borrowing funds to finance expansion or modernization is a very positive strategy if the terms of the loan are not too burdensome. We certainly don't want the interest rate to be too high. Perhaps more important, we want the cash flow benefits of the investments to be received before the debt becomes due. Many companies have run into financial problems because their bank debts came due before their investment projects achieved their forecasted benefits. In such cases, when the loans come due, the company has yet to generate the cash flow needed to repay them, and as a result, it finds itself in a very uncomfortable financial position. The term of the loan is usually more critical than the actual interest rate paid. If a company can achieve an after-tax return on investment of 25 percent on a project that will reach fruition in three years, whether the cost of the money needed to finance that project is 6.0 percent or 6.5 percent, is not going to change the decision to invest in the project as long as the loan has a maturity of more than three years. If the financing is a one-year bank loan, the company will not have the cash to repay it and may be forced to cut back the project and reduce expenses at exactly at the wrong time. It will probably be able to refinance that loan with the bank, but under terms and conditions that are favorable to the bank. The company will have few options. So while the cost of funds is important, you should focus on the repayment schedule, as well.

Debt/Equity Ratio

The debt/equity ratio measures risk from the perspective of both the company and existing and potential lenders. The primary risk to the company is that both principal and interest payments on debt are fixed costs. They must be paid even if the company's business and its cash flow decline. The other risk to the company is that if its ratios decline, it might violate its loan agreements. This might trigger higher interest rates, or worse, the bank requiring immediate repayment of the loan.

$$\frac{\text{Long-Term Debt}}{\text{Stockholders' Equity}} = \text{Debt/Equity Ratio}$$

Short-term bank debt is also a source of financial risk. Repayment of this debt is also a fixed cost, and its due date is more immediate than that of long-term debt. Remember that short-term debt is due in less than one year. Some analysts redefine the debt/ equity ratio to include bank debt, as follows:

$$\frac{\text{Bank Debt} + \text{Long-Term Debt}}{\text{Stockholders' Equity}} = \frac{\text{Funded Debt}}{\text{Stockholders' Equity}}$$

Funded debt refers to funds of all maturities borrowed from financial institutions. For most manufacturing companies, a debt/ equity ratio of more than 0.5 is perceived to be on the borderline of being risky. This would not be true if the company were a public utility or a very high-quality commercial real estate company. For manufacturing or service businesses, a funded debt/equity ratio in excess of 0.6 or 0.7 to 1 is interpreted as definitely approaching the "risky" stage.

Most private equity transactions, especially when a public company is taken private, involve a debt/equity ratio in excess of 5:1. These are very risky situations with high degrees of financial leverage. There are two circumstances that mitigate this risk. The first is that the subject companies usually generate a lot of cash and will generate more after layoffs and other efficiencies. The second is that very often the providers of the debt financing and the equity investors are the same organizations. They use their funds to finance the acquisition via debt because being repaid their principle is a tax-free event.

As the U.S. economy entered a very high-risk phase in the 2007–2009 time period, debt ratios of 1:1 and 2:1 had the appearance of being somewhat safe, at least within the context of companies with debt/equity ratios in the range up to 5:1 or worse. When the economy essentially crashed in late 2008 into early 2009, lenders went to the other extreme, becoming extremely very risk-averse. Credit availability was severely limited, and interest rates approached the range of 3 to 4 percent, if you could find funding at all. The only companies that were viewed positively during this period were those that were cash-rich and relatively debt-free. These included Apple, Dell, Oracle, and Microsoft.

In the 2011–2014 time period, companies expanded success-fully but usually in high-value-added businesses. Much of this expansion was accomplished with outsourced resources, minimiz-ing the need for debt financing. The higher-margin businesses have generated rather than consumed considerable cash to the point that by early 2015, companies had accumulated more free cash and had less debt perhaps than ever before.

Interest Coverage

This describes the cushion that the company has between the amount of cash it generates before interest expense and taxes and the amount of interest it must pay on its debt. This margin of safety is usually prescribed by the lending institutions as a condition of making the loan. The desired coverage ratio is based upon:

> The quality of the assets used as collateral, if any
> The profitability history of the company and its industry
> The predictability of the company's earnings

The greater the predictability and certainty of the company's earn-ings and the higher its growth, the lower the required interest cov-erage ratio will be. The figure used to measure the amount of cash available to pay interest expense is EBITDA.

$$\frac{\text{EBITDA}}{\text{Interest Expense}} = \text{Interest Coverage}$$

Sometimes the company is required to make regular payments of principal along with the interest. The payment of principal plus interest is called *debt service.* Such payment structures are exactly the same as the monthly payments that individuals make to the bank on a home mortgage, which include both principal and interest. When a company is required to repay its bank in this manner, some analysts and financial institutions will calculate the coverage ratio to include the principal payments as well as the interest. This is called *debt service coverage*. Still another version of this ratio also includes lease payments on the premise that long-term leases are in fact a form of equipment financing. Using the same version consistently once the methodology has been selected is very important.

Metropolitan Manufacturing Company Financial Leverage Ratios

Debt/Equity:

	2016	2015	
Long-Term Debt	$300,000	$350,000	(line 17)
Stockholders' Equity	$2,004,000	$1,894,000	(line 22)
Debt/Equity Ratio	15%	18.5%	

$$\frac{\text{Long-Term Debt}}{\text{Stockholders' Equity}} =$$

Metropolitan's debt/equity ratio is very low. A ratio below 50 percent would probably be perceived as comfortable. Also, notice that Metropolitan paid off $50,000 in long-term debt. We know that this was voluntary because, by definition, long-term debt is not due in the upcoming year. Not only is low debt a favorable condition from a risk perspective, but the lenders will look upon reinvested net income as a very positive event. Metropolitan's interest rate is probably not too high.

Interest Coverage:

$$\frac{\text{EBITDA (line 27a)}}{\text{Interest Expense}} = \frac{\$368,000}{\$48,000\ [8\% \times (\$300,000 + \$300,000)]}$$
$$= 7.7\ \text{times}$$

An interest coverage of 4 to 5 times is considered acceptable. A coverage ratio of 7.7 times is well within the comfort level. When this information is combined with a debt/equity ratio of 15 percent, it appears that Metropolitan Manufacturing is not at all at financial risk. It certainly has the capacity to borrow more funds.

Debt/Equity Ratio and Return on Equity

Exhibit 6-1 clearly demonstrates the risks and rewards that companies experience as they increase their levels of debt. The reward is an improved return on equity. The risk is higher interest expense and debt service requirements that become increasingly difficult to meet.

Using earnings before interest and taxes (EBIT), this company is achieving a return on assets of 20 percent, as follows:

$$\frac{\text{EBIT}}{\text{Assets}} = \frac{\$200,000}{\$1,000,000}$$

To simplify the example, we make the following assumptions:

The interest rate is 10 percent.
The tax rate is 50 percent.

The interest coverage calculation is shown in Exhibit 6-1.

The *Return on Equity* calculation is:

$$\frac{(\text{EBIT} - \text{Interest})/2 = \text{Net Income}}{\text{Stockholders' Equity}}$$

The *Interest Coverage Ratio* is:

EBIT/Interest Expense

1. $\dfrac{(\$200,000 - 0) = \$200,000}{\$1,000,000} = 20\%$

2. $\dfrac{(\$200,000 - 10,000)/2 = \$95,000}{\$900,000} = 11\%$ $\$200,000/\$10,000 = 20.0$ times

3. $\dfrac{(\$200,000 - 30,000)/2 = \$85,000}{\$700,000} = 12\%$ $\$200,000/\$30,000 = 6.7$ times

6. $\dfrac{(\$200,000 - 90,000)/2 = \$55,000}{\$100,000} = 55\%$ $\$200,000/\$90,000 = 2.2$ times

For a given level of earnings before interest and taxes, the more debt the company takes on in its capitalization structure, the greater the return on equity will be. However, the higher the debt/equity ratio, the greater the possibility that a downturn in earnings

Exhibit 6-1. How Debt Affects ROE

EBIT	Assets	Debt/Equity	ROE	Interest Coverage
1. $200,000	$1,000,000	0	10%	—
2. $200,000	$1,000,000	100/900	11%	20.0 times
3. $200,000	$1,000,000	300/700	12%	6.7
4. $200,000	$1,000,000	500/500	15%	4.0
5. $200,000	$1,000,000	700/300	22%	2.9
6. $200,000	$1,000,000	900/100	55%	2.2

will leave the company unable to meet its interest payment obligation. If a company with the capital structure shown in line 1 has a severe earnings downturn, this will cause extreme unhappiness among management and shareholders. But the company will still remain in business. If a company with the capital structure shown in line 6 experiences a similar earnings downturn, it will be in default on its loans.

Companies with very predictable, high-quality earnings can afford the risk of a high debt/equity ratio. This is especially true if they have a considerable amount of fixed assets to provide collateral for the loans. Economic conditions and current events aside, examples are commercial real estate and power utilities. Start-up and high-tech research companies often have no earnings at all, or at best very erratic earnings. They generally do not qualify for loans from financial institutions, and in fact depend on venture capital as a major source of financing.

The economic turmoil of the 2008–2009 period worked against the exact type of investment that generally was accustomed to having the greatest level of financial leverage, real estate. Between 1995 and 2005, many companies and individuals purchased real estate with very low down payments. As real estate inflation created a real estate bubble, those with 90 percent or higher debt levels made huge amounts of money if they sold the properties soon after purchasing them. A 20 percent return on assets with 90 percent debt financing produced a 200 percent return on equity. This became known as

flipping, where the properties were sold soon after they were purchased. Those who participated in this financial equivalent of musi-
cal chairs were very successful until the music stopped and there
were no more buyers. Some of those who were left holding properties lost everything. In the United States, the term *underwater* is
used to describe the situation where the mortgage on the property
exceeds the value of the property, if a buyer could be located.

As of 2015, many of the properties that went underwater in 2008
have still not recovered, even to a breakeven point. A new industry
emerged in 2010, as private equity firms purchased thousands of
single-family homes that were loan-defaulted, from the banks that
sadly held the paper. These properties were then rented out to families that had lost their homes in 2008. Because new home construction in the 2014–2015 time period was far below levels previously
achieved prior to 2008, the private equity firms are now in the process of selling off this real estate, usually at a great profit.

Revenue per Employee

This is a very valuable ratio that does not fit into the other categories we have discussed in this chapter. It is calculated as follows:

Annual Corporate Revenue / Total Employees

This an overall measure of the company's performance, efficiency,
profitability, and the value-added nature of its business.

To explore this issue, we examine the experience of one very
successful high-quality company, Johnson & Johnson. They produce pharmaceuticals, medical products, and a wide variety of
consumer products, all on a global scale.

In 2001 Johnson & Johnson required 101,000 employees to produce $32 billion in annual revenue. In 2011, 118,000 employees
produced revenue of $65 billion. In 2001 this represented a reve-
nue per employee of $317,000. In 2011 the equivalent number was
$550,000 per employee. This represents a doubling of revenue with

less than an 18 percent increase in employees over the 10-year period. What does this mean?

Revenue per employee is an all encompassing metric that is reflective of every aspect of the business. It can be improved by:

> Raising prices (but global competition inhibits this)
> Economies of scale (achieving more revenue with the same productive capacity)
> Becoming more efficient
> Improving the product mix (toward the most profitable businesses)
> Outsourcing to others who can do it better (mostly in the United States)
> Investing in technology
  • to become even *more* efficient
  • to accelerate throughput by creating capacity and reducing cost
  • to reduce working capital investment

Johnson & Johnson had revenue per employee of approximately $550,000; we reached this number by dividing its annual revenue by the total number of employees ($65 billion / 118,000 = $550,847)

Had Johnson & Johnson remained at revenue per employee of $317,000 (its prior experience), it would have required—using our same formula—205,047 employees ($65 billion / $317,000 = 205,047 employees). They would have needed the full 205,000 employees *had productivity not improved.* But it did, dramatically—and because of the many improvements, the company actually had only 118,000 employees, a savings of approximately 80,000 employees. The additional expenses that Johnson & Johnson would have incurred would have essentially destroyed its profitability. Most corporations have had similar achievements over the years, although Johnson & Johnson's performance is exceptional.

Did Johnson & Johnson create jobs? Yes it did. Approximately

18,000 new employees during these ten years. How did their im-proved employee productivity impact our economy?

The 80,000 additional workers would have driven up wages and their inflationary impact. Its corporate profits (and resulting tax payments) would have essentially been eliminated. Its ability to compete internationally would have been severely impaired. It would not have developed and/or purchased large amounts of new technology.

Now multiply this experience by the one thousand companies represented by the Fortune 1000. This provides a good description of our current economic situation and its near-term future.

The loss of some jobs in recent years has not resulted from the recession or from U. S. government economic policies. The recession certainly caused serious problems but it also accelerated a secular trend that was already well in place. This "loss" (really the absence of part of the theoretical gain) is the result of our econ-omy's incredible advancement in the use of technology and its im-proved management methods that together have led to greater efficiency and profitability.

When you take the ratio matching test in Exhibit D, note the differences among the companies in their revenue per employee ratios. They are very different among industries from as low as $200,00 per employee (supermarkets, lower end retail stores) to over a million dollars per employee for oil drilling and refineries. The one clear conclusion for using this as a benchmark (and you should) is that for your company, it should improve every year.

Ratios: Quick and Dirty

Here are four ratios to look at if you want to scan the financials, get a quick overview of the story they tell, and then later, at your leisure, do all of the detailed ratio calculations.

The current ratio: If it is less than 1.0, the company is probably having liquidity issues and is having difficulty paying its bills. If, however, the ratio is greater than 1.0, as we said earlier in this chapter, no significance can be attached.

Days' sales outstanding (DSO): If it is more than 60 days and getting longer, the company is having serious cash flow issues and is probably hesitant to pressure its customers for payment out of fear of losing customers.

Gross profit: If the gross profit percentage is declining, inefficiencies in production might be getting worse. If the percentage is declining but revenue is growing, the company is using selling price to get more business. If the percentage is improving but revenue is flat or declining, the company is improving cash flow by getting rid of its least desirable businesses. None of these are desirable.

Debt/equity ratio: If this ratio (long-term debt divided by equity) is less than 1.0 maybe up to 1.5, the company is not seriously in debt as long as it is growing. A ratio higher than 2.0 implies that the company will have to constrain investing to get the cash to pay off debt. This is more severe if the current ratio is less than 1.0.

CHAPTER SEVEN

Using Return on Assets to Measure Profit Centers

The use of return on assets is extremely valuable in the management of profit centers. A profit center is a business entity that is dedicated to a specific market, distribution channel, or set of customers. It has its own strategy and perhaps even its own business model, the one that is best suited to making that type of business successful and profitable. These profit centers may be called *strategic business units* (SBUs). Each has its own balance sheet, for which the unit's management is responsible.

These businesses need not be legal entities, nor do they need to have complete balance sheet responsibility. In many cases, SBUs are responsible only for the asset side of the balance sheet. The corporate parent remains responsible for the liabilities and any stockholder issues. The SBU's mandate is to achieve a profit and to use the assets for which it is responsible with maximum effectiveness.

The analytical model for return on assets that we are going to use is called the DuPont formula. Its roots go back at least 75 years. But its age does not diminish its value. In fact, its durability says much about its usefulness. The formula can be found in the archives of the DuPont Chemical Company. However, like most analytical techniques, it was probably an adaptation of other formulas that existed before its time. Nothing is totally new. Techniques and formulas evolve and are adapted over time to take advantage of newer ideas and business developments. The formula for return on assets (ROA) is:

$$\text{ROA} = \frac{\overset{(4)}{\underset{(3)}{\text{After-Tax Cash Flow (ATCF)}}}}{\text{Revenue}} \times \frac{\overset{(2)}{\text{Revenue}}}{\underset{(1)}{\text{Assets}}} = \frac{\overset{(5)}{\text{ATCF}}}{\underset{(6)}{\text{Assets}}}$$

It is summarized here, and we will then analyze it in detail.

1. Assets: The profitability of any business depends on how much money is invested in the business.
2. Revenue: The amount of revenue that is generated with those assets.
3. Revenue (again): The represents the same amount of revenue generate.
4. After-tax cash flow: How much cash remains after taxes and all expenses are paid.

In the calculation of ROA, revenue (#2) and revenue (#3) cancel out resulting in the simplified ROA formula:

$$\text{ROA} = \frac{\overset{(5)}{\text{After Tax Cash Flow}}}{\underset{(6)}{\text{Assets}}}$$

Assets

The profitability of any business is certainly affected by the amount of assets that are dedicated to that business. These assets include cash, accounts receivable, inventory, and fixed assets.

Cash

The size of the working cash balances needed by the business depends on its managers' overall ability to predict and manage cash inflows and outflows. In some larger companies, profit centers do not manage their cash balances at all. Instead, cash is consolidated at the corporate level to provide a maximum return on the cash invested. The SBUs will be provided with cash as needed.

Accounts Receivable

What are the credit terms that the SBU offers when it sells its products or services to its customers? The answer to this question depends on the type of business the SBU is in and the competitive environment. The accounts receivable on the SBU's books will also be affected by how well the SBU communicates these credit terms to its customers and how effectively it enforces those policies.

Inventory

There are a multitude of issues that affect this investment, including supply-chain management, how vertically integrated the operation is, and how efficiently the operation is run.

The degree of vertical integration refers to how much of the overall production process is done by the company itself rather than being outsourced. The more vertically integrated the business is, the greater the amount of the value-adding process that is performed by the company. A vertically integrated oil company drills for petroleum, owns and operates the pipelines and refineries, stores the finished product, and has a major chain of retail gas stations on our nation's highways. In contrast, there are companies that own and operate chains of retail gas stations, purchasing the gasoline they sell from outside sources—perhaps from distributors, but often from the fully integrated oil companies. (Yes, they may buy from their competitors.) Generally, with some exceptions, the more vertically integrated the company's operations are, the more inventory investment it will have for longer periods of time.

Fixed Assets

The previous discussion of vertical integration discussion also applies to the business's investment in fixed assets. A company that is vertically integrated will require a tremendous investment in fixed assets and a commitment to maintaining them.

The type of business a company is in and how the company chooses to conduct that business will also greatly affect its investment in fixed assets. A three-shift operation requires less equipment than a two-or one-shift operation producing the same amount. The question, then, is: Why would a company run a one-shift operation, with all the extra equipment it requires, when it can operate with less equipment on a three-shift basis? The answer is that it would not unless other factors were involved.

A three-shift operation is most applicable to a machine-driven mass-production operation where the products are the same or similar and value-added labor input is not that critical. Examples are chemical, steel, and paper companies. A business that requires very highly skilled labor or that requires extensive supervision may be most profitable if it runs a one-shift operation. There may not be enough high-quality labor or supervision available to operate around the clock. Custom-designed products require considerable management attention. Also, the businesses for which around-the clock operations are desirable are often those for which it is prohibitively expensive to stop the machines, and so they must run continuously. A steel furnace cannot be economically shut down at 5 p.m. and restarted the next morning. If a chemical plant were shut down, it would take weeks to clean up the kettles before they could be restarted, and it could be done that quickly only if the exact same mixture was being produced.

Three-shift operations can be very efficient if the quality and efficiency of the process is consistent. When very highly skilled workers are required, the efficiency and quality of the work done on the second and third shifts might be unacceptable. Every factor affecting the decision to run a one-, two-, or three-shift operation will have an impact on the product's profit margin. It is in evaluating this issue and making this and other similar decisions that the DuPont formula is so valuable, as we shall see.

The 2015 automobile manufacturing business is highly technologically sophisticated, employing advanced technology and robotics. Because production operations are so technology-driven, these manufacturing companies are able to use a three-shift operation with great success. They also avoid the inefficiencies associated with a one-shift operation. The old automobile manufacturers were notorious for their inconsistent quality. When operations were labor-driven, quality was highest on cars made Tuesday to Thursday and lowest on cars made on Fridays. Friday was the day of highest labor absenteeism, when temporary, less skilled workers were used. The absenteeism manifested itself in quality differentials, well known to senior management and eventually the public.

Revenue

Given the assets dedicated to the profit center, how much business can it generate? The issues here include efficiency, how much value added is built into the product, and how much of the process is outsourced. Companies that outsource the total production process, such as warehouse distributors, can expand their revenues significantly with minimal additional investment in fixed assets. Only inventory and accounts receivable will need to be increased to produce the higher revenue.

After-Tax Cash Flow (ATCF)

Given the revenue generated by the business, how much profit is achieved? This is related to the type of business, economies of scale, capacity utilization, and operating efficiencies. It is greatly affected by the degree of vertical integration and value-added processes.

Return on Assets: Its Components

The return on assets ratio is really a combination of two ratios: revenue/assets and ATCF/revenue.

Revenue/assets is called *asset turnover.* It is conceptually the same as inventory turnover, except that it encompasses all assets. The second ratio, ATCF/revenue, is known as the *margin.* Multiplying asset turnover times margin yields the return on assets. The value of the DuPont formula far exceeds its individual components, however. Many business decisions cause the two ratios, asset turnover and margin, to move in opposite directions. So not only are the two ratios valuable tools for measuring the performance of the SBU, but they also give the managers of the SBU a tool that they can use in making decisions.

Here are some examples:

> ➤ Outsourcing improves turnover but reduces the margin, as profit that was formerly kept in-house now must be paid to the supplying vendor.

> ➤ Vertical integration improves margins because the company keeps the profit that is achieved at each step of the operation. However, asset turnover declines because additional equipment will be needed to produce the product.

> ➤ Continuous 24-hour operation reduces the amount of equipment needed; hence asset turnover improves. Interestingly, margins may also improve because having fewer machine start-ups may improve efficiency. However, if sales don't keep pace with the continuous output, inventory may build up dangerously, and margins may then deteriorate as a result of price cutting to get the product out the door.

Using the DuPont formula helps in the two main business activities:

1. Measuring performance
2. Management decision making

However, it does not *make* the decision. Valuable as it may be, it is merely a tool. Management must make its judgments based on what the expected result will be if the decision is made.

As the next phase of developing the use of this tool, we will look at three SBUs within a company in order to get a better understanding of the DuPont formula. Their respective results for the past year are given in Exhibit 7-1.

> *Line 1: Revenue.* All three businesses achieved significant revenue gains in the most recent year. The Flanagan Company is the largest of the three, with $50 million in annual revenues, while the Joseph Company is the smallest, with revenues amounting to $10 million.
>
> *Line 2: After-tax cash flow.* This is each business's net income plus depreciation expense, which is added back to calculate the cash flows generated.
>
> *Line 3: Total assets.* This identifies the total assets dedicated to each business. Ideally, common property is excluded from this measure and no overhead expenses are allocated to the individual businesses.

Exhibit 7-1. Measurement of Profit Centers Using Return on Assets ($000)

	Wilson	Flannagan	Joseph
1. Revenue	$27,000	$50,000	$10,000
2. After-Tax Cash Flow	$1,810	$3,000	$500
3. Total Assets	$20,272	$50,000	$5,000
4. Cash Flow as a % of Revenue (margin)	6.7%	6.0%	5.0%
5. Asset Turnover	1.33×	1.00×	2.00×
6. Return on Assets (line 4 × line 5)	8.9%	6.0%	10.0%

Line 4: Margin. This is ATCF/revenue. As we have discussed, this measures efficiency and reflects all of the operating decisions made by the SBU management team. Notice that Wilson has the highest (which does not necessarily mean the best) margin.

Line 5: Asset turnover. All three of these businesses are quite asset-intensive. Any asset turnover ratio below 2.0 indicates a considerable investment in assets relative to the amount of revenue generated with those assets.

Line 6: Return on assets. This is line 4 multiplied by line 5. It can also be calculated by dividing line 2 by line 3. Wilson has the highest margin (line 4) and an asset turnover of 1.33. Its asset intensiveness is compensated for by the higher margin.

Corporate management now has a tool that it can use to evaluate the performance of these three SBUs. The SBU management teams also have a decision-making tool that is congruent. The consistent use of this tool provides both clear measurement and an understanding of whether particular decisions will improve the performance of the company.

Let us be very clear that we are not trying to compare the three SBUs with one another. We do not know what businesses they are in or even if they are in related industries. Flanagan Company's performance within its industry may be superior to Joseph Company's performance in its industry. The corporate team, however, may use these measures in deciding how much money to allocate to each company in the future.

There are many adaptations of the ROA formula, but they are conceptually the same. Here are some of them:

- ➢ Return on capital employed (ROCE)
- ➢ Return on invested capital (ROIC)
- ➢ Return on assets managed (ROAM)
- ➢ Return on net assets (RONA)

In Exhibit 7-1, after-tax cash flow was used. Net income would have been almost as good. Operating income is often used as the measure of achievement. This is helpful if corporate management wants to remove interest expense and taxes from the equation. The premise is that SBUs are not responsible for debt financing or corporate income taxes. Therefore, measurements of them should not include these corporate expenses. Gross profit is a very useful measure when individual products or product lines are being analyzed as profit centers. Some companies and analysts use EBITDA as the measure of operating performance. This is a pretax cash flow number that recognizes that financing and taxes are issues to be dealt with at the corporate level rather than by the SBU.

Sales Territories

The DuPont formula can also be applied to the management of sales territories within a profit center. It gives each sales team the opportunity to make certain decisions in response to the specific competitive pressures that it faces. It allows for dissimilarities of strategy if this is appropriate. Company policies that limit the decisions that the SBUs may make can be developed in order to protect the company. Within these limits, each sales team remains totally accountable for its decisions and performance. A financial relationship is created between the sales organization and the manufacturing operation. In this example, there are three sales territories and one manufacturing entity. To keep the example simple, it is a one-product business. Exhibit 7-2 shows the actual results for a recent year.

1. Actual revenue results are reported.
2. The sales territories "purchase" the product for a predetermined price of $1.00. This is a market-oriented price that provides the factory with a profit. Within guidelines set by the company, the territory purchases the amounts that it believes it will need. Customer service issues and the size and logistics of the territory have a great deal of impact on that decision.

Exhibit 7-2. Sales Territories as Profit Centers

	Full Year Results 2015			
	North	Central	West	Factory
1. Revenue	$3,600	$2,400	$1,500	$1.00/unit
2. − COGS ($1.00/unit)	2,592	1,600	1,125	0.60
3. Gross Profit	$1,008	$ 800	$ 375	$0.40
	(28%)	(33%)	(25%)	
4. Less: Specific Expenses:				
Sales Compensation	$ 400	$ 250	$ 150	
Travel and Entertain-				
ment	75	75	25	
Field Sales Office	50	50	25	
Bad Debts	—	25	—	
Total Expenses	$ 525	$ 400	$ 200	$
5. Profit Center Earnings	$ 483	$ 400	$ 175	$
Invested Capital:				
6. Accounts Receivable	$1,200	$ 800	$ 300	$
7. Finished Goods				
Inventory	600	800	250	$
8. Total Assets	$2,400	$1,600	$ 550	$
9. Earnings as a %				
of Revenue	13.4%	16.7%	11.7%	
10. Asset Turnover	2.0×	1.5×	2.72×	
11. Return on Assets	26.8%	25.0%	31.9%	

3. The gross profit is reported. Although each territory paid the same purchase price of $1.00 (line 2), the selling prices are different, and therefore the gross profit percentages are also different. The West territory probably sells larger quantities per order, resulting in lower pricing and therefore lower margins. Central has higher margins than the other two territories. This may be explained by superior performance, less competition, or a combination of these factors.

4. Territory management expends the funds that it feels are necessary to sell to and service the marketplace. North may have more salespeople and/or may pay higher commis-

sions because of competitive issues. Notice that Central has been charged with bad debts. Because an individual territory may use easier credit terms as part of the marketing mix, it is held accountable if the customers do not pay.

5. Profit center earnings are reported. This is:

$$\text{Revenue} - \text{Cost of Goods Sold} = \text{Gross Profit} - \text{Specific Expenses} = \text{Profit Center Earnings}$$

6. Accounts receivable: Each territory is responsible for the credit that it grants to its customers. The corporate accounting department can do all the credit checking and administration, but the territory makes the final decision about a potential customer's creditworthiness, subject to some debate. Therefore, the territory is held accountable.

7. Inventory: Based upon their sales forecast, territories order product from the factory. The sales territories are responsible for their forecasts. The inventory that they have on their books is a combination of products that they have not sold and products that they want available for fast delivery. Territories must determine the amount of inventory that they must maintain in order to keep their level of delivery service competitive. Each territory is responsible for this strategy. This approach does not require sales territories to physically manage the product in the warehouse. It does, however, hold them accountable for the levels and mix of inventory that are maintained on their behalf.

8. Total assets: This is the working capital (accounts receivable plus inventory) managed by the territory.

What is accomplished here is:

➢ A clear measure of achievement

➢ Strategies that are appropriate for each marketplace

➢ Limitations on extremes to protect the company

> ➤ Accountability for those resources used by each SBU that are identified as being competitively desirable.

Using the DuPont formula, achievement and accountability can now be measured. Management teams have a decision-making tool that can really help them.

9. Margin: Earnings as a percentage of revenue (line 5 divided by line 1
10. Turnover: Revenue/assets (line 1 divided by line 8)
11. Return on assets: Earnings/assets (line 9 multiplied by line 10 or line 5 divided by line 8)

The West territory has the highest return on assets, 31.9 percent. While its margins are lower than those of the other territories, its investment in accounts receivables and inventory is very low. However, while West has a higher ROA, we cannot be sure that it is "better" than the others. There are other issues that need to be considered, including: What is the current market share and potential in each territory? Is North more successful in a very competitive marketplace, while there is less competition in West's marketplace? The DuPont formula is clearly a valuable profit-oriented resource. It can be a key tool for intelligent sales management.

Notice that the factory is also a profit center. It sells to the sales territories at a predetermined, market-oriented price, so that it is given credit or held accountable for positive or negative efficiencies. The factory is responsible for its own assets and is measured as an SBU by margin, turnover, and return on assets. It is accountable for its own inventory, so that it can plan production runs to maximize its own efficiency.

A Business with No "Assets"

This extension of the Return on Assets discussion focuses on a business that, in an accounting sense, has no assets. Think about a CPA firm, a management consulting firm, or a company that performs pharmaceutical research. The only "accounting assets" may be computers and office furniture. The "real assets" are the billable professionals and their support staff who constitute the value of the business.

The key ratio that helps to evaluate these businesses are different versions of revenue per employee.

We reviewed this ratio earlier in Chapter 6 but it's worth doing so again in this context.

The simple ratio Billed Revenue per Employee / Total Number of Employees is a function of the value-added nature of the business, the relationship between billable and non-billable employees, and the overall efficiency of the firm.

For each billable employee the firm needs to bill two to three times the total cost of the employee. This covers all direct costs plus overhead plus the firm's profit.

CHAPTER EIGHT

Overhead Allocations

C orporations are required by generally accepted accounting principles to allocate (mathematically distribute or apportion) their overhead expenses to individual profit centers when they prepare their information for the Internal Revenue Service (absorption accounting in LIFO/FIFO calculations), the Securities and Exchange Commission, and certain industry-specific regulatory authorities. There are numerous criteria that may be used for this calculation, including revenue, direct cost, units produced, direct labor dollars or hours, and square footage consumed.

It is often presumed, incorrectly, that the methodology that must be used for regulatory compliance is also appropriate for intelligent management decision making. Nothing could be further from the truth.

Problems That Arise from Cost Allocation

The process of allocating overhead charges to individual businesses can lead to several problems within a company.

It Fosters Politics

The process of allocating overhead charges to individual businesses fosters political infighting. When the management team of a strategic business unit shines as a result of its contribution to the improved profitability of the business, this is a positive result, and the company as a whole wins. However, when costs are allocated, a manager who knows how to manipulate the allocation methodology can make his department look better by getting charges assigned to other operating units. When one profit center looks good at the expense of another, without the company benefiting at all, that's politics.

It Inhibits New Product Introductions

When analyzing the profitability of a new product, traditional accounting methodology assigns a portion of the existing overhead to that product. This inflates the cost of the new product and causes the estimates of its contribution to profit to be severely understated. The analysis of a new product should include only costs that are incremental for that new product. Existing overhead that is not affected should not be included in the analysis.

It Understates the Profitability of Business Beyond Budgeted Volume

Overhead allocations are assigned to all products, regardless of volume. When sales surpass budgeted expectations, the accounting department will continue to charge these overhead allocations to the individual products, even though the company has already generated enough business to pay for the actual corporate overhead. These fictitious charges will continue to be added until the end of the fiscal year. This leads to a severe understatement of the actual profits of each business that has had sales above the budgeted number and may cause the company to under reward unit managers who surpass their sales budgets. When the company's books are closed for the year, this excess overhead will be removed from the costs. In accounting terminology, this is referred to as being "overabsorbed." This correction, however, does not remove the business distortion that has occurred up until that time.

It Inhibits Marketplace Aggressiveness

Incremental business is really more profitable than the accounting information reveals. Larger customer orders permit longer production runs and more efficient raw material purchasing. Traditional accounting information does not recognize this.

The potential profitability of giving price breaks on larger customer orders (volume discounting) because of these advantages may not be recognized because overhead charges are assigned to the products regardless of volume.

It Overstates Savings From Eliminating "Marginal" Products

A company should never eliminate products from its mix except in the following situations:

1. The product achieves a negative contribution margin, and there is no opportunity to correct the situation.
2. The product is a quality disaster that will impair marketplace perceptions of the entire business.
3. The company is near capacity and needs the space, people, and machine time for more profitable offerings.

Eliminating a product that has a positive cash flow results in the loss of that cash flow. Why is there confusion about this? Because our accounting systems tell us that eliminating a product will save the variable labor costs and the corresponding overhead assigned to the product. Labor costs, as anyone who has ever managed an operation will tell you, are more fixed than variable. They will not be reduced appreciably, if at all, when volume declines. And overhead will not be reduced because the building does not get smaller, nor do the staff departments (including accounting).

If overhead spending is too high, then appropriate actions should be taken on their own merits. But to assume that all costs will decline because a product is eliminated is too simplistic and usually not true.

What About the IRS and GAAP?

Companies should continue to comply with their accounting responsibilities. Nothing that we are advocating here addresses regulatory issues at all. However, marketing and operating managers should receive the product and performance information that they need if they are to make intelligent business decisions and judgments. Accounting compliance and management information are not conflicting goals.

Effect on Profits of Different Cost Allocation Issues

To explore these issues, let's look at a company with three profit centers. Exhibit 8-1 shows the annual results achieved by the Middlesex Products Company. The company is very profitable and serves its customers well. Each of the three profit centers focuses

Exhibit 8-1. Middlesex Products Company Income Statement
Full Year 2015

Product / Brand	A	B	C	Total
Units Sold	100,000	100,000	100,000	300,000
Average Price	$15.00	$20.00	$10.00	
Revenue	$1,500,000	$2,000,000	$1,000,000	$4,500,000
Direct Costs	900,000	1,300,000	800,000	3,000,000
Gross Profit	$ 600,000	$ 700,000	$ 200,000	$1,500,000
	(40%)	(35%)	(20%)	(33%)
Corporate Overhead				$1,000,000
Corporate Profit				$ 500,000

on a distinct marketplace and performs as a semi-independent unit.

Revenue

Each profit center has developed a pricing structure that fits with what is necessary and desirable in its marketplace. Some profit centers might sell direct, whereas others might sell through distributors or reps. Their product mixes will certainly be different. For purposes of convenience, we will assume that each strategic business unit has sold 100,000 units of product.

Direct Costs

This includes all profit center costs and expenses. To be considered *direct expenses*:

1. These costs must be *specifically identifiable* to an individual profit center. They include the costs of producing the product or providing the service, operating and staff expenses, and the costs of any services or functions that the profit center outsources to others.

2. The expenditures must be *incremental* to the profit center. They are not shared among the profit centers, and so they would disappear if the responsible profit center were not in business.

3. These costs may be *fixed* or *variable*. They can be part of the product, or they can be support costs. They could include costs for engineering, product design, and accounting, if those costs were dedicated to an individual profit center.

4. The profit center management team must have some ability to *control* the costs for which it is responsible. While the management team does not control the purchase price of a natural resource, it can control the quantity purchased, the mode of transportation, the product source, and whether there is any value added to what is purchased.

Corporate Overhead

This includes all of those support efforts that are necessary if the entire organization is to function, such as accounting, legal, corporate staff, and management information systems. It also includes all spending that supports all of the profit centers combined and is really not divisible among them. For example, if all the profit centers were housed in a single building, this building would be considered part of the corporate overhead.

Profit

Gross profit percentages are gross profit dollars divided by revenue.

Corporate profit is the cumulative gross profit of all of the businesses less corporate overhead. An examination of how overhead allocations affect the perceptions of performance will be very valuable at this point.

Overhead Allocation

If the corporate overhead is allocated by revenue, the result will be:

	A	B	C	Total
Gross Profit	$600,000	$700,000	$200,000	$1,500,000
Overhead	333,000	444,000	223,000	1,000,000
"Profit"	$267,000	$256,000	($ 23,000)	$ 500,000

Because Profit Center A provided one-third of corporate revenue, it is charged for the same proportion of the corporate overhead. Remember that these corporate charges are not based upon the services that each profit center receives. The amounts allocated support the entire organization collectively.

Notice that on this basis, Profit Center C is now losing money. This profit center contributed $200,000 cash flow to pay for corporate overhead and achieve corporate profit. It now must revise its strategy to eliminate the losses that it neither caused nor can control. A more damaging conclusion is the feeling on the part of corporate management that this unit will never be "profitable" and therefore must be eliminated. If the allocation were based upon units sold, Profit Center C would have looked even worse:

	A	B	C	Total
Gross Profit	$600,000	$700,000	$ 200,000	$1,500,000
Overhead	333,000	333,000	334,000	1,000,000
"Profit"	$267,000	$367,000	($134,000)	$ 500,000

"Turning around" Profit Center C is clearly impossible. While remedies for its problems will be proposed, its days are numbered.

If corporate allocations are based upon direct labor (which is part of direct costs), all three of the profit centers will be profitable, as follows:

	A	B	C	Total
Gross Profit	$600,000	$700,000	$200,000	$1,500,000
Overhead	450,000	400,000	150,000	$1,000,000
"Profit"	$150,000	$300,000	$ 50,000	$ 500,000

With this method of overhead allocation, all three profit centers have achieved a "profit."

Which method is correct? Is Profit Center C profitable or not? The answer depends upon which method of allocation the accounting department happens to have selected. All are acceptable in terms of GAAP requirements. The accounting department will study the company's operations and attempt to select the method or formula that it perceives as being the most accurate. However, the results will be the same: Decisions will be based upon the statistical method selected. Will these decisions improve the business, as many expect they will? Let's look at some of those decisions and focus on what solutions would be in the best interest of the Middlesex Products Company.

1. **Are all profit centers contributing to the profitability of the business?**
   Absolutely yes. Each of the three has a positive contribution

margin. Each is more than covering all of the costs and expenses associated with its individual business.

2. **How should Middlesex management respond to excessive corporate overhead?**

Not by passing it on to the profit centers and asking them to figure out a way to pay for it. The best strategy for eliminating excessive overhead is to hold those departments accountable for their own performance and reduce their budgets and/or expect them to increase their achievement. Allocating excessive spending to operating units does not solve the problem. Instead, it asks the profit center teams to solve problems that they did not create and cannot control. Increasing selling prices and compromising on product quality to compensate for others' inefficiencies are remedies that are no longer available.

Because product quality and high levels of service are no longer negotiable, during the 2007–2009 time period, companies were forced to hold corporate managers accountable for their performance. Many of the millions of people who lost their jobs during that time period were middle- and higher-level managers who became expendable when the companies could no longer afford the luxury of having them on the payroll. These jobs will not be replaced. Economic pressure is increasing accountability at all levels, and all of those corporate staff jobs have ceased to exist.

3. **In which business should Middlesex management expect improved profitability?**

Why not all of them? We do not know, however, if each of the profit centers can improve its profitability to the same degree. Perhaps 20 percent profit growth would be very easy for Profit Center B but absolutely impossible for Profit Center C. A 20 percent gross profit in Profit Center C's market might be relatively better performance than the 40 percent in Profit Center A's market. We would have to benchmark each profit center against its respective competitors to determine what are feasible expectations. Achievement must be evaluated against potential. Learning management techniques from other businesses is very helpful. However, you cannot benchmark financial ratios among dissimilar businesses and reach decisions that will help the company overall.

4. **In theory, what would be the most favorable product mix?**
   If Profit Center A achieves a gross profit of $6.00 per unit ($600,000/100,000 units) and Profit Center C achieves a gross profit of $2.00 per unit, expanding Profit Center A's business at the expense of Profit Center C would improve gross profit by $4.00 per unit (the gross profit differential). Keeping these numbers very simple, the ranking of these profit centers by gross profit dollars is:

   > Profit Center B: $7.00 per unit
   > Profit Center A: $6.00 per unit
   > Profit Center C: $2.00 per unit

   However, if you rank the profit centers by gross profit percentage, the ranking changes:

   > Profit Center A: 40%
   > Profit Center B: 35%
   > Profit Center C: 20%

   If you check your company's financial statements, you will notice that in most cases, accountants rank product profitability by percentages, although it is their dollar impact that is most critical.

5. **Should the fact that Profit Center C has a gross profit percentage that is below the average for the entire Middlesex Products organization be a cause for divestment?**
   Middlesex Products Company should never eliminate a business with a positive gross profit unless:
   a. The lower quality of its products is damaging the company's other businesses.
   b. Productive capacity is limited and can be used for more profitable businesses.

c. Supporting the product requires too much, less profitable investment.

6. **If these three businesses are all profitable, why make choices at all?**

We do not have to make choices among these businesses if:

a. There is adequate capacity to allow all of them to grow.

b. The company can afford to provide sufficient financing to permit all of them to prosper.

c. The ROI for this funding exceeds the company's discounted cash flow hurdle rate (see Chapter 10).

If Middlesex does not meet any of these three condition, then product mix choices should be made soon. These become strategic issues with long-term answers. Perhaps one of the profit centers should be sold to finance the others. Perhaps the profit center with the most promising future should be financed by the cash flow generated by the more mature businesses.

7. **How do we evaluate the profitability of a proposed new business?**

Middlesex Products Company is considering the addition of Product D. The annual forecast for this new business is:

Annual Sales	100,000 units
Price	$4.00 per unit
Direct Cost	$3.00 per unit
Incremental Gross Profit	$1.00 per unit

Capacity is more than sufficient to allow both this product and the other three to grow for the foreseeable future. Product D is a very good product that has tested well. There might be some cross-selling and other synergistic benefits with the other businesses, but these have not been included. Depending on the measure of profitability you use, you will have different outcomes. We look at the three most common below.

a   If the company measures product profitability by gross profit percentage, the proposal for Product D will be rejected.

	Company Average	Product D
Price	$15.00	$4.00
Direct Cost	10.00	3.00
Gross Profit	$5.00	$1.00
Gross Profit Percentage	33%	25%

The gross profit percentage for Product D is below the average for the company as a whole. Therefore, adding Product D will bring down the average.

Prioritizing products by their gross profit percentage may be helpful if the company is near full productive capacity and outsourcing opportunities are not available. In such a case, Product D will bring down the average and will not be acceptable.

b. If the company allocates nonincremental overhead and does so by units, the proposal to add Product D will be rejected.

Product D Forecast

Revenue	$400,000
Direct Cost	300,000
Gross Profit	$100,000

The company overhead of $1,000,000 will now be reallocated as follows:

Corporate Overhead	$1,000,000
Units Sold (including D)	400,000
Overhead per Unit	$2.50
Charge to Product D	$250,000
Projected "Loss" on Product D	$150,000 ($100,000 − $250,000)

The projected loss is calculated as gross profit of $100,000 minus the overcharge of $250,000.

c. If the Middlesex Products Company is most concerned about the cash flow that will be generated by its decisions, the proposal to introduce Product D will be approved.

	Company Without Product D	Product D	Company With Product D
Units	300,000	100,000	400,000
Revenue	$4,500,000	$400,000	$4,900,000
Direct Cost	3,000,000	300,000	3,300,000
Gross Profit	$1,500,000	$100,000	$1,600,000
Corporate Overhead	$1,000,000	—	$1,000,000
Corporate Profit	$ 500,000	$100,000	$ 600,000

Implementing Product D will improve corporate profitability to $600,000. Notice that an increase in revenue of slightly less than 10 percent results in a 20 percent increase in bottom-line profitability. This is true even though Product D has a gross margin percentage that is below the corporate average.

When Middlesex Products Company is reporting its results to others, adhering to generally accepted accounting principles is both required and desirable. It promotes the uniformity and integrity of the numbers. This is especially helpful to bankers, security analysts, and others who rely on the company reports that they receive in order to carry out their responsibilities. However, the decisions that will improve the performance and financial health of the company are those that will improve its cash flow. The methodologies that are best for achieving this objective are different from but not necessarily inconsistent with GAAP. These issues should be explored in your company.

Decision Making for Improved Profitability

CHAPTER NINE

Analysis of Business Profitability

The discussion in this chapter will focus on the factors that determine the profitability of individual products and help us to improve the decisions that we make concerning these products. We will measure and evaluate the factors that determine the profitability of a product, including:

- ➤ Product price
- ➤ Unit volume sold
- ➤ Costs, both fixed and variable
- ➤ Profitability

The financial tool used to achieve these goals is called *breakeven analysis.*

We begin our discussion by looking at the operating budget for Raritan Manufacturing Company, which is presented in Exhibit 9-1. Raritan has established revenue, spending, and profit targets.

Exhibit 9-1. Raritan Manufacturing Company Annual Budget

Revenue (10,000 units × $50 per unit) $500,000

Costs:

	Fixed	Variable Per Unit	Total	
Direct Material	$ —	$ 5	$ 50,000	
Direct Labor	—	10	100,000	
Factory Overhead	40,000	15	150,000	
Administration	45,000	2	20,000	
Distribution	50,000	3	30,000	
Total	$135,000	$35	$350,000	$485,000
Operating Profit				$ 15,000

To Summarize:		
Revenue	($50 × 10,000)	$500,000
− Variable Costs	($35 × 10,000)	− 350,000
= Gross Profit	($15 × 10,000)	150,000
− Fixed Costs		− 135,000
Operating Income		$ 15,000

Note that the costs are divided into major categories and also separated into their fixed and variable components. Identifying which
costs are fixed and which are variable is very valuable for effective
decision making. To keep things simple, we will assume that Raritan Manufacturing Company is a one-product business. All of the
basic principles of this analysis are equally valid for a multiproduct
business. Most of these principles are also applicable to a service
business; some of the terminology and processes differ, but conceptually the analyses are the same. The analysis that a manufacturing company develops is called a *standard cost system.* This is
an accounting-oriented mechanism that attempts to identify how
much the company will spend during the budget year under different volume assumptions. In the financial services industries, this
process is called a *functional cost analysis.*

After the business has been analyzed using the concepts of breakeven analysis, the actual performance is evaluated as it takes place. This is often called *variance analysis.* Variance analysis provides management with the ability to evaluate actual results against what was expected when the budget was prepared. This both provides performance accountability and contributes to the learning process. It enables management to determine who is and who is not accomplishing the desired goals. Also, budget assumptions and forecasts can be retroactively evaluated.

Chart of Accounts

Almost every company has a numerically based accounting system that assigns a series of code numbers to every department. This is very helpful for analytical purposes, and is also necessary to comply with generally accepted accounting principles (GAAP). This system ensures that all similar expenses are recorded in the same manner. When accounting transactions are added up at the end of the month or the year, the company can be confident that all direct labor has been recorded in one account, all travel expenses in another, and so on for trade shows, advertising, and every other expense. There is no other mechanism that will help us determine how much is actually being spent in each category, which is certainly necessary information. Also, one of the GAAP requirements is consistency. The chart of accounts provides that as well. Note that the five categories that Raritan Manufacturing Company uses in its budget are summaries of perhaps one or two hundred cost and expense codes. And they are only examples. Your company will probably use different categories and may even use somewhat different terminology.

Once the chart of accounts has been established, the accountants will examine each and every individual cost category in order to attempt to determine whether the cost is fixed or variable. They will often reach simplifying conclusions.

Fixed Costs

Fixed costs are costs that will be the same regardless of the volume of products produced. They are regular and recurring. The amount spent will not change if volume increases or decreases during a given period of time. Among the costs included in this category are staff expenses, administration, rent, machinery repair, and management salaries. Note that just because a cost is identified as fixed, this does not mean that it cannot change. Rent can change, as can salaries, employee benefits, and even advertising. These are fixed costs because the amount spent is not volume-driven, although it may be volume-motivated. Advertising and trade shows create revenue, presumably. If this is true, then perhaps a forecast of weak sales should lead to an increase in these marketing investments. Telephone and travel are examples of other expenses that may increase when business is soft. Customers may be called and visited more frequently.

Development of Fixed-Cost Estimates

It is estimated that during the budget year, Raritan Manufacturing Company will spend a total of $135,000 for costs that are identified as fixed. This includes:

Factory Overhead	$40,000
Administration	45,000
Distribution	50,000
Total Estimated Fixed Costs	$135,000

Variable Costs

These costs are volume-driven. They will increase or decrease in response to changes in production and distribution volume. Some of the costs in this category are direct labor (production labor), materials (components of the product), and some administrative and distribution costs.

Development of Variable-Cost Estimates

Estimates of variable costs are developed with the assistance of manufacturing and engineering analyses of the production facility and administrative departments. Each of the per-unit costs is then multiplied by the expected number of units to determine the estimates of variable costs, by category and in total. This is described as follows.

Material estimates are based upon engineering specifications, some analysis of production efficiencies, and product mix. Levels of waste and quality rejects are based upon past experience, subject to hoped-for and engineered improvements. After consultation with manufacturing staff and, preferably, even the people who actually build the product, it is estimated that the material cost per unit will be:

$$\$5 \times \text{budgeted } 10{,}000 \text{ units} = \$50{,}000 \text{ materials budget}$$

Direct labor is a very complex cost to estimate. Total expenditures in this area may be affected by:

➤ The use of manual labor versus technology in production

➤ Outsourcing versus internal manufacture/assembly

➤ Efficiency

➤ The number of shifts planned

➤ Employee training and turnover

➤ Forecast length of production runs

➤ Whether the product is market-driven (made to order) or production-driven

➤ Planned overtime and weekend shifts

➤ Premium pay for performance agreements

Other Expenses

The expenses other than direct labor and materials—factory overhead, administration, and distribution—have both fixed and variable components. The basic premise espoused by the accounting department and others is that while a portion of these expenses is fixed, the balance will increase or decrease along with the volume experienced by the company.

There is serious controversy concerning this conclusion, especially during an individual budget year, when the managers responsible will argue that their costs are essentially fixed. The accounting department would not increase or decrease the number of its own people on a week-to-week basis depending on the number of invoices that have to be sent out. Trucks must complete their delivery routes, whether they are entirely or partially full. Managers should examine the standards used by their company and evaluate whether the behavior assumed by the cost system agrees with their perception of how their costs really behave.

Taking these issues into account, Raritan Manufacturing has made the following estimates of the variable-cost portion of these expenses.

Cost Category	Cost per Unit	Forecast Volume (units)	Variable Budget
Factory Overhead	$15	10,000	$150,000
Administration	2	10,000	20,000
Distribution	3	10,000	30,000

In summary, Raritan Manufacturing's budget is as follows:

Variable cost: $35 per unit × 10,000 units = $350,000

$135,000 (estimated fixed costs)
+350,000 (estimate of variable costs at 10,000 units)
$485,000 Total costs in budget

The budget is summarized at the bottom of Exhibit 9-1. Notice that the per-unit price, variable costs, and profit are identified at the bottom of the exhibit. The per-unit profit is called *contribution margin.*

Breakeven Calculation

Companies should know the volume they need to achieve in order to reach breakeven. This information should be available by product, or at least by class of product. The breakeven point may be of purely academic interest, or it might have strategic importance, either at present or in the future. It is particularly significant for very new and, at the other end of the life-cycle spectrum, very mature products. Before we get to mathematical formulas, some theory will be helpful.

Conceptually, if Raritan sold no product, it would lose $135,000, which is the fixed-cost commitment. Each time it sells a single unit, it generates $50 in cash. However, before the unit can be sold, it must be manufactured at a cost of $35. The difference between the selling price and the variable cost per unit is called the *contribution margin.* Therefore, the number of units necessary to break even is the number of "contributions" necessary to cover the fixed cost. The formula is as follows:

$$\frac{\text{Fixed Cost}}{\text{Price} - \text{Variable Cost per Unit}} = \text{Unit Volume}$$

The formula can be adapted to calculate the number of units that need to be sold to achieve any desired amount of profit by including profit in the formula, as follows:

$$\frac{\text{Fixed Cost} + \text{Profit}}{\text{Price} - \text{Variable Cost per Unit}} = \text{Unit Volume}$$

The breakeven point for Raritan Manufacturing is:

$$\frac{\$135,000 + 0}{\$50 - \$35 = \$15} = 9,000 \text{ units}$$

At 9,000 units, the income statement will be:

Revenue	(9,000 × $50)	$450,000
− Variable Cost	(9,000 × $35)	− 315,000
= Contribution Margin	(9,000 × $15)	$135,000
− Fixed Cost		− 135,000
= Profit		$ 0

Now that we know the breakeven volume, there are many valuable observations that we can make.

Analysis 1

Every unit sold will result in a gross profit (the same thing as contribution margin in this discussion) of $15. At 9,000 units, the company has generated enough gross profit to pay for the fixed cost of $135,000.

$$\$135,000 = 9,000 \times \$15$$

Above 9,000 units, since the fixed costs are already paid for, every additional unit sold results in a profit increase of $15. Therefore, if volume were 9,500 units, profit would be $7,500, as follows:

$$500 \text{ units (above breakeven)} \times \$15 = \$7,500$$

The complete income statement would be:

Revenue	(9,500 × $50)	$475,000
− Variable Cost	(9,500 × $35)	− 332,500
= Gross Profit	(9,500 × $15)	142,500
− Fixed Costs		− 135,000
= Operating Income		$ 7,500

Analysis 2: Price Reduction

This formula can assist in answering a number of business questions. For example, the company forecasts that it could achieve a volume of 11,000 units (up from the budget of 10,000 units), but to do this, it would have to reduce the selling price from $50 to $47. Would such an action improve profits? The numbers will tell the tale.

Revenue	($47 × 11,000)	$517,000
− Variable Cost	($35 × 11,000)	− 385,000
= Gross Profit	($12 × 11,000)	$132,000
− Fixed Costs		− 135,000
= Operating Profit		($ 3,000)

Lowering the selling price to $47 per unit in order to increase the number of units sold to 11,000 units is clearly not the correct decision. Operating income would decline from a profit of $15,000 to a loss of $3,000.

Analysis 3: Business Opportunity

Let us once again assume a budgeted volume of 10,000 units. Raritan has the opportunity to sell an additional 1,000 units (above budget) through a distributor into a market that it does not currently serve. The selling price to the distributor would be $42 per unit. The distributor would then resell the product at $50. Think through the issues of selling through a distributor as opposed to selling direct. Quality of service might be an issue, as might productive capacity and competitive strategies. Costs per unit and fixed costs will remain as budgeted. With these facts in mind, would it be profitable for Raritan to sell these 1,000 units at $42 (assuming that without this sale, it will achieve budget)? This kind of analysis, the analysis of proposed business opportunities, is called *financial analysis.* It involves forecasting the future in order to evaluate opportunity.

Financial Analysis Solution

FORECAST

	Without	With	Proposed Opportunity
Revenue	$500,000	$542,000	$42,000
− Variable Cost	− 350,000	− 385,000	− 35,000
= Gross Profit	$150,000	$157,000	$ 7,000
− Fixed Costs	− $135,000	− $135,000	
= Profit	$ 15,000	$ 22,000	$ 7,000

This example brings up a number of important business issues. As businesspeople, we think *incrementally.* We analyze a business opportunity in terms of how much profit will be added, in this case as a result of the sale of an additional 1,000 units. However, a problem may arise if the analysis that the accounting department has prepared is not incremental. Traditional standard cost systems would present the budget in the following way:

Variable Cost per Unit: $35.00

Fixed Cost per Unit:

$$\frac{\text{Budgeted Fixed Costs}}{\text{Budgeted Units}} = \frac{\$135,000}{10,000} = 13.50$$

Total Cost per Unit $48.50

This accounting practice is called *absorption accounting.* The $13.50 of fixed cost per unit is called the *burden.* If the financial analysis of this sale of 1,000 additional units were done using this accounting convention, the conclusion would be to reject the opportunity as being unprofitable. The analysis would show the following:

Absorption Accounting Solution

Proposed Selling Price	$42.00
− Cost per Unit	48.50
= Profit (Loss)	($6.50)

How can a deal that adds $7,000 to Raritan's bottom line, increasing it from $15,000 to $22,000, create a loss of $6.50 per unit? This is a question that often causes considerable unease, and even strife, and leads to distrust between the accounting department and the rest of the company. The explanation lies in something that we described in the introduction to this book. Accounting is the reporting of the past. GAAP accounting *requires* a manufacturing company to use absorption accounting. Therefore, in calculating the burden rate, the accounting department is complying with required practices. The mistake is the accountants' belief that a GAAP technique is necessarily applicable to business decision making.

Incremental Versus Absorption

The issue of incremental decision making versus absorption accounting continues to this day, with mixed results. On the issue of too much inventory versus not enough, some companies have recognized that they can protect their brand but still sell excess inventory "off-market." Overstock.com, for example, has a quite comprehensive online catalog of almost any type of product, some of them branded. The retail chains Marshalls and T.J.Max sell branded products at discount prices. The goods may be out of season or out of style, but the deep discounts provide an exciting opportunity for consumers to save money and for brand name manufacturers to sell excess inventory. It might also be argued that the inventory was not really excess but produced specifically for these discount markets.

Nordstrom is a high-end, luxury retail chain. They have their own discount distribution which they have named Nordstrom Rack. Some of these products may be excess inventory from Nordstrom's own stores. Some might be specifically produced for this discount outlet. Brooks Brothers is a retail chain of higher-end business clothing. They too have outlet stores. The problem with branded outlet stores is that much of the product is made specifically for these outlets and the quality along with the price may be "discounted," which is not necessarily good for the brand.

Here is an example of how overhead allocations, discussed in Chapter 8, can lead companies to made poor decisions. Consider this high-tech products company:

	Product	Consulting	Total
Revenue	$20,000	$4,000	$24,000
− Direct Cost	− 14,000	− 2,000	− 16,000
= Gross Profit	6,000	2,000	8,000
− Allocated Overhead	− 2,000	− 2,000	− 4,000
= "Profit"	$4,000	0	$4,000

This company designed and manufactured a line of highly engineered electronic products. It also provided consulting support to its customers for which it charged a fee. It failed to realize that the consulting support helped it to sell product and also that the overhead was associated with the entire business and not to its two individual segments. It eliminated the consulting segment because it refused to operate a business at a "breakeven." Its cash flow from the consulting business disappeared. Its product sales diminished. Its margins declined because it had to sell on retail price point rather than value-adding support. To stem the decline in sales, it had to begin offering value-adding advice *for free*, as part of the sale. All because it allocated non-divisible overhead.

Analysis 4: Outsourcing Opportunity

Raritan is considering hiring an outside firm to do its product warehousing, a function that it is finding to be very expensive. The warehousing company under consideration, Warehouse Inc., is an expert in that function; it has an excellent reputation and is interested in handling Raritan's product line. Outsourcing this function will also provide systems support and related services that Raritan is finding difficult. Keeping the numbers very simple, the following information is provided:

Current Warehousing Expense. Raritan's budget includes a fixed warehousing expense of $20,000, which is part of the distribution budget. Raritan is doing a decent job and has the capacity to handle up to 12,000 units, compared to its budget of 10,000 units.

Proposal from Warehouse Inc. If Raritan outsources this function to Warehouse, it will save the $20,000 fixed cost. However, the proposed fee from Warehouse is $2 per unit.

The original budget cost structure is:

$$\$135,000 \text{ (fixed)} + \$35 \text{ per unit}$$

Removing $20,000 from the fixed cost and adding $2 per unit to the variable cost gives a revised cost structure of:

$$\$115,000 \text{ (fixed)} + \$37 \text{ per unit}$$

At 10,000 units, the profit with the revised cost structure will be:

Revenue	10,000 × $50	=	$500,000
− Variable Cost	10,000 × 37	=	− 370,000
= Gross Profit	10,000 × 13	=	$130,000
− Fixed Costs			− 115,000
= Profit		=	$ 15,000

At the budgeted volume of 10,000 units, the profit will remain at $15,000 regardless of whether the warehouse cost is fixed or variable. At 12,000 units and 8,000 units, however, the profits will be as follows:

Units		12,000	8,000
Revenue	($50)	$600,000	$400,000
− Variable Cost	($37)	− 444,000	296,000
= Gross Profit	($13)	$156,000	$104,000
− Fixed Costs		− 115,000	− 115,000
= Profit		$ 41,000	($11,000)

On the other hand, if the warehouse cost were fixed (that is, if the company did not outsource the warehouse function), the profit at 12,000 units would have been $45,000. At 8,000 units, the loss would have been ($15,000). At this juncture, it is worthwhile to look at the profits if the warehouse cost is fixed at $20,000 compared to those if the cost is variable at $2 per unit.

	Profits if the warehouse cost is:	
Volume	Fixed	Variable
7,000	($30,000)	($24,000)
8,000	(15,000)	(11,000)
8,846	(2,310)	0
9,000	0	2,000
10,000	15,000	15,000
11,000	30,000	28,000
12,000	45,000	41,000

These are the profits if the warehouse cost is fixed at $20,000 or variable at $2 per unit, with every other element of the forecast remaining exactly the same. This includes selling price and all other costs. There are a number of valuable lessons to be learned from these observations in a variety of business circumstances.

General Observations

Minimize Losses. At low volumes, the more variable costs there are, the less the amount of the loss experienced by the company will be. At 7,000 units, there will be a loss of $30,000 if the warehouse cost is fixed compared with a loss of $24,000 if the warehouse cost is variable. Outsourcing is a definite strategy when volumes are weak, such as during a recession, or when the company is relatively new and the breakeven volume has yet to be achieved.

This describes the strategies employed by companies in the 2007–2009 time period. Millions of people unfortunately lost their jobs during these years, and hundreds of plants and offices were closed. Many of the functions performed by the people who were let go are now provided by outsourcing firms. Quite a few of the unemployed are finding jobs with these vendors or starting up businesses that provide the same services. The former employers are now customers of these companies. What they accomplished was reducing fixed costs in favor of variable costs, generating considerable cash flow because they have fewer facilities to support, and probably receiving better levels of service because they are now customers rather than employers. Hundreds of thousands of the formerly unemployed are gaining new careers in this manner.

Technology, as we know, is creating extraordinary opportunity as well as greater complexity in the business world. Outsourcing has seriously expanded as economic conditions have warranted. Technology has expanded outsourcing benefits by enabling and perhaps requiring firms to seek the best solutions available to solve product and business issues. Rather than providing databases and data storage for their own use, firms are outsourcing these functions to cloud-based solutions. This concept of providing "solutions" to issues has freed firms to deal with finding multiple sources for their resources. Outsourcing used to be anathema to firms that felt they could do everything better internally. Vertical integration as a strategy is disappearing as firms are seeking the best solutions and resources available, regardless of where they come from.

The Internet has contributed greatly to the outsourcing trend. Most outsourcing used to come from local suppliers because they were known to the potential customer. The global Internet has created the art of the "supply chain"; we can now identify a plethora of suppliers—of any imaginable resource—anywhere in the world.

Breakeven. The greater the proportion of the costs that are variable, the lower the volume necessary to achieve breakeven will be. If the warehouse cost is fixed, Raritan will have to sell 9,000 units in order to break even. If the warehousing function is outsourced, the breakeven volume is reduced to 8,846 units. This becomes even more critical if the budgeted project has to break even within a fixed time period or be closed, or if the company has debt or cash flow obligations that require a positive cash flow by a specified point in time.

Economies of Scale. The benefits of size will begin to be achieved when Raritan's volume surpasses 10,000 units. Opportunities to bring outsourced functions inside can be explored at that time. Before any investments are made, however, all outsourcing contracts should be renegotiated to take advantage of the company's enhanced buying power. Being the low-cost producer is always a desired corporate objective. This can be achieved by continuing to outsource, but at the same time, skillfully taking advantage of expanded purchasing power. Below the breakeven point, the cost per unit of outsourcing will almost always be less than the cost per unit if the same function is performed internally. This is because of the additional overhead and support that may be necessary if the functions are performed internally.

There are no economies of scale when the volume sold is below breakeven.

Financial Strategy for New Businesses

The profitability impact of what we refer to as the fixed cost/variable cost mix is directly applicable to the financial strategy that is appropriate for new business start-ups. Observe how profits and losses behave with changes in volume from below the breakeven point to well above it. Within the context of profitability (read cash flow) behavior, consider the following truisms:

1. The more funds that are dedicated to the core competencies of the new business, the greater the start-up's chances for success. This strongly suggests outsourcing as many as possible of those functions that are not part of the business's core competencies. Outsourcing reduces overhead (read fixed costs) and permits the company to pay for only what it needs. The more the company tries to accomplish itself during these early stages, the greater its fixed costs will be, and the greater the negative cash flows that will surely result.

2. During the early stages of development, the more functions that are outsourced, the faster the start-up can begin to

deliver its product. An early-stage company that attempts to provide for its own needs (that is, to vertically integrate) must order machinery, hire and train workers and staff, install the machinery, work out the problems—and only then can it begin production and delivery. To outsource much of its needs, the company must create relationships with reliable vendors at reasonable prices. Once this is accomplished, outsourcing in areas that may not be part of the company's core competencies is much faster and presents fewer potential problems. The outside vendors already have efficient, smooth-running businesses. This permits the start-up's critical focus to be on the customer.

3. When functions are outsourced in the early stages, the costs will be highly variable. Having mostly variable costs rather than fixed costs at these early stages results in minimizing cash outflows at a most critical time. This allows additional cash to be devoted to marketplace opportunities and the company's core competencies.

4. Outsourcing at the early stages usually results in a higher-quality product. Outside vendors have experience and a track record of excellence. The company's only excellence is in its core competencies and, we hope, its marketing and sales of its expertise. All other responsibilities should be left to outside experts.

5. Keeping costs variable at the early stages expedites the achievement of breakeven. Remember that in the profit table for Raritan Manufacturing, a higher level of variable costs results in a lower breakeven point (8,846 units versus 9,000 units).

6. What happens about four or five years after the start-up period, when having a lot of variable costs appears to be counterproductive? In our example, beyond 10,000 units, fixed costs permit the company to achieve economies of scale. This issue should be considered during the planning process once breakeven volume has been permanently achieved. Prior to that time, the best financial strategy for a start-up business is to focus its cash and management

attention on its core competencies. All other functions should be outsourced to those vendors who are best equipped to provide an excellent product and service at reasonable prices.

Let's look at building a management consulting firm, from business plan to a fully developed global management consulting and training business.

The Wrong Way. Lease a large office in a really nice building; 15,000 square feet would be nice. Have it decorated by a top designer; insist on really impressive furniture and classy paintings on the walls. Make sure there are many desks occupied with computer terminals attached to servers in the back room, loaded with up-to-date operating systems and software. Hire between 10 and 15 really top people and don't forget to supply them with plenty of support staff. Then hire expensive consultants to develop some literature and build a snazzy website. When all this is to your satisfaction, you begin the process of looking for clients.

Analysis. In the context of earlier fixed cost/variable cost discussions, you have now entered a new business with no revenue and a monthly cash outflow of maybe $50,000 or more. Unless you have an impressive amount of funds, you will consume whatever cash you have before you have had the opportunity to build the business.

The Right Way. Examine your own core competence. What is it that you know how to do that companies will pay you to share with them? Perform a S.W.O.T analysis (see Chapter 12) on yourself. Through networking, find a client who will hire you. Hire one or two other experts for the project, if they can help you succeed. Work from home (the rent is free). Meet with your clients at their offices. It is a more effective way to get the project accomplished because all of their key players will be available for feedback and discussion.

Get more clients and repeat the above. Rent an office in a shared facility with services only when you need a space.

Analysis. You are not in business until you have a revenue-producing customer. So get the customer before you make any serious commitment to spend funds. You are keeping cash outflows to a minimum and working very hard to grow revenue faster than expenses. Hire full-time people with great reluctance. I had a 15-person consulting business and never paid rent. I hired the best experts on a contract basis for each project, paid them very well, and always had satisfied clients.

Variance Analysis

Analyzing the variances or differences between budgeted and actual performance provides the company with the ability to:

➤ Evaluate past assumptions and forecasts.
➤ Make adjustments in the business when circumstances change.
➤ Provide accountability for performance.
➤ Revise plans for the future in response to current realities.

Variance analysis is a management process that involves comparing the actual achievements of the business during a period of time with the budget for that same time period. This process should generally be performed monthly, with more extensive quarterly reviews. The annual review should encompass strategic issues and have a longer-term perspective. To illustrate this process, we return to the budget for the Raritan Manufacturing Company and compare it with Raritan's actual performance for the same time period (see Exhibit 9-2).

Raritan Manufacturing Company budgeted revenue of $500,000 and achieved $547,250. Profits achieved were $45,000 versus a budgeted $15,000. Raritan clearly sold more product and made more profit than was expected. Notice that the third column

Exhibit 9-2. Raritan Manufacturing Company
Full Year Actual vs. Budget

	Budget	Actual	Difference
Volume (units)	10,000	11,000	1,000
Price	$ 50.00	$ 49.75	$ 0.25
Revenue	$500,000	$547,250	$47,250
Costs:			
Direct Material	$ 50,000	$ 52,250	$ 2,250
Direct Labor	100,000	111,000	11,000
Factory Overhead	190,000	195,000	5,000
Administration	65,000	64,000	1,000
Distribution	80,000	80,000	—
Total Costs	$485,000	$502,250	
Profit	$ 15,000	$ 45,000	$ 30,000

is labeled difference, not variance. Variance sometimes takes on a negative connotation, although the event may not be negative at all. The column also has no label of better (worse) because that also has a negative association that may or may not be valid. All differences should be analyzed to find out what actually happened; then it can be determined whether the event was "good" or "bad."

Price and Volume

The product was sold at a price of $49.75 versus a budgeted price of $50.00. On the surface, this would appear to be an unfavorable event until you add in the fact that 11,000 units were sold compared with the budget of 10,000 units. While a higher price surely would be preferable, the additional units might not have been sold if the price had not been lowered. In fact, if the selling price had been held at $50.00, actual volume might have fallen below the budgeted amount. The price charged and the volume sold are not separate, isolated events. We therefore cannot evaluate them independently, out of context. Revenue amounted to $547,250, $47,250 above budget. While this in itself is certainly a positive outcome, the real analysis involves the determination of how this affected the rest of the business and whether the company's strategy (if there was one) improved the company's overall business perform-ance (it did).

Direct Material

Direct material was budgeted at $50,000, or a variable cost of $5 per unit. Had the cost per unit remained at the budgeted level, the actual material cost would have amounted to $55,000.

$$\text{Actual Volume} \times \text{Budgeted Cost per Unit} = \text{Expected Cost}$$
$$11,000 \times \$5.00 = \$55,000$$

Since the actual cost per unit was $4.75 ($52,250/11,000), Raritan was apparently able to reduce its average material cost per unit by $0.25 compared with the budgeted level. Thus the company re-duced cost and improved profit in this cost center by $2,250 be-cause of efficiency. The explanations for how this may have been accomplished include the following:

➤ Purchasing larger quantities of product from vendors may have reduced acquisition costs.

➤ Longer production runs may have reduced the occurrence of machine setups, improving efficiency and reducing product waste.

Direct Labor

Direct labor is also budgeted as a variable cost. The company ex-pected to spend $100,000 in this category but actually spent more, $111,000. Had the direct labor cost per unit remained at the bud-geted level of $10.00, the company would have spent $110,000. It actually spent $1,000 more than that amount.

$$\text{Actual Volume} \times \text{Budgeted Cost per Unit} = \text{Expected Cost}$$
$$11,000 \times \$10.00 = \$110,000$$

Actual cost per unit was $111,000/11,000, or $10.09. This $0.09 un-favorable difference cost the company $1,000.

This negative event is certainly undesirable. The following factors should be considered and evaluated.

1. If higher volumes resulted in longer production runs, this should have reduced the number of machine setups. If this were true, average labor cost per unit should have been lower than budgeted rather than higher.

2. If the additional volume was gradual and anticipated, production planning should have provided for the increase and the cost overrun should not have occurred.

3. If the demand for higher volumes was met by reducing finished goods inventory, then labor cost should not have been different from the budget at all.

4. If the increased volume was a sudden surge, especially if it came from one or two customers placing orders with short lead times, overtime or weekend work might have been necessary if the company was to respond in a timely manner.

5. If the additional volume came from new customers, delivery lead times might have been artificially shortened to make a good impression. If these new customers placed smaller orders in order to test Raritan's quality or its commitment to customer service, then labor efficiency would be expected to decline somewhat, but only for a short period of time.

6. Since direct material costs were down and direct labor costs were up, another possible explanation is that the lower material cost is the result of using lower-quality materials. If this is true, then extra labor might have been required to compensate for the cheaper material. Some product may have had to be redone or repaired manually to ensure a high-quality finished product. The lesson here is that looking for "bargains" is rarely effective. Also, the days of compromising quality are gone. Quality of product is no longer negotiable.

Intelligent analysis requires that no judgments be made until the cause of an event has been determined. While differences should be explained, the effort should not be limited to negative variances, and no value judgments should be made until the facts are known. Much of the cost of direct labor is really fixed. Higher volumes are therefore expected to reduce the average cost per unit. The so-called efficiency explanations are really attributable to better utilization of a relatively fixed cost. This was not Raritan's experience.

Factory Overhead

This expense category has both fixed and variable components. Based on a production budget of 10,000 units, Raritan expected to spend $190,000 on this category. Breaking that amount into its fixed and variable portions, the budgeted amount was

$$\$40,000 + \$15 \text{ per unit}$$

With actual volume at 11,000 units, it would be reasonable to expect that expenditures in this category would amount to $205,000, as follows:

$$\$40,000 + \$15(11,000) = \$40,000 + \$165,000 = \$205,000$$

Actual expenditures were $195,000. This suggests efficiency greater than what was reflected in the budget and a positive variance of $10,000. Explanations for this and other categories must include the possibility that more of the costs than the standards suggest are really fixed. Other explanations include the benefits of economies of scale associated with the higher volumes. Further examination of the details of the components of this category is required. Surface appearances do not suggest any major problem issues.

Administration

Raritan expected to spend $65,000 in this category based upon the budgeted volume of 10,000 units. The actual budget is:

$$\$45,000 + \$2(10,000) = \$65,000$$

If this category truly has a variable component, it would be expected that at 11,000 units, spending would have amounted to $67,000, calculated as follows:

$$\$45,000 + \$2(11,000) = \$45,000 + \$22,000 = \$67,000$$

The actual spending of $64,000 is even below the originally budgeted amount. We know that technology is improving the efficiency of support departments, especially accounting. This might be a factor here.

Distribution

There are opportunities for significant efficiencies and economies of scale in this category, which includes warehousing and trucking. Loading additional volume on delivery trucks costs very little more, especially if the product is destined for the same customers. An efficiently organized and managed warehouse should be able to handle significant increases in volume with very little additional spending. This would not be true, of course, if the additional volume was not anticipated, but was very sudden and had short lead times. Disruptions can be very expensive, however worthwhile they may be. The company expected to spend $80,000 in this category. The budget is:

$$\$50,000 + \$3(10,000) = \$80,000$$

At an actual volume of 11,000 units, total spending in the distribution categories could have been $83,000, as follows:

$$\$50,000 + \$3(11,000) = \$50,000 + \$33,000 = \$83,000$$

Actual expenditures in this category amounted to $80,000. This represents an efficiency variance of $3,000.

Further analysis of Raritan's performance requires us to dig deeper into the details. All categories should be reviewed periodically to identify both positive and negative events. Then the negative events should be corrected, and the positive events should be reinforced. The quarterly reviews should be more extensive than the monthly review meetings, unless it is determined at a monthly meeting that the actual results are a significant departure from budget assumptions.

Total actual spending amounted to $502,250. Had the actual variable costs per unit been the same as the budgeted costs, this amount would have been $525,000. The conclusion here is that Raritan generally handled the additional business well, functioned efficiently, and enjoyed some economies of scale that were not necessarily reflected in the budget formulas.

CHAPTER TEN

Return on Investment

A n investment is an exposure of cash that has the objective of producing cash inflows in the future. The worthiness of an investment is measured by how much cash the investment is expected to generate compared with how much investment is required.

The analysis of return on investment is a financial forecasting tool that assists the business manager in evaluating whether a proposed investment opportunity is worthwhile, given the context of the company's business objectives and financial constraints.

What Is Analyzed?

The investments to be analyzed have some of the following characteristics:

- ➤ A major amount of money is involved.
- ➤ The financial commitment is for more than one year.
- ➤ Cash flow benefits are expected to be achieved over many years.

➤ The strategic direction of the company may be affected.

➤ The company's prosperity may be significantly affected by making—or not making—the investment.

Why Are These Opportunities Analyzed So Extensively?

Investment decisions should be analyzed carefully because such analysis assists the decision-making process. These decisions are irreversible, have long-term strategic implications, provide considerable uncertainty as to their success, and involve serious financial risk.

Forecasting the future performance of a proposed investment requires the analyst to identify all of the issues and effects, both positive and negative, associated with the investment. While this does not eliminate risk, it does produce a more intelligent, better informed decision-making process. Facts and expectations based upon research and strategic thinking are incorporated into the forecast. The results of the financial analysis do not make the decision. People make decisions based upon the best available information. A capital expenditure requires significant funds and corporate commitment. It is vital that these decisions be well informed.

Irreversible

Operating decisions, such as scheduling some overtime or purchasing larger amounts of raw materials, can be changed if the environment or circumstances change. Adjustments can also occur when it becomes obvious that a mistake was made. With these decisions, the need for correction can be readily determined, and the correction can be implemented soon thereafter, with minimal financial penalty. A capital expenditure decision, such as the purchase of machinery, can also be changed. In this case, however, the financial penalty can be substantial. Having installed equipment sit idle because customer orders dried up or never materialized can be severely damaging. Changes in customer preferences that are not recognized before assets are purchased and installed can be even more damaging if the company cannot or is unwilling to admit the mistakes and take corrective actions. The discipline of analysis and forecasting should minimize the occurrence of this type of event.

Long-Term Strategic Implications

Locating an operation in a certain part of the country or the world, building a factory in a certain configuration, and deciding what kind of machines are needed and how many are all decisions that will affect the way the company conducts its business for many years to come. These decisions may very well contribute to the company's future prosperity, or the absence of it. Companies have experienced all of the following problems:

- Depletion of critical raw materials
- Termination of rail transportation service
- Manpower and/or skills shortages

The discipline of the forecasting process forces companies to identify, evaluate, and resolve these risks and vulnerabilities.

Uncertainty

Predicting the future is becoming more complex for businesses. Markets, customers, competitors, and technology have made the need for strategic discipline more critical than ever before. This becomes even more difficult when you add global sourcing; economic turmoil; the growth of China, Brazil, and India; and communications advances that make us all one major marketplace.

Technology has caused additional complexity in developing competitive strategy. Few if any retailers considered Amazon a competitive threat twenty years ago. Today, few independent booksellers remain afloat, and Barnes and Noble is suffering. Most companies that print checks for bank customers never contemplated online bill payment. How often do you turn to a new checkbook? Once or twice a year? Most newspaper companies have had to separate content from delivery of information. Do you still have a paper delivered to your door? Newsweek Magazine, once a prominent player in weekly magazines, has disappeared from your dentist's waiting room and now distributes its content solely on its website.

Financial Exposure

In addition to the uncertainties and risks involved, the sheer amount of funds involved in a major investment requires that all available facts and issues be identified and evaluated. If additional debt is directly or indirectly involved, the analytical process becomes even more critical. Involving banks or other sources of external financing is often very helpful. Despite current economic events, banks are risk-averse businesses. They will not lend money unless they are convinced of the merits of the proposed investment. Lenders often protect their clients by identifying risks that the clients have not identified or have underemphasized. In this situation, the forecast becomes a selling document as well as a decision-making tool.

Discounted Cash Flow

The financial tool that is used to evaluate investment opportunities is called *discounted cash flow (DCF)*. The different measurements used to evaluate investment opportunities that use this tool in some way are:

- ➤ Internal rate of return
- ➤ Net present value
- ➤ Profitability index
- ➤ Payback period

The types of investments that can be evaluated with this tool are:

>   Capital expenditures
>   Research and development
>   Major advertising and promotional efforts
>   Outsourcing alternatives
>   Major contract negotiations (price, payment terms, duration, specifications)
>   Evaluating new products and businesses
>   Buying another business
>   Strategic alliances
>   Valuing real estate

Let's start out by identifying a number of key conceptual premises of DCF.

0 means period zero, or the starting point of the project.
1 means one year from the start of the project.
2 means two years from the start of the project, and so forth.

A simple example is:

0. ($1,000) cash outflow (represented within parentheses)
1. $1,020 cash inflow

This is a profitable investment because the cash inflow exceeds the cash outflow—but only by $20 (2 percent). This is not a particularly attractive investment, therefore, because if the money were put in a local bank, the return might be 5 percent:

0. ($1,000)
1. $1,050

The bank deposit is also risk free because the deposit is insured by the FDIC.

Therefore, we have already established three basic principles of DCF:

1. It is measuring profitability.
2. Risk issues are incorporated into the analysis.
3. There is an opportunity cost. Projects are judged against alternatives.

Profit $ = Interest $

Now consider the following financial relationship:

0. ($1,000)
1. $1,200

If this were a stock purchase and sale one year later, the profit would be $200. If this were a bank loan, where you borrowed $1,000 and repaid $1,200 after a year, the bank's profit (interest) would obviously be $200.

These are the same concepts; the only differences are semantic.

ROI % = Interest %

The return on investment (ROI) on the stock purchase and sale would be 20 percent. The interest rate on the loan would also be 20 percent, as follows:

$$\frac{\text{Profit}}{\text{Investment}} = \frac{\$200}{\$1,000} = 20\% = \frac{\$200}{\$1,000} = \frac{\text{Interest}}{\text{Loan}}$$

The interest rate is the annual fee that the banker charges for the loan. The ROI is the annual "fee" (ROI requirement) that we impose on an investment.

Annual Concept

Consider the following:

0. ($1,000)
2. $1,200

While the dollar amount of interest and profit remained at $200, the ROI and the interest rate declined to approximately 10 percent. Therefore, ROI and interest rate are annual concepts.

Time Value of Money Concept

Discounted cash flow is based upon the *time value of money* concept. What this means is that not only do we value how much cash flow is generated, but we are also very concerned with when it is received. Sooner is better. The faster the cash flow is received, the sooner it can be reinvested.

Principal First

The following two investments are not the same:

	A	B
0.	($1,000)	($1,000)
1.	$1,200	$ 200
2.		$ 200

Notice that the ROI in alternative B is negative. In fact, the figures for alternative B show a loss of $600. For an ROI to be achieved at all, a return of the investment itself must come first. In the case of the loan, the banker wants the principal to be repaid before the interest is recognized.

Present Value

The basic premises of discounted cash flow have now been identified.

1. This is a measure of profitability.
2. Risk issues are incorporated into the analysis.
3. There is an opportunity cost. Projects are judged against alternatives.
4. Profit $ = Interest $.

5. ROI % = Interest %.

6. This is an annual concept.

7. Principal must be returned first.

While these key points are all interdependent, the critical one is that interest rate and ROI are calculated in the same way. The basis of the discounted cash flow technique is to use the interest rate or present value tables to calculate ROI. Interest rate tables and present value tables use the same mathematics. They are just constructed differently. Focus on the analysis in Exhibit 10-1. Each lettered item in the exhibit is addressed individually.

(a) The company is considering an investment of $15,000. It wants to buy a machine that will help it to increase revenue and the resulting cash flow by adding more features and benefits to its products,

(b) The company estimates that this opportunity will benefit it for four years. This might be determined by the physical life of the machine, the market life of the features and benefits that the machine will make possible, or the market life of the product line itself. Alternatively, the company's forecasting horizon may be four years. The time period used in the forecast may well be determined by the company's comfort level.

(c) The company has determined that the minimum required return on investment for this particular opportunity is 15

Exhibit 10-1.

	Present Value	
Cash Flows	Factors @ 15% (c)	Amount (e)
0. ($15,000) (a)		
1. $ 6,000	× 0.86957 (d) =	$ 5,217
2. 6,000	× 0.75614 =	4,536
3. 6,000	× 0.65752 =	3,945
4. 6,000 (b)	× 0.57174 =	3,430
	2.8550 (f)	$17,128 (e)

percent. The company may or may not require the same ROI of all projects. Some companies call the required ROI the *hurdle rate* (that must be "jumped over" by the project). The hurdle rate may or may not be the same as the company's cost of capital. There are many different versions of this terminology, so be careful. ROI and interest rate are the same. Therefore, 15 percent is also the *interest rate.* The annual fee that the company will "charge" the project for the use of the company's money is the equivalent of the annual fee that a bank charges for a loan. The 15 percent is also the *time value of money* (TVOM) of that annual fee. In terms of the discounted cash flow technique, the 15 percent is called the *factor.* These four terms—*ROI, interest rate, TVOM,* and *factor*—are synonymous.

(d) These decimals are the present value factors. The decimal given for each year is 15 percent less than the decimal given for the previous year. These factors can all be found in Table 10-1, under the column for 15 percent.

(e) The annual cash flow forecast is multiplied by the present value factors. The results are the present value amounts. Through this procedure, each year's forecast cash flow is penalized by 15 percent times the number of years the company will have to wait for that cash inflow. We are in fact "discounting the cash flows"—hence the name of this technique. The four discounted cash inflows add up to $17,128. This is called the *present value of the cash inflows.* It is, in fact, the value of the deal. If this company invested $17,128 and achieved cash inflows of $6,000 per year for four years, the ROI would be exactly 15 percent. In this case, the machine cost less than $17,128. Therefore, the return on investment is greater than 15 percent.

(f) Notice that in Table 10-1, we multiplied $6,000 times each individual annual factor. As an alternative, we can add up the four annual factors, giving us 2.855, and multiply this number by the annual cash flow. Except for differences caused by rounding decimals, doing one summary multiplication will give the same result as the individual annual calculations. The sum of the annual factors (2.855) is called

Table 10-1. Present Value of $1 Due at the End of n Periods.

Period	1%	2%	3%	4%	5%	6%	7%	8%	9%	10%	12%	14%	15%	16%	18%	20%	24%	28%	32%	36%
1	.9901	.9804	.9709	.9615	.9524	.9434	.9346	.9259	.9174	.9091	.8929	.8772	.8696	.8621	.8475	.8333	.8065	.7813	.7576	.7353
2	.9803	.9612	.9426	.9246	.9070	.8900	.8734	.8573	.8417	.8264	.7972	.7695	.7561	.7432	.7182	.6944	.6504	.6104	.5739	.5407
3	.9706	.9423	.9151	.8890	.8638	.8396	.8163	.7938	.7722	.7513	.7118	.6750	.6575	.6407	.6086	.5787	.5245	.4768	.4348	.3975
4	.9610	.9238	.8885	.8548	.8227	.7921	.7629	.7530	.7084	.6830	.6355	.5921	.5718	.5523	.5158	.4823	.4230	.3725	.3294	.2923
5	.9515	.9057	.8626	.8219	.7835	.7473	.7130	.6806	.6499	.6209	.5674	.5194	.4972	.4761	.4371	.4019	.3411	.2910	.2495	.2149
6	.9420	.8880	.8375	.7903	.7462	.7050	.6663	.6302	.5963	.5645	.5066	.4556	.4323	.4104	.3704	.3349	.2751	.2274	.1890	.1580
7	.9327	.8706	.8131	.7599	.7107	.6651	.6227	.5835	.5470	.5132	.4523	.3996	.3759	.3538	.3139	.2791	.2218	.1776	.1432	.1162
8	.9235	.8535	.7894	.7307	.6768	.6274	.5820	.5403	.5019	.4665	.4039	.3506	.3269	.3050	.2660	.2326	.1789	.1388	.1085	.0854
9	.9143	.8368	.7664	.7026	.6446	.5919	.5439	.5002	.4604	.4241	.3606	.3075	.2843	.2630	.2255	.1938	.1443	.1084	.0822	.0628
10	.9053	.8203	.7441	.6756	.6139	.5584	.5083	.4632	.4224	.3855	.3220	.2697	.2472	.2267	.1911	.1615	.1164	.0847	.0623	.0462
11	.8963	.8043	.7224	.6496	.5847	.5268	.4751	.4289	.3875	.3505	.2875	.2366	.2149	.1954	.1619	.1346	.0938	.0662	.0472	.0340
12	.8874	.7885	.7014	.6246	.5568	.4970	.4440	.3971	.3555	.3186	.2567	.2076	.1869	.1685	.1372	.1122	.0757	.0517	.0357	.0250
13	.8787	.7730	.6810	.6006	.5303	.4688	.4150	.3677	.3262	.2897	.2292	.1821	.1625	.1452	.1163	.0935	.0610	.0404	.0271	.0184
14	.8700	.7579	.6611	.5775	.5051	.4423	.3878	.3405	.2992	.2633	.2046	.1597	.1413	.1252	.0985	.0779	.0492	.0316	.0205	.0135
15	.8613	.7430	.6419	.5553	.4810	.4173	.3624	.3152	.2745	.2394	.1827	.1401	.1229	.1079	.0835	.0649	.0397	.0247	.0155	.0099
16	.8528	.7284	.6232	.5339	.4581	.3936	.3387	.2919	.2519	.2176	.1631	.1229	.1069	.0930	.0708	.0541	.0320	.0193	.0118	.0073
17	.8444	.7142	.6050	.5134	.4363	.3714	.3166	.2703	.2311	.1978	.1456	.1078	.0929	.0802	.0600	.0451	.0258	.0150	.0089	.0054
18	.8360	.7002	.5874	.4936	.4155	.3503	.2959	.2502	.2120	.1799	.1300	.0946	.0808	.0691	.0508	.0376	.0208	.0118	.0068	.0039
19	.8277	.6864	.5703	.4746	.3957	.3305	.2765	.2317	.1945	.1635	.1161	.0829	.0703	.0596	.0431	.0313	.0168	.0092	.0051	.0029
20	.8195	.6730	.5537	.4564	.3769	.3118	.2584	.2145	.1784	.1486	.1037	.0728	.0611	.0514	.0365	.0261	.0135	.0072	.0039	.0021

an *annuity factor*. Annuity factors can be used accurately only when the annual cash inflows are the same amount. When annual cash inflows differ, the present value factors for each individual year must be used. The annuity factors are already calculated and can be found in Table 10-2.

Discounted Cash Flow Measures

The specific measures of profitability that can be used to evaluate this investment are:

➤ Net present value
➤ Profitability index
➤ Internal rate of return

Net Present Value

The *net present value (NPV)* is a dollar amount. It is calculated as follows:

Present Value of the Cash Inflows	$17,128	
− Present Value of the Cash Outflow	− 15,000	(the investment)
= Net Present Value	$ 2,128	

A net present value that is a positive amount means that the actual return on investment exceeds the target rate, in this case 15 percent. An NPV that is a negative dollar amount means that the actual ROI is below the target. If the NPV is equal to zero, the ROI percentage used to do the calculation is the actual ROI.

Profitability Index

The *profitability index (PI)* is a comparison of the actual ROI to the target ROI. Its calculation is:

$$\frac{\text{Present Value of the Cash Inflows}}{\text{Present Value of the Cash Outflows}} = \text{Profitability Index}$$

$$\frac{\$17,128}{\$15,000} = 1.14$$

Table 10-2. Present Value of an Annuity of $1 per Period for n Periods.

Period	1%	2%	3%	4%	5%	6%	7%	8%	9%	10%	12%	14%	15%	16%	18%	20%	24%	28%	32%
1	0.9901	0.9804	0.9709	0.9615	0.9524	0.9434	0.9346	0.9259	0.9174	0.9091	0.8929	0.8772	0.8696	0.8621	0.8475	0.8333	0.8065	0.7813	0.7576
2	1.9704	1.9416	1.9135	1.8861	1.8594	1.8334	1.8080	1.7833	1.7591	1.7355	1.6901	1.6467	1.6257	1.6052	1.5656	1.5278	1.4568	1.3916	1.3315
3	2.9410	2.8839	2.8286	2.7751	2.7232	2.6730	2.6243	2.5771	2.5313	2.4869	2.4018	2.3216	2.2832	2.2459	2.1743	2.1065	1.9813	1.8685	1.7663
4	3.9020	3.8077	3.7171	3.6299	3.5460	3.4651	3.3872	3.3121	3.2397	3.1699	3.0373	2.9137	2.8550	2.7982	2.6901	2.5887	2.4043	2.2410	2.0957
5	4.8534	4.7135	4.5797	4.4518	4.3295	4.2124	4.1002	3.9927	3.8897	3.7908	3.6048	3.4331	3.3522	3.2743	3.1272	2.9906	2.7454	2.5320	2.3452
6	5.7955	5.6014	5.4172	5.2421	5.0757	4.9173	4.7665	4.6229	4.4859	4.3553	4.1114	3.8887	3.7845	3.6847	3.4976	3.3255	3.0205	2.7594	2.5342
7	6.7282	6.4720	6.2303	6.0021	5.7864	5.5824	5.3893	5.2064	5.0330	4.8684	4.5638	4.2883	4.1604	4.0386	3.8115	3.6046	3.2423	2.9370	2.6775
8	7.6517	7.3255	7.0197	6.7327	6.4632	6.2098	5.9713	5.7466	5.5348	5.3349	4.9676	4.6389	4.4873	4.3436	4.0776	3.8372	3.4212	3.0758	2.7860
9	8.5660	8.1622	7.7861	7.4353	7.1078	6.8017	6.5152	6.2469	5.9952	5.7590	5.3282	4.9464	4.7716	4.6065	4.3030	4.0310	3.5655	3.1842	2.8681
10	9.4713	8.9826	8.5302	8.1109	7.7217	7.3601	7.0236	6.7101	6.4177	6.1446	5.6502	5.2161	5.0188	4.8332	4.4941	4.1925	3.6819	3.2689	2.9304
11	10.3676	9.7868	9.2526	8.7605	8.3064	7.8869	7.4987	7.1390	6.8052	6.4951	5.9377	5.4527	5.2337	5.0286	4.6560	4.3271	3.7757	3.3351	2.9776
12	11.2551	10.5753	9.9540	9.3851	8.8633	8.3838	7.9427	7.5361	7.1607	6.8137	6.1944	5.6603	5.4206	5.1971	4.7932	4.4392	3.8514	3.3868	3.0133
13	12.1337	11.3484	10.6350	9.9856	9.3936	8.8527	8.3577	7.9038	7.4869	7.1034	6.4235	5.8424	5.5831	5.3423	4.9095	4.5327	3.9124	3.4272	3.0404
14	13.0037	12.1062	11.2961	10.5631	9.8986	9.2950	8.7455	8.2442	7.7862	7.3667	6.6282	6.0021	5.7245	5.4675	5.0081	4.6106	3.9616	3.4587	3.0609
15	13.8651	12.8493	11.9379	11.1184	10.3797	9.7122	9.1079	8.5595	8.0607	7.6061	6.8109	6.1422	5.8474	5.5755	5.0916	4.6755	4.0013	3.4834	3.0764
16	14.7179	13.5777	12.5611	11.6523	10.8378	10.1059	9.4466	8.8514	8.3126	7.8237	6.9740	6.2651	5.9542	5.6685	5.1624	4.7296	4.0333	3.5026	3.0882
17	15.5623	14.2919	13.1661	12.1657	11.2741	10.4773	9.7632	9.1216	8.5436	8.0216	7.1196	6.3729	6.0472	5.7487	5.2223	4.7746	4.0591	3.5177	3.0971
18	16.3983	14.9920	13.7535	12.6593	11.6896	10.8276	10.0591	9.3719	8.7556	8.2014	7.2497	6.4674	6.1280	5.8178	5.2732	4.8122	4.0799	3.5294	3.1039
19	17.2260	15.6785	14.3238	13.1339	12.0853	11.1581	10.3356	9.6036	8.9501	8.3649	7.3658	6.5504	6.1982	5.8775	5.3162	4.8435	4.0967	3.5386	3.1090
20	18.0456	16.3514	14.8775	13.5903	12.4622	11.4699	10.5940	9.8181	9.1285	8.5136	7.4694	6.6231	6.2593	5.9288	5.3527	4.8696	4.1103	3.5458	3.1129

A profitability index greater than 1.0 means that the actual ROI exceeds the target. A profitability index lower than 1.0 means that the actual ROI is below the target. If the PI is exactly 1.0, the ROI percentage used in the calculation is the actual ROI.

In this example, it is now known with certainty that the actual return on investment exceeds 15 percent. The NPV is a positive amount, and the PI exceeds 1.0. The profitability index and the net present value will never provide conflicting signals, nor will there ever be conflicting signals between the NPV and PI and the actual return on investment. Within the realm of normal business forecasting, a conflicting signal is impossible.

Internal Rate of Return

Consider the following formula:

$$PVCO = PVCI \times Factor\ (\%, yrs)$$

This is the formula for the internal rate of return, which is the actual ROI based upon the discounted cash flow technique. This formula is in all computer software dealing with this technique. In words, it reads:

The present value of the cash outflows (PVCO, or investment) will be equal to the present value of the cash inflows (PVCI) when multiplied by the correct factor. Correct means the factor corresponding to the right percentage and the right number of years.

We now have a critical formula in which three of the four parameters are known. Returning to the example:

PVCO (investment)	$15,000	$15,000 = $6,000 × F (%, 4 yrs)
Cash Inflows	$ 6,000	
Number of Years	4	

Solving for the factor using algebra, we get $15,000/$6,000, or 2.5. Now we search in Table 10-2 (the annuity table) in the row for

Year 4 until we find the factor 2.5. Notice that for Year 4, the factor for 20 percent is 2.588 and the factor for 24 percent is 2.404. Therefore, the actual return on investment is between 20 percent and 24 percent. In fact, it is approximately 21 percent. Remember that Table 10-2 can be used only if the annual cash inflows are the same amount. If the annual cash inflows are different, the method described here will work, but since the formula will include each annual cash flow amount multiplied by the present value factor for that amount and year, more trial and error and number crunching will be necessary.

Payback Period

The payback period is the amount of time that it takes for the cash inflows from the investment to be exactly equal to the investment. It is a cash flow breakeven. While it is not a measure of profitability, it is a measure of risk. Consideration of the payback period is especially valuable for companies with tight cash flow situations. While the company does not want to shut off investment completely, it needs to focus on those opportunities that will have the greatest positive effect on its tight cash position. For the opportunity that has been analyzed here, the payback period is calculated as follows:

$$\frac{\text{Investment}}{\text{Annual Cash Inflows}} = \frac{\$15,000}{\$6,000} = 2.5 \text{ years}$$

This measure is sometimes the only tool that companies use to evaluate an investment opportunity. The problem with this payback-only approach is that, in addition to the fact that it is not a measure of profitability, it treats all cash inflows within the payback period equally, without regard to their time value, and it ignores all cash flows after the payback period.

Risk

The psychology of corporate investment risk is very different from that of personal investment risk. When we as individuals are contemplating an investment, such as a stock purchase, our perception of the risk of the investment focuses on the possibility of our losing the funds invested. In a corporate environment, investment risk involves not achieving the profitability improvement that was forecast to justify the investment and gain budget approval for it.

If an ROI of 20 percent is forecast and the ROI actually achieved is 8 percent, there is a corporate credibility problem and an opportunity cost issue. The next time this manager asks for funds, his "failure" will be incorporated into the decision. The manager didn't "make the numbers." Someone higher up will be wondering what other investments were not made because of the manager's ROI forecast of 20 percent and actual achievement of 8 percent.

Personally, if we invested in a stock hoping for a 20 percent return and achieved 8 percent, we would be somewhat disappointed, but we would still feel somewhat satisfied because we "made money." We as individuals don't have the corporate perspective and don't have to deal with political issues.

Given these factors, there are ways in which a company can incorporate risk into its investment analysis. These include combining the payback period and the ROI hierarchy.

As mentioned earlier, the payback period is a reflection of risk. The longer the time required to reach the cash flow breakeven point, the greater is the uncertainty associated with forecasting the future. A new machine that reduces manufacturing labor and materials could have a payback period of six months. Expanding production based upon a forecast of new products and customer opportunities involves considerable risk. This type of investment might have a payback period of three years. While the investment may turn out to be wonderfully profitable, there is a considerable amount of uncertainty associated with it. Risk can be incorporated into the ROI analysis by creating an ROI target with the payback period as the guiding factor, as follows:

Payback Period	ROI Target
2.0 years or less	15%
2.0–3.0 years	20%
3.0–4.0 years	25%

The ROI target reflects expectations, risk, cash constraints, and opportunity cost. Using the payback period helps the company to incorporate risk into the analysis.

Another means of incorporating risk is to classify the projects. The company can then create a hierarchy of ROI targets based upon these classifications. An example is:

Classification of Project	ROI Target
Process Improvement	15%
New Product	19%
New Market	21%
Corporate Acquisition	25%

Capital Expenditure Defined

As stated at the beginning of this chapter, an investment is an exposure of cash that has the objective of producing cash inflows in the future. Therefore, the amount used for a capital expenditure should include:

- ➤ Capital equipment, including installation
- ➤ Additional inventory to support the project
- ➤ Additional accounts receivable to finance increased revenues
- ➤ Software and systems to support production and warehousing

It is quite conceivable that capital expenditures that improve the manufacturing process will make a significant contribution to the reduction of inventory. This will be attributable to:

- ➤ Improved communication between the company and its suppliers
- ➤ Faster delivery times that reduce the need for raw materials inventory
- ➤ More efficient production that reduces work in process inventory

> ➤ Overall efficiencies that reduce the need for safety stock
> ➤ Higher quality that permits a reduction in finished goods inventory

The Cash Flow Forecast

All of the incremental revenues and expenses that will be created if the investment is made should be included in the forecast. The key term here is incremental. No existing expenses or overhead amounts should be allocated to the project. They already exist and will not be affected.

> Revenue
> − Cost of Goods Sold
> = Gross Profit
> − Incremental Overhead
> = Operating Income
> − Depreciation
> = Net Income Before Tax
> − Income Tax
> = Net Income
> + Depreciation
> = After-Tax Cash Flow

As mentioned previously, many investments that will improve manufacturing processes will also have the very positive effect of reducing inventory. Making the process more efficient, especially through the use of technology, will drastically reduce processing time, almost eliminating work in process inventory. More predictable, higher-quality production can reduce requirements for safety stock of raw materials and finished products.

Characteristics of a Quality Forecast

A forecast is a reflection of the future. An executive who uses the information to make a major decision involving a commitment of substantial resources and feels comfortable doing so has been working with a quality forecast. Does the forecast contain all of the available information that is pertinent to the decision being evaluated? Here are some of the characteristics of a forecast that may provide comfort to both the analyst and the decision maker.

Incrementality

All benefits, expenses, and investments that will change as a result of the decision should be included in the financial forecast. That is the concept of incrementality. This includes indirect expenses and the cost of additional support staff. The cost of an engineer who must be added to the team to support the product is incremental. So is the cost of marketing research that is necessary to make some marketplace decisions. Any spending is incremental as long as it results from implementing the decision and will not occur if the decision is to not implement the project.

The financial forecast should not include allocations of existing corporate overhead. The purpose of the forecast is to identify the financial impact that the project will have on the company. The existing corporate overhead will be the same regardless of the decision.

Forecast Time Frame

With a few exceptions, most forecasts should provide a maximum of five years of cash inflows. Major advances in technology and global economic turmoil are making predicting the future more difficult than ever. Even though we hope that the new business will last forever, we know that this is not likely to happen. If five years of cash inflows do not justify the investment and permit the company to achieve its ROI targets, the risk factors increase substantially.

Adding years to the forecast can be a form of analytical manipulation, whether intentional or not. Adding more years of cash inflows will increase the ROI. Therefore, using a set number of years lends credibility to the forecast and ensures comparability and objectivity.

Exceptions to the five-year guideline include calculating the

ROI on such things as pharmaceutical research or the construction of major oil pipelines and nuclear power plants. Even here, any new oil refineries or investments made in drilling during the 2011–2014 time period were based on the $100 price per barrel of oil at the time. Oil actually hit a peak of $140 per barrel during that time. Incredible advances in drilling technology have dramatically improved access to oil and allowed for cheaper extraction costs. Recent calming of political turmoil in Libya, Nigeria, and other major oil-producing countries has made the supply of oil even greater. In 2015 the price of a barrel of oil went below $45. All of the forecast assumptions made in and after 2011 have proven to be ruinously incorrect. And investments that were being made in nuclear power all have stopped since the Fukushima nuclear power facility melted down in 2011 following the magnitude 9.0 earthquake, as have plans for future construction. These types of investments may very well have to have time horizons of 10 years or more and should be analyzed accordingly.

Accounting Rules

The forecast should respect the accounting rules and practices that will govern the company's reporting over the period for which the forecast is made. This is particularly important as it relates to tax reporting, which will have significant cash flow effects. However, adhering to the requirements of the accounting format is not critical except insofar as cash flow will be affected. After all, the analysis is forecasting the future, not reporting the past.

External Financing

Cash flow forecasts should assume that the investments will be all cash, and they should be included in the forecast at the point when the commitments to acquire assets are made. This should be done even if the company expects to get financing for the project from a bank or even from the equipment vendors. The project and the underlying risk begin when the commitments are made, which may be long before the cash is disbursed. While the use of external financing sources may be favorable and in fact may be necessary, external financing increases risk. Debt service payments are a fixed cost that increases the company's breakeven point.

If external financing is decided upon, the first analysis should reflect the now hypothetical up-front cash investment. This is called the *base case*. The ROI calculated on this basis should exceed the company's ROI hurdle rate. Analyses of financing alternatives can then be compared to this base case. Thus, discounted cash flow analysis becomes a tool for evaluating proposals from banks and other lenders. When the external financing is included in the analysis, the ROI will increase significantly. Financing is in fact postponing cash outflows. The cost of that financing will be included in the revised forecast. The before-tax cost of borrowing should be substantially below the after-tax ROI, thus improving the ROI on the project in its entirety.

Working Capital Investment

As we have said, an investment is an exposure of cash that has the objective of producing cash flow benefits in the future. If a project involves business expansion, additional inventory will be needed to produce the additional products, and additional accounts receivable will be needed to finance the sales that will be made. Additions to inventory and accounts receivable are investments just like the purchase of fixed assets. They should be an integral part of the project analysis.

Economics and Pricing

Forecasts should reflect current product prices and operating costs. The company should never rely on higher future selling prices to justify current investments for three reasons:

1. Technology is causing prices to be lower rather than higher as business expands. Competition on a global scale makes every business vulnerable to increased pricing pressures.
2. If the project implementation is successful, potential

competitors will be attracted to the market and will soon be actual competitors. As a result, prices will not be higher. Computers, computer software and operating systems, and pharmaceuticals are prime examples of this. It is very dangerous to invest in a business on the premise that selling prices in the future will be higher.

3. You should look at the annual economic forecasts published in the major business publications. These are surveys of the country's top 50 economists. The divergence of their expert analyses is eye-opening. The range between the most optimistic and the most pessimistic forecasts of GNP, inflation, and unemployment is extreme. Most of these forecasts will be wrong. Incredibly, these economists are forecasting only one year in the future. If these econo-mists cannot forecast one year accurately, how can we novices superimpose our economic forecasts on an ROI analysis and expect to be reasonably accurate? The most effective method of dealing with this uncertainty is to assume that the current economic situation will continue, perhaps adjusting it for known events extending into the next year.

Establishing the ROI Target

Determining what the company defines as an acceptable return on investment is a very important process. The target ROI may be the result of intense mathematical modeling or, at the other extreme, it may be simply a continuation of things that have worked in the past. We will use the phrase *hurdle rate* for this ROI target. Using both the term *hurdle rate* and the term *cost of capital* could be seriously misleading. The ROI target used should reflect:

- ➤ The cost of raising debt and equity funds, past and future
- ➤ The expected risk and the company's ability to tolerate it
- ➤ Alternative uses of the funds, such as debt reduction and dividend payments

➤ The improved profitability necessary if the company is to attain its future goals

Exhibit 10-2 outlines a method of establishing a company ROI target (hurdle rate). It incorporates the factors just stated. The sequence of events is described by the numbers in parentheses.

1. The company currently has a 10 percent return on assets. Notice that it uses a version of the ratio that uses after-tax cash flow rather than the traditional net income. The calculation is in Exhibit 10-2.

2. The company is developing a strategic plan that will include a financial forecast covering the same time period. It does this for a number of reasons, including getting answers to the following questions:
   a. What investments can it afford?
   b. Does the plan achieve the targets?
   c. How profitable must those investments be?
      Targeted return on assets for 2018 is determined to be 11 percent. This is a significant improvement from the level

Exhibit 10-2. Establishing Return on Investment Target Using the Management by Objectives Concept ($000)

	2015 Actual	3-Year Internal Improvements			3-Year Capital Budget	2018 Plan
		Volume	Efficiency	Total		
Revenue	$10,000	$500	—	$500		
Costs/Expenses	9,400	460	($25)	435		
Net Income	$ 600	$ 40	25	$ 65		
After-Tax Cash Flow	$ 1,000			$ 65	$ 90	$ 1,155
	(7)			(8)	(9)	(6)
Assets	$10,000				$500	$10,500
	(4)				(3)	(5)
Return on Assets	10%			18%		11%
	(1)				(10)	(2)

achieved in the current year. It should be benchmarked against competitors' returns and should reflect cash requirements for debt service and dividend payments.

3. The capital budget for the three-year period amounts to $500,000. This should incorporate all of the investments needed to implement the strategic plan.

4. The current asset base amounts to $10 million. This includes cash, accounts receivable, inventory, and the gross book value of the fixed assets. Using the gross book value rather than the net book value in this analysis is preferable. It avoids the appearance of year-to-year ROA improvement that results from assets being depreciated, making the denominator smaller.

5. Since the company has assets of $10 million and plans to add an additional $500,000 over the three-year period, it is forecasting an asset base of $10.5 million in the year 2018.

6. Since the company's target ROA for the year 2018 is 11 percent, and it is forecasting an asset base of $10.5 million, it will have to generate $1,155,000 in after-tax cash flow in order to achieve that target. The calculation is:

$$\text{ROA:} \quad \frac{\$1,155,000}{\$10,500,000} = 11\%$$

7. The company is currently achieving a cash flow of $1 million annually, and this is certainly expected to continue. There are two sources of improvement in this performance, internal and external. Internal improvements are those actions that the company can take to improve upon its existing performance that do not require investments or additional capacity. External improvements are the benefits resulting from additional investments.

8. Internal improvements are estimated to add $65,000 annually to after-tax cash flow. This results from the margins on additional sales volume and improved process efficiency.

9. Cash flow in 2018 must amount to $1,155,000. Subtracting from this amount the cash flow already achieved and the cash flow to be achieved from internal improvements leads to the conclusion that the annual cash flows generated by capital investments must amount to $90,000, as follows:

Target Cash Flow	$1,155,000
− Amount Already Generated	− 1,000,000
− Internal Improvements	− 65,000
= Amount to Be Generated by Capital Investments	$ 90,000

10. To achieve this amount of cash flow from the capital budget, the return on investment required of all projects must be at least 18 percent. The calculation is:

$$\frac{\text{ATCF}}{\text{Capital Budget}} = \frac{\$90,000}{\$500,000} = 18\%$$

This is not a mathematically perfect model, although its flaws do not diminish its value as a decision-making tool. Projects that are implemented in the first year of this three-year plan will probably reach their cash flow potential by Year 3. However, larger projects that are implemented in the third year of this plan may actually detract from the company's ability to attain the ROA requirement of 11 percent. A project that is implemented in the third year will add to the asset base but possibly will not yet be adding to the cash flow. Issues such as this will have to be resolved. However, using the 18 percent hurdle rate as a guide will result in quite effective decision making.

Analytical Simulations

The internal rate of return formula can help managers answer many business questions and evaluate reward/risk issues. To review:

$$\text{PVCO} = \text{PVCI} \times \text{Factor (\%, yrs)}$$

Example 1: Number of Years

A company is considering an investment of $10,000 and expects it to produce annual cash inflows of $4,000. If the company's ROI target is 20 percent, for how many years must these cash inflows continue if the company is to make this investment decision?

Using the formula:

$$\frac{\$10,000}{4,000} = \frac{\$4,000 \times F\ (20\%,\ yrs)}{4,000}$$

We now search Table 10-2, under the 20 percent column until we find a factor that is near 2.5. Notice that at three years, the factor is 2.106, and at four years, the factor is 2.59. Therefore, this investment opportunity must produce cash flows at this level for almost four years if the company is to achieve its 20 percent ROI target.

This investment model might describe a very high-tech investment, where the life of the technology itself is in question. If the technology will not continue to be state of the art for more than three years, then the company may not achieve its investment requirements and should invest its funds elsewhere. This model can also be used to evaluate fashion items or other investments with uncertain futures.

Example 2: P&L Components

A company is considering an investment of $10,000. The company requires an ROI of 24 percent and expects the investment to produce cash flows for four years. What annual cash flows are necessary to justify the investment?

$$\$10,000 = \text{Annual Cash Flows} \times \text{Factor (24\%, 4 yrs)}$$
$$\$10,000 = \text{Annual Cash Flows} \times 2.404$$
$$\text{Annual Cash Flows} = \$10,000/2.404 = \$4,160$$

Using the cash flow forecasting model, we can now determine whether the product's selling price, volumes, and cost structure will result in annual cash flows of $4,160.

Example 3: Corporate Acquisition

A company is considering the purchase of another company. It is a "friendly" acquisition in that the buyer and the seller are sharing information and negotiating. How much should the buyer be willing to pay if it is to achieve its required return on investment of 24 percent? The company's time horizon is 10 years with no salvage value.

1. After-tax cash flows forecast by seller	$ 9,000
2. Reduction by buyer because seller is optimistic	− 2,000
3. Synergistic benefits buyer will experience after takeover	+ 3,000
4. Benefits of improved efficiencies that buyer will implement	+ 2,000
5. Forecast cash inflows achieved by buyer after takeover	$12,000

We then apply the ROI formula:

6. Investment = $12,000 × F (24%, 10 yrs)
7. $12,000 × 3.6819 = $44,183

The maximum financial exposure that the company can afford if it is to receive all of the benefits of owning the subject company and still achieve an ROI of 24 percent is $44,183. This is not the recommended purchase price, however. The recommended purchase price is calculated as follows:

Maximum financial exposure	$44,183
Investment necessary to achieve synergies	− 7,000
Investment necessary to achieve efficiencies	− 3,000
Maximum purchase price	= $34,183

Some additional notes and comments:

Sellers tend to be optimistic because they are trying to sell something. Therefore, the forecasts that they provide have to be discounted, as is done here on line 2. The biggest reasons for the failure of an acquisition are:

➢ The buyer paid too much.
➢ The benefits were not achieved as soon as expected.

> ➤ Unknown problems surfaced after the takeover, suggesting
>   that the due diligence process was not adequately thor-
>   ough.

Reducing the amount of cash paid up front improves the ROI. Paying for the business over many years both improves the ROI and reduces risk. This improvement can be greatly enhanced through the use of an "earn-out" provision, which involves tying the payments to the achievement of the cash inflows that were forecast. If the seller forecast cash inflows of $9,000 per year, this is in fact what the buyer is paying for. Tying the buyer's payments to the achievement of that cash flow ensures that the buyer will pay for only the cash flows that are actually achieved. It also challenges the credibility of the seller and ensures the seller's efforts should the seller remain part of the buyer's team.

See Appendix E for a comprehensive case study providing practice in cash flow forecasting and ROI analysis using this discounted cash flow technique.

PART 4

Additional Financial Information

CHAPTER ELEVEN

Financing the Business

Borrowing money is a very positive corporate strategy. It helps the company to increase its growth, finance seasonal slowdowns, and invest in opportunities that will ensure its future. However, while the proper financing strategy will support these objectives, the wrong financing strategy will make what otherwise would be excellent corporate programs vulnerable to failure.

Business and our global economy are very dynamic. They are constantly changing, and the rules are always being redefined. Therefore, financing strategies must also be dynamic. What was appropriate for the company six months ago may be very undesirable now. So, like most other aspects of the business, the company's financing strategy requires constant monitoring and revision.

Those members of the management team who are responsible for marketing, operations, human resources, and technology have no direct responsibility for the company's relations with the financial community, although in a smaller company they may participate in this process when a major project is involved. All senior executives of public companies will be called upon to answer questions posed by stockholders and the financial community.

Every major project of the company will ultimately be affected by the existence, form, and quantity of the financing that the company secures. Budgets are expanded and people are hired because of new financing. Budgets and headcounts are reduced when financing is not obtained or the terms are onerous.

This chapter is included in this book because every businessperson has a serious vested interest in financing and financial strategy. The main issues affecting financing are its:

- Maturity
- Cost
- Conditions and restrictions
- Payment schedule
- Collateral

There are two classes of financing, debt and equity.

Debt

A company that uses debt to finance its business can engage in either short-term or long-term borrowing. Short-term borrowing involves loans with a maturity of one year or less. It is used to cover current cash needs, such as financing growth, seasonal cash flow needs, and major customer orders. The loans in this category are often called working capital loans, because that is what they finance.

Long-term loans have maturities of longer than one year. Companies borrow long term to finance major capital expansions, research and development projects with longer time horizons, and real estate.

Short-Term Debt

There are a number of types of both short-and long-term debt, and a number of related elements. We first cover those having to do with short-term debt:

1. Accounts receivable financing
2 Factoring
3. Inventory financing
4. Floor planning
5. Revolving credit
6. Zero-balance accounts
7. Lines of credit
8. Credit cards
9. Compensating balances

Accounts Receivable Financing. This is an excellent form of short-term financing that helps the company manage its cash flow. It involves using part or all of the company's accounts receivable as collateral for short-term loans. The collateral might include only specific invoices if some of the invoices are over 90 days old or if some customers' credit is not of high quality. (If the latter is true, perhaps these customers shouldn't be given credit at all.) By refusing to lend against these invoices, the bank is protecting itself from lending against the receivables of customers with low credit ratings. At the same time, it is giving the company some sound advice regarding its dealings with these customers.

With accounts receivable financing, the company retains the credit risk if its customers do not pay, and the company is responsible for collecting on its customers' accounts. Repayment schedules for this type of financing are highly negotiable. The company should make certain that undesirable inflexibilities are not built into the repayment terms. There are critical "shades of gray" between financial discipline and bank-imposed restriction. Banks and other lenders will typically create a line of credit equal to between 70 and 90 percent of qualified accounts receivable.

Factoring. In this financing alternative, the company actually sells its qualified accounts receivable to a bank or to an independent factoring company at a discount from their face value. The company receives immediate cash for its invoices. The invoices will direct the customers to pay the funds directly to the bank or factoring company (the factor).

This form of financing is expensive compared with alternative forms. In addition, it may lead customers to misjudge the company's financial position and conclude that it is having financial difficulties. The factor may have the right to take the initiative and call overdue accounts directly.

Factoring can cost between 2 and 5 percent per month. This could significantly cut into margins, especially if the borrower is in a low-margin business. However, if the terms of sale are currently 2/10, n/30, factoring may be a desirable alternative. Selling on terms of 2/10, n/30 means that the customer can take a 2 percent discount off the invoice amount if the invoice is paid within 10 days of the invoice date, and payments are expected within 30 days in any event. With these terms, customers will either take the 2 percent discount or delay payment for up to 30 days. If factoring costs 2 percent and the company can get its cash immediately, this is an attractive alternative.

Accounts receivable can be sold to a factor either with or without recourse. If the sale is without recourse, the buyer of the accounts receivable (the factor) assumes the full credit risk. If the customer does not pay, the factor loses the money. If the sale is with recourse, the company assumes the ultimate responsibility for credit losses if the customer does not pay. Selling without recourse is very expensive. Because only very high-quality receivables qualify for this form of financing, there is rarely a credit loss. Thus, selling without recourse is rarely advantageous. Companies can actually buy credit insurance that protects them against credit loss.

Inventory Financing. Usually only finished goods and raw materials inventory qualify as collateral. There is no market for work in process. Lenders will usually provide financing in the amount of one-half of the collateral that qualifies. This is a good form of financing to cover the cost of fulfilling a very large order from a high-quality customer, or perhaps, in a seasonal business, to cover a period of high cash needs that will be followed by a period of high cash inflows.

Using inventory as collateral requires fairly sophisticated inventory control methods, including systems support. This imposes corporate self-discipline, which the company should have anyway.

Floor Planning. Floor planning is a special form of inventory financing that is very common in the retail sale of very high-priced products, such as boats, cars, and appliances. With this form of financing, it is the vendor and its products that must be credit-qualified. The lender buys the products from the manufacturer and places them in the retailer's store and supporting warehouse, in effect lending them to the retailer.

The lender retains title to the products. When the retail dealer sells a product, the dealer must first pay the lender in order to get title to that product, which it can then transfer to the purchasing customer. This may be a simultaneous transaction, so that the retailer just receives the difference between the selling price and the loan amount.

Floor planning is often provided by a finance company owned by the manufacturer. The manufacturer and its associated finance company will provide various "bargains" to induce the retailer to overload on inventory. This smooths out the manufacturing process and places a lot of product in the dealer's showroom, which presumably will help sales. Slow-moving product is often provided to the dealer at zero financing cost as a way for the manufacturer to handle excess inventory.

As a business lesson, count the number of cars in a dealer's lot, calculate the estimated value of those cars (maybe the number of cars $\times$ \$20,000), and multiply that by 1 percent per month (the interest the dealer has to pay on the loan). It may very well be lower than 1 percent per month but it's an easier mental calculation. You can get an idea of how many cars a dealer must sell each month just to cover its floor plan interest expense.

Revolving Credit. This is basically a working capital loan with accounts receivable and inventory as collateral. The maximum amount of the loan is based on a formula tied to high-quality inventory and accounts receivable. For example, the maximum amount might be 75 percent of accounts receivable less than 60 days old and 50 percent of finished goods and raw materials inventory less than 60 days old. This formula forces the company to make regular payments and reduce the outstanding debt when the inventory is used and the receivables are collected.

Because of the pressure to repay and the constant monitoring of working capital, it would be very dangerous for a company to use this form of funding to support long-term projects. Some banks require what is known as a "cleanup" period. This means that for some period of time, perhaps one month per year, the loan balance must be zero.

Zero-Balance Accounts. This type of account may very well be required by another loan agreement. In a "regular" loan, the borrower collects funds from its customers, deposits the funds in the company checking account, and makes some sort of payment to the lender for principal and interest on the loan. With a zero-balance feature, the loan and the checking account are connected. When customer payments are deposited in the checking account, the funds are automatically used to reduce the loan balance and pay the interest that is due. Since the account balance is therefore zero, when the company writes checks, these checks increase the loan balance.

This feature is very similar, conceptually, to the overdraft privileges attached to individuals' checking accounts (although individuals usually decide how much of the funds they deposit should be used to reduce the loan balance, subject to a minimum monthly payment). This feature can be very beneficial to the company because float is reduced to zero. Customer payments automatically reduce the loan balance. The interest rate may also be advantageous because the bank knows that as the company receives payments from its customers, the loan will be repaid. Also, the company borrows only the exact amount it requires.

Lines of Credit. A line of credit is not a loan; it is a very favorable method of securing a loan. The cliche' describing this arrangement is "borrow when you don't need it so that you will have it when you do."

Suppose that a company is considering expansion plans or a major expenditure that will take place sometime within the next six months. The company's balance sheet is strong, and its need for the loan is uncertain, or at least not immediate. The company can go to the bank and arrange for a line of credit. This is an advance reservation that makes funds available, to be used only if and when they are needed.

The advantages of a line of credit are:

> The loan is arranged at a time chosen by the borrower.
> The funds are available; they can be used or not, at the choice of the borrower.
> The company is in a position to make major purchase commitments, knowing that this and maybe other financing options are available.
> It provides considerable purchase price bargaining power.
> Interest payments do not begin until the funds are actually used.

The company will pay a reservation fee, probably somewhere around 1 percent of the total line. Payment terms, interest, and other fees and collateral requirements will be the same as those on any other loan and are always negotiable. This is conceptually the same as a homeowner's equity line of credit.

Credit Cards. More and more customer orders are being placed by phone or by computer over the Internet. Allowing the customer to pay by credit card accomplishes a number of things:

> It eliminates accounts receivable, thus eliminating the wait for the money and the associated paperwork.
> The customer's creditworthiness need not be evaluated.

➤   There will be no overdue receivables.

➤   The customers can take as much time as they want to pay.

For smaller orders, waiting for customer payments and making the often inevitable collection phone calls can eliminate the profit. Although the company must pay the credit card fee, which is approximately 2 percent, accepting credit cards will make small orders profitable. This form of payment was often resisted. With the expansion of debit cards, point-of-sale payment systems tied to smart phones, PayPal and other Internet mechanisms, individuals and companies are becoming more comfortable with automatic payment systems. This transfers credit risk from the selling company to the credit company, which is usually better qualified to evaluate credit riskiness anyway. It also diminishes, if not eliminates, expensive invoicing, bad debts, and waiting for your money.

Compensating Balances. Requiring compensating balances is a bank strategy that increases the effective cost of borrowing money without increasing the stated interest rate. A compensating balance means that the borrower is required to keep a certain minimum balance in the checking account at all times.

If a company borrows $1,000,000 for one year at 10 percent, the interest rate is obviously 10 percent. However, if a 10 percent compensating balance is required, the borrower has the effective use of only $900,000. This results in an effective rate of about 11 percent. If the borrower really needs $1.0 million, it must borrow approximately $1.1 million. Like loan origination fees, collateral audit fees, search fees, and other such charges, compensating balances are a cost of borrowing and can be negotiated.

Long-Term Debt

The following types of long-term debt are covered here:

1. Term loans
2. Bonds

3. Debentures
4. Mortgage bonds
5. Convertible bonds
6. Senior debt
7. Subordinated debt
8. Junk bonds

Term Loans. This is the form of long-term debt that businesses use most frequently. It is a loan from a bank to a company that is used to finance expansion efforts. It has a fixed maturity date, frequently five to seven years from the date of the loan. The company will repay the loan in monthly installments of principal and interest. Spreading the payment of the principal over the life of the loan is called *loan amortization.* The monthly payments of principal and interest are called *debt service.* The amortization of the principal can also take place over a period that is longer than the loan period. With this arrangement, the remaining principal is due at the end of the loan period. That ending balance is called a *balloon payment.*

Bonds. A bond has many characteristics similar to those of a term loan. There are two differences:

1. A bond is a negotiable instrument that can be bought and sold like common stock.
2. A bond is usually sold to the public through a public offering registered with the Securities and Exchange Commission.

Bonds are usually sold in units of $1,000. A bond that is selling at its face value is said to be selling at par. The interest rate is called the coupon. After these securities are issued, their prices fluctuate in accordance with economic conditions. The prices of many bonds are quoted daily in major financial publications. Bonds usually make interest payments only, with the principal being repaid at maturity.

Debentures. A debenture is a bond that has only "the full faith and credit" of the company as collateral. Other than the credit rating and creditworthiness of the debtor, there is no specific collateral. The owners of these bonds, therefore, are classified as unsecured creditors.

Mortgage Bonds. A mortgage bond differs from a debenture only in that there is specific collateral to back up the security. Owners of these bonds are known as secured lenders. Because of this collateral, the interest rate should be lower than that on a debenture.

Convertible Bonds. This is a type of debenture with a very interesting feature. If a company does not have a high credit rating and therefore does not qualify for a reasonable interest rate, it would be prohibitively expensive for that company to sell bonds. Remember that investors and lenders have very different views on risk and reward. An investor may take a very high risk in the hope of experiencing a very high reward. A lender can never make more than the interest rate, and thus a lender that takes a very high risk may lose everything, but does not have the prospect of a high reward. The convertible bond changes the risk/reward relationship for the lender.

The bond is sold at a relatively low interest rate, perhaps 7 percent rather than the 12 percent that the company would otherwise have to pay. The owner of the bond has the right to convert the bond into shares of common stock at a predetermined price called the *strike price* (which is higher than the stock price at the time the bond is issued) at a later date. The company enjoys an affordable interest rate and can now expand its business. The owners of the convertible bonds get some interest and share in the rewards of success if the company does well and the price of the stock increases to above that strike price. Prices of convertible bonds are listed in the bond price tables in major financial publications with the extra symbol CV.

Senior Debt. This is a debenture issue that gives its holders priority over the holders of all other debenture issues in receiving interest payments and access to the company's assets in the event of a bankruptcy.

Subordinated Debt. Holders of this type of debt have priority below that of the holders of senior debt. Because of this secondary position and the resulting higher risk, holders of this debt will receive a higher interest rate than the holders of senior debt.

Junk Bonds. The creditworthiness of most companies and their securities is rated by various agencies, such as Standard & Poor's and Moody's. Bonds with the three or four highest ratings are generally classified as investment grade. Bonds in this category are recommended for pension funds and very conservative investors.

Bonds that do not qualify for these high ratings have a much smaller pool of available buyers. As a result, they must pay considerably higher interest rates, and so they are referred to as "high yield." As a company's creditworthiness declines, the yield on its bonds increases at an increasing rate because of the incrementally greater risk. When bonds reach a very high-yield, lower-quality status, they are known as "junk" bonds.

Equity

Selling common and preferred shares is essentially a permanent form of financing. It is also a form of financing that requires no repayment. In addition to raising funds, equity may also be issued for the purpose of expanding ownership of the stock, reducing concentration of voting power, and making the stock more liquid for stock market purposes.

There are three particularly important categories under the general heading of stockholders' equity that deserve attention here:

1. Venture capital
2. Preferred stock
3. Common stock

Venture Capital

Investors who supply venture capital are usually financing not much more than an idea, perhaps supported by a business plan. To obtain this type of financing, the founders of a company must be people who have some sort of track record or credentials indicating that they can effectively span the gap between an idea and a marketable product. Venture capital financing is most frequently available to high-tech ideas. Venture capital financiers are a very valuable source of early-stage investment funds. The companies they finance are not candidates for any sort of bank borrowing unless the principals or their backers are high-net-worth individuals who are willing to personally guarantee the loans.

People who are seeking venture capital financing will have a number of fundamental issues to deal with. Venture capital investors will want a large piece of the equity so that if the company is successful, the reward for its success will cover the cost of their probable other failures. They will be also intimately involved in deciding how their money will be spent. On the other hand, the company founders may very well not have any alternative, and they also may not have the managerial and marketing skills needed to create a viable business. Therefore, unless the company founders have an "angel" investor, venture capital is a very valuable option.

An "angel" investor is usually a high-net-worth individual who finances start-ups that may not appear attractive to more traditional investment firms. Such an investor often mentors the start-up's management team and provides necessary management and marketing skills.

Preferred Stock

Preferred stock is a hybrid class of equity that is usually associated with mature businesses that have considerable, predictable cash flow. The company may have very large amounts of investment in fixed assets and limited ability to raise money through debt issues. Preferred shareholders receive an indicated, but not guaranteed dividend. In periods when cash is tight, holders of preferred stock receive their full dividend before common shareholders can receive any dividend. Preferred stockholders generally are not entitled to vote for members of the board of directors or on any other proxy matters, unlike common shareholders, but they may have an option to convert their stock into common stock. While interest payments on debt are tax-deductible for the issuer, preferred dividends are not. Thus, this is a fairly expensive form of financing for the company.

Common Stock

A company that is going public for the first time will do an *initial public offering*, or IPO. By going public, the company can both raise a considerable amount of cash and create a market for the stock. This means that the stock held by the existing owners (the company's founders and venture capitalists) will become a liquid asset, enabling them to eventually sell some of it. Going public is very expensive. SEC filings and legal expenses can cost many hundreds of thousands of dollars. In addition, the equity of the existing owners of the company will be diluted, possibly to the point where they will lose effective control of the company.

Many public companies issue additional shares to investors over the years to raise funds or to improve the liquidity of the stock, and many also make shares available to their employees.

Some Guidance on Borrowing Money

Whenever a company borrows money, whether it is to finance an expansion, to cover working capital needs, or to acquire another business, preparation is required. It is important to understand that payments of principal and interest will often be required each month.

1. Interest payments are a tax-deductible expense and will appear on the income statement. Repayments of principal

are not an expense, will not appear on the income statement, and are not tax-deductible.

2. Only the principal portion of the unpaid balance will appear on the balance sheet; it will appear as a current liability if it is due within one year or as long-term debt if it is due in more than one year, or it may be split between the two categories. Interest is never a liability on the balance sheet unless a payment is overdue or unless, in the case of bonds, the balance sheet date falls between coupon payments and the amount applicable to the period before the balance sheet date is recorded. This will be referred to as an accrued liability.

3. As previously mentioned, the key issues to be negotiated when arranging a loan are:

> *The amount.* When the company is planning the project, a cash flow forecast is necessary, both for analytical purposes and also to present to the bank. Don't ask for less money than you really need. This may impair rather than improve your negotiating ability. Some people believe, incorrectly, that asking for a smaller amount will increase their chances of having the loan approved. In addition, being inadequately funded will hurt the project and may require you to cut back at a time when you are trying to build the business. This is very counterproductive.

> *The interest rate.* Evaluate the issue of a fixed rate versus a variable rate. A variable rate may be tied to the London interbank offered rate (LIBOR) or the prime rate. For example, it may be quoted as "prime + 2," which means two percentage points above the prime rate. If it is tied to a prime rate, make sure that you know whose prime rate will be used. Will it be your bank's prime rate or the rate quoted by the large money center banks, such as Citi, Chase, or Bank of America? Understand that when interest rates are moving higher, they

generally move quickly. This is in the bank's best interest. When interest rates are declining, however, they are often "sticky," meaning that they are slow to move.

The years of payments. The questions involved here are, "What is the maturity date of the loan?" and "Over how many years will the loan be amortized?" The first of these questions indicates how many years of principal and interest payments you will have to make. Make sure that the project being financed will achieve its potential before the maturity date of the loan. Also, if the project is expected to achieve a positive cash flow in three years, where will the company get the cash it needs to make the required payments in the first and second years? Payments must be scheduled (read minimized) in such a way that they are very low in the early years and then increase in the later years. This permits the loan to be repaid with the cash flows generated by the project itself. If the maturity and the number of years of amortization are not the same, a balloon payment will be required, as mentioned previously.

Fees, compensating balances, and restrictions. Incorporate all fees into the loan. That saves cash for the project and postpones the payments over the life of the loan. Remember that a compensating balance reduces the amount that is actually available for the project.

Collateral. Keep it to a minimum. Try not to pledge all of your assets. Doing so restricts your future flexibility and creates greater vulnerability should cash flows not grow as fast as expected. Banks usually have loan/collateral formulas. Find out what these formulas are early in the discussions.

4. When negotiating, use your banker as an adviser. Her advice is free, and she is often very knowledgeable.

Bankers' conservatism serves as a protective mechanism. Your company has needs and will make substantial profits after your project succeeds. The bank has needs, as well. However, its upside profitability is limited to the interest rate it can achieve on the loan.

5. Learn how to use the amortization schedule. An example follows:

Loan Amount	$100,000
Time to Pay	5 years
Interest Rate	8.5%

The monthly payment will be $2,051.65. Total payments over the 60 months will be $123,099, broken down as follows:

Principal	$100,000
Interest	23,099
Total	$123,099

The payments during the first two years will be mostly interest. In fact, after the first year, the amount of principal still owed will be more than $83,000.

The number of years of amortization can be more critical to success than the actual interest rate. If the same $100,000 loan has an interest rate of 9.5 percent (100 basis points or 1 percentage point higher) but is for a seven- rather than a five-year term, the monthly payment will be reduced to $1,634.40. To improve cash flows during the early years, a higher interest rate but a longer term will be beneficial.

Consider a twenty-year amortization with a seven-year balloon. This means that the monthly payments of principal and interest are calculated as if this were a twenty-year loan. If this loan had a 10 percent interest rate, the monthly payment would be reduced to $965.02. What this means, however, is that after seven years, the principal amount will still be $84,072.45, and this balloon payment will be due at that time. This could be dangerous if the company has the cash to repay the loan in the early years but diverts the funds to other uses rather than preparing to repay. When the balloon comes due, the company's negotiating power will be limited or nonexistent. The best strategy might be to arrange the twenty-year amortization and then begin to prepay after a year or two. The company can also prearrange a schedule of two years of reduced payments and then extra payments for years three through seven, after which the loan will be fully paid off.

CHAPTER TWELVE

Business Planning and the Budget

The planning process is a cohesive management effort that organizes management knowledge, mobilizes the company's resources, and focuses those resources on achieving the company's goals. The first phase of this annual effort is somewhat strategic in nature. It might be best done off site because it requires managers to think about the business and to brainstorm ideas. A database of past information is helpful because there is a great deal to be learned, both positive and negative, from what has happened in the past. Considerable research is required in the areas of:

- Markets
- Technology
- The economic environment
- Competition
- Human resource issues
- Organizational development

S.W.O.T. Analysis

S.W.O.T. stands for *s*trengths, *w*eaknesses, *o*pportunities, and *t*hreats. It is a form of management self-examination to ensure that all of the issues facing the company have been brought to the surface. The results of this self-examination should be action plans that identify:

1. *Strengths:* The best opportunities available to the company. Is the company dedicating adequate resources to these opportunities? Are marketing and operational efforts synchronized? The company must make certain that its strengths are translated into competitive advantage and improved profitability.
2. *Weaknesses:* Issues that make the company vulnerable to loss of market share and reduced profitability.
3. *Opportunities:* Actions that the company can take to improve its performance and achieve its goals.
4. *Threats:* The internal and external vulnerabilities that can damage the company's future.

The S.W.O.T. analysis should cover a variety of areas, including:

- Management
- Products
- Financial strength
- Market position
- Technology
- Operations
- Distribution
- The economic environment

In summary, this effort is a corporate self-examination of where you are, where you want to go, and how you will get there. On the basis of this analysis, action plans indicating what steps should be taken now in order to attain the desired future should be developed. The planning process does not eliminate risk. It attempts to ensure that the right risks are taken for the right reasons to attain the desired goals. Resource allocation is a key component of this effort. Will the most important projects be properly funded? Can crises be anticipated and unforeseen events dealt with?

Planning

There are a number of reasons why planning is necessary:

> The future is not an extension of the past.
> The rate of change in the marketplace will continue to accelerate.
> Technological progress is taking place at an extraordinary rate.
> Regulatory issues require constant attention.
> Population changes, demographics, and geographic shifts require constant adjustment of marketing strategies.
> Global competition is common in almost every industry.
> Organizations and the workforce are becoming more complex.

Types of Planning

Here are the five types of planning that companies engage in and some key issues involving each:

1. *Strategic.* What businesses is the company in, and what businesses should it be in?
2. *Marketing.* Why do customers buy the company's products, and why should they? This should also include discussions of pricing, quality, and service strategies.
3. *Sales effort.* Should the company sell through a dedicated organization, through distributors, or via the Internet? How can marketplace awareness of the company's products be improved?

4. *Operations.* What is the supply-chain strategy? How can technology improve customer service and reduce inventory at the same time? What functions can be more efficiently outsourced? How will demographic changes affect the workforce in the future?

5. *Financial.* How much free cash flow does the company expect to generate? What are the internal (capital expenditures) and external (debt service) demands made upon these funds?

Requirements for Effective Planning

There are a number of elements that are required if planning is to be effective.

1. Management must provide conspicuous support and active participation.
2. Goals must be quantifiable. In addition, if they are to be useful, goals must be:
   - Time-related
   - Measurable
   - Attainable
   - Simple to calculate
   - Realistic
3. This is a profit center effort with staff support.
4. Performance expectations should be reflected in the budget.
5. The effort should be relatively flexible and simple. It should not constrain creativity, judgment, and risk taking.

Planning and Management

For planning to be effective, profit center managers need to have:

- A clear understanding of their job responsibilities
- Good leadership through constant, clear communication of plans, goals, and direction

- ➤ The opportunity to participate in planning and decision making
- ➤ Recognition of their achievements
- ➤ A performance appraisal system that gives them the opportunity to discuss advancement
- ➤ Professional working conditions that are conducive to productivity and effectiveness
- ➤ Compensation that is related to their accomplishments and responsibility
- ➤ The opportunity to take normal business risks in a nonpunitive environment, without fear of excessive reprisals

Human Tendencies in Planning

There are a number of human tendencies that can interfere with or restrict the company's planning process.

- ➤ *Optimism:* The belief that performance will improve over the next few months
- ➤ *Short-term orientation:* An emphasis on quarterly and monthly goals and reviews, with the period beyond the first year being deemphasized
- ➤ *Oversimplifying the environment:*
  - Not anticipating competitive reactions to the company's moves
  - Assuming that the past will extend into the future
  - Point forecasting rather than forecasting a range of outcomes
- ➤ *Unwillingness to face tough issues:*
  - Postponing corrective actions in the hope that the problem will disappear
  - Devoting attention to issues that are interesting but not critical
- ➤ *Ambiguity in strategic definition:*
  - Overstating cash flow expectations

- Understating capital needs
- Having inadequate strategic coordination
➢ *Minimizing the difficulty of change:*
  - Entering new, relatively unknown marketplaces
  - Not planning and testing new ventures adequately

Reasons Why People Resist Planning

There are a number of reasons why people resist the planning process:

➢ They have an unclear understanding of the benefits that can result.

➢ Planning is time-consuming.

➢ Planning requires intuitive thinking rather than simply doing.

➢ The process requires writing plans and sharing them with others.

➢ The process involves accountability; it creates an environment in which people will be measured and critiqued.

➢ People often define themselves by what they do rather than by how they contribute to the organization's profitability and success.

Significant Planning Guidelines and Policies

Planning guidelines and policies are statements or ground rules that provide a framework for management decisions and actions that are related to the achievement of organizational objectives.

The framework established by these guidelines and policies also affects decisions made within the context of the strategic plan. It is not concerned with day-to-day decisions as long as those decisions are consistent with the strategic objectives.

This framework, in general, serves three important purposes: It (1) provides guidelines, (2) establishes limitations, and (3) focuses direction. The framework is important for planning in a number of ways:

1. It helps to sharpen and define the organization's mission and focus.
2. It eliminates the need to make the same decisions repeatedly.
3. It ensures that efforts are not directed toward areas that are not acceptable to senior management.
4. It provides measurable parameters for performance that cannot be violated without triggering a managerial response.

What follows are some examples of policies and policy statements from a variety of corporate perspectives that help to illustrate these points and can serve as models for anyone whose job it is to create and draft policies.

Financial

The company will reinvest at least 60 percent of its net income in the business.

It is the company's objective to pay a regular dividend to common shareholders on a quarterly basis.

Corporate Development

The company will not enter any business in which the market growth rate is less than 15 percent.

All acquisitions of other companies, whether in whole or in part, must have the approval of the board of directors.

Companies will be acquired only if their markets are known to senior management and there are synergistic benefits to the relationship.

Our corporate image and purpose shall always be maintained. We will consider only opportunities for investment or acquisition that will maintain or enhance our corporate image of progressiveness, technical excellence, customer commitment, and merchandising preeminence in the sale of quality products and services. New opportunities will not be considered if they will

in any way compromise the reputation for being an ethical
company with due regard to human and social responsibilities
that we have worked so hard to achieve and maintain. Our
employees command respect for their business abilities,
integrity, fairness, and humanity.

Investment, whether capital expenditure or corporate acquisition,
requires a return on equity of 20 percent or greater. This serves
to enhance our current expectations for corporate performance.

Corporate

The company will prepare a three-year strategic plan and an
annual budget.

The company will establish goals for each of these documents,
measure the performance of its staff against these parameters,
and incorporate these evaluations into its compensation plans.

It is company policy to comply with all OSHA and EPA regulations.
We will develop training programs that will assure compliance
without the need for outside audit. The company will make
certain that employee safety is always emphasized and is never
compromised in any of its activities.

It is the company's policy to comply with generally accepted
accounting principles in the preparation of information for any
regulatory agency, financial institution, or other party that may
receive this information.

Some Additional Issues

Budgets should be developed by those who have the responsibility
for meeting them, subject to the requirements and expectations of
the organization.

A budget need not be completely detailed in every respect in
order to be effective and valuable. The level of detail should be
governed by the value of the information being developed.

Every excellent plan is almost out of date by the time it is being used. The value of the planning process is the thinking, research, and communication that it fosters.

The coordinator of the budget process should have considerable knowledge of the business, its products, and its markets. While a knowledge of accounting and finance is important, developing the budget is a management challenge rather than an accounting responsibility.

A Guide to Better Budgets

Here are some steps that will help you in preparing a budget:

➢ Start simple.

➢ Have each function and area of responsibility prepare its own budget, consistent with the corporate goals, objectives, constraints, and policies.

➢ Recognize that effective budgets require senior management approval and the endorsement of the organization.

➢ Understand that having a budget improves the performance of the entire organization and each of its parts—really.

➢ Understand that a budget is developed to ensure that every department head is working toward the same goal and knows the department's resources and constraints.

➢ Recognize that the budget department does not create the budget. It is simply a coordinator, consultant, and adviser.

➢ Arrange educational meetings to ensure that everyone involved has an understanding of the process and the expectations for it. Do this at least twice during the process.

➢ Make certain that interdepartmental relations are coordinated. Departments cannot perform well without the cooperation of other departments. Make certain that these interdependencies are properly documented.

➤ Ensure that expenditures above a specific threshold amount that are included in the budget are supported with proper documentation and financial analysis.

➤ Incorporate into the budget procedure specific requirements covering approval for nonbudgeted expenditures and cost overruns.

➤ To sell the budget concept, select one department or profit center manager to convey the value of developing an intelligent budget. Demonstrate how the budget has improved the performance of this manager's organization. The word will spread among the manager's peers.

➤ Express budget procedures in writing. Document corporate targets, policies, and constraints, and convey them to everyone who is involved in the process. Update this documentation frequently.

➤ Provide each involved department with information on the department's past financial and statistical history, known economic factors, and the accounting chart of accounts in order to properly prepare the department for effective participation.

➤ Classify the expenditures of individual departments carefully. Do not arbitrarily allocate common costs to individual profit centers.

➤ Budget product and service costs on a per-unit basis, if possible. Be realistic.

➤ Do not create theoretical models that make accountability unachievable.

➤ Prepare budgets that incorporate alternative environments and competitive factors. Have a fallback plan available for emergencies; identify best-and worst-case scenarios. This enhances the thought process.

➤ Base the sales forecast on realistic expectations. Like all other elements of the budget, it should be achievable, but a challenge.

➤ Establish production plans in accordance with a detailed forecast. Incorporate purchasing and inventory strategies and product pricing expectations.

> ➤ Incorporate the cash flow improvements from the capital expenditure budget into the operating budget. These are interrelated parts of the planning process.

> ➤ Develop and share the positive and negative elements of past budget efforts, and incorporate them into the current process. Learn from both the successes and the mistakes.

> ➤ Make sure that reports of actual performance are provided to responsibility centers in a timely manner, with the appropriate level of detail.

> ➤ Never forget that a budget and its forecast components are estimates.

> ➤ Precision does not count.

> ➤ Improve the quality and effectiveness of the process continuously. Make sure everyone knows that you are focusing on this issue. Solicit and accept feedback from participants.

Preparation of the Budget

Sales Planning

Consider the historical patterns of behavior for your customers, your markets, your products, and your competitors. The success of your company depends on the success of your customers.

Your company's sales will be affected by the economy. Identify how future economic events will affect your business. This includes looking at the consumer outlook, inflation, taxes, political events, and the business cycle.

Ask the sales organization for its input. The salespeople know their customers and markets better than anyone else. Salespeople are optimistic, by their stereotypical nature. On the other hand, they have been known to "low-ball" forecasts in order to minimize their quotas. Somehow, given the balance between these two forces, a consensus forecast by the sales team usually provides very usable information.

Identify all known or anticipated events that will affect your market during the upcoming year. This should include competitors entering or leaving the market and product additions and eliminations. Industry trade shows are an excellent source of this information: Look at what is and what is not being featured. What shows companies take booths at is often an indication of those companies' perceived strategic identity.

The sales and marketing teams should identify the level of customer service that is necessary if the company is to achieve a competitive advantage. Strategies involving inventory and the entire supply chain should be based upon customer service expectations.

For companies that do business on a global basis, it would have been almost impossible to forecast the strength of the U.S. dollar in the 2014–2015 time period. This has seriously improved the prospects of those companies that import their raw materials, components, and products because foreign purchases are 10 to15 percent less expensive. However, companies that export to Europe have experienced a serious competitive disadvantage as their products are now between 10 and 15 percent more expensive. You would have had to be clairvoyant to have known this in 2012—or to know when the pendulum will next swing in the other direction—but currency issues should certainly be part of the S.W.O.T. analysis discussed earlier in this chapter.

Operations Planning

Capacity should be defined based upon the expected product mix. This will provide insights into pricing decisions and decisions concerning whether to pursue marginal business.

Product mix capability and flexibility are very important. How rapidly machinery can be changed between products will provide guidance for determining the required minimum orders and the extent to which discounts should be offered for very large orders.

The company should consider the number of shifts to be operated. This depends on both the relative efficiency of each shift and the size of an ideal production run. If machine changeover is expensive, working four 10- or 12-hour shifts will be more cost-effective than working five 8-hour days. Overtime can be built into the schedule.

Technology can make a major contribution to improving the efficiency of the overall operation. Establishing computerized hookups among customer orders, machine and workforce schedules, and raw material logistics will:

> Improve customer service.

> Accelerate billing and cash flow.

> Reduce work in process inventory and time.

> Reduce raw materials inventory.

> Usually pay for itself in less than a year.

The capital budget can be prepared after all of the previously mentioned analyses have been performed. Return on investment analysis and the capital budget are discussed at some length in Chapter 10.

You should consider outsourcing less important resource-consuming operations. This will free up assets, cash, and people for more important activities in which your company provides more value-added contribution.

CHAPTER THIRTEEN

Final Thoughts

The two topics discussed in this chapter are an extension of the planning and budget process described in Chapter 12. They discuss a number of issues that can surface during the development of the budget. While Chapter 12 describes many practices that make the process work successfully in corporations, the articles in this chapter identify in greater analytical detail what the outcomes of the budget process should be.

Many companies are managed from an accounting-oriented perspective. You would think that the 2008–2010 financial crisis would have been a wake-up call for clear thinking. Sadly, strategic thinking is not universal. There are certain characteristics, such as conservatism and being risk-averse, that are appropriate for the accounting department but may be less so for other areas. In those other areas, nontraditional management styles are often desirable and necessary. Many of the techniques of financial analysis that are described in this book support the more contrarian corporate strategies. But these articles are of particular interest because they advocate management thinking that is outside the box, nontraditional, and contrarian.

"Profitability During Tough Times" offers some insights into how to thrive in a highly competitive environment. It advocates contrarian thinking and strategy development, and it offers some specific insights into how to focus on the real issues and break out of the traditional mold.

"Do the Right Thing" recognizes that companies sometimes need to retrench on expenses and redirect their focus. It suggests some specific actions that companies can take that will enable them to respond to difficult periods successfully without damaging the core competencies of the organization.

Profitability During Tough Times

Many of the strategies that were appropriate and effective in the past are no longer above reproach. In fact, we have learned over the years that the global marketplace is a dynamic place, full of turmoil—the growing value of the dollar against the euro and the 50 percent decline in oil prices are only two examples examples; therefore, rethinking past assumptions and engaging in outside-the-box thinking is always required. Organizations need to address this constant change. They must focus on the state of the world, both as it exists now and as it may be in the future, and raise their performance to new levels of effort and achievement.

Recent Progress

Product quality is no longer an issue. It is almost impossible to justify a multilevel pricing structure by offering different levels of product quality. Market segmentation now focuses on differences in features and support. Differences in product performance are acceptable. Differences in performance quality are not. Being the low-cost producer is still valuable, especially when sales are price sensitive. Moore's Law, which states that in technology every three years the capability of the technology will double while the prices decline by half, still applies. Being vertically integrated is no longer the path to becoming the low-cost producer as supply chain management becomes more and more efficient.

Responsive Service

You will gain competitive and profit advantages if you can compress the supply chain from your suppliers to your company to your customers. The amount of time required for this sequence of events has a substantial effect on your inventory, your accounts receivable, your profitability, and ultimately your cash flow. Service levels are affected as well, which may in turn affect your market share and sales growth.

Competitive Pricing

In many cases, competitive pricing means price reductions. Pricing pressure is not going to end any time soon. Asking our customers to pay for our inefficiencies is not an option. Many industries are experiencing price deflation and will continue to do so. This means that companies must find new ways to maintain their profit margins. The successful ones will become more efficient, find more value-added features to add to the product, and focus on new markets and distribution channels in order to remain competitive. Differentiation is becoming the new normal. Have you priced out a personal computer lately? Have you even considered purchasing a desktop computer now that there are so many other alternatives? Why buy a GPS for your car when you have the app on your smartphone?

Companies will need to make a great effort to distinguish themselves from their competition. The new realities include very low interest rates, economic turmoil in Asia and elsewhere, essentially zero inflation, and a single global economy. However, a company's profitability can be enhanced, even during tough times. These realities can serve as a competitive advantage if you refocus the attention of the organization on the fundamental realities of a successful business. You must find *your* company's answers to the following questions:

1. Why are we special?
2. Why do we deserve to exist?
3. Why should customers buy our products?
4. Why do we deserve to have our customers' money?

Attitudes and Strategies for Success

We exist to help our customers sell their products to their customers at a significant profit for both of us. This is called *strategic partnering.*

We need to help our customers solve problems and focus on their opportunities rather than merely providing products, since anyone can sell products. This is called *consultative selling.* This means we don't need a store to sell retail products to consumers and don't need warehouses to sell product to commercial customers.

Our prosperity is enhanced as we improve our customers' ability to compete in their marketplace. We should know enough about our *customers'* businesses and markets to enable us to provide products and ideas that will make our customers special.

We must know no limits to our efforts.

Specific Action Strategies

The fundamental ingredients have not changed; only the environment in which we need to make things happen is different. Not only is thinking outside the box necessary, but I am no longer certain that there are many "boxes" remaining. Here are some strategies that are available to you:

> Invest in sales professionals and their training and support. High-quality marketplace visibility is the most profitable investment your company can make.

> Accelerate the development of innovative products and services. Focus your company's resources, both people and money, on those products and services that offer the opportunity for significant financial reward. Persistence is

valuable—but not when it implies refusing to change direction when success will elude you if you continue as you are.

➤ Use the strategic planning matrix developed by the Boston Consulting Group to measure the desirability of businesses relative to the resources dedicated to those businesses. This classifies your businesses into "cash cows," "stars," "dogs," and "question marks." It puts these into the context of markets with opportunities spanning from terrific to poor. GE is currently divesting itself of its financial businesses using their own version of this matrix. Finance was as much as 40 percent of their businesses during the peak of the financial crisis in 2008 and will be reduced to less than 10 percent by 2018.

➤ Learn more about the current global economic environment and persistent worldwide turmoil. How can you benefit? What are the risks? This has implications for buying, selling, and the supply chain throughout. Change is good because it creates opportunity for those who are prepared and ready to take action.

➤ Expand your marketplace support to include participation in trade shows and industry showcases, advertising in well-directed journals and use of other media to communicate with existing and potential customers. Keep your customers aware of your constantly improving capabilities. If you have nothing new to say to your customers, your competitors will. You must become your own fiercest competitor.

➤ Streamline the performance of your administrative support. Use technology in ways that let you derive its maximum value. Use experts to fill in and eliminate the knowledge gaps in your organization.

Do the Right Thing

Companies have worked hard at restructuring themselves in response to the dramatic changes that have occurred in the economy and in their marketplaces in recent years. Even those that were very resistant to change were forced by the financial crisis that began in 2008; they finally had no choice. Fortunately the U.S. government imposed "wake-up" conditions on companies that it bailed out, including General Motors and AIG Insurance.

Here are seven of the most serious mistakes that companies have made in their efforts to change—and how to avoid them.

Mistake #1: Laying Off Only Lower-Level Support Staff

Personnel decisions are made by senior and middle management —who, of course, are not going to choose themselves for outplacement. As a result, the company ends up with many chiefs and not enough Indians. Six-figure executives spend their time typing, photocopying, and faxing when they should be meeting with customers and planning strategies.

Executives should prioritize entire programs, products, and markets based on their profitability and opportunity. Maintaining or even increasing the number of support staff and expanding their responsibilities makes more time available to executives to develop the business. Leave the more routine tasks to those who are best trained (and appropriately paid) to perform them.

Mistake #2: Seeing the Future as an Extension of the Past

During times of marketplace turmoil and uncertainty, some companies focus on those programs, strategies, and attitudes that worked well in the past. This provides a level of organizational comfort and eases the tensions associated with change. However, sticking to what has always worked well may, in fact, be perpetuating approaches that are no longer valid as a result of new market conditions.

There should be no sacred cows when the company underachieves. Reexamine and reprioritize all of the company's operations and activities.

Mistake #3: Not Recycling Past Ideas That Merit Current Consideration

Whether an idea is profitable or not depends on both the timing of its implementation and the management support it receives. Something that did not work seven years ago may have considerable merit now.

The market may need some products and services today that it did not need in the past. List, explore, and give consideration to all ideas. With input from everyone concerned, make a list of *all* possible courses of action. Some resurrected fundamentals or past failures may in fact save the day. Imagine a company deciding in 2001 that selling on the Internet was not a good idea—and being unwilling to reconsider the decision in 2015. For example, certain large bulky products are not conducive to Internet sales. But the sales can be made through the website with the actual delivery made to the store for customer pickup or delivery. Home Depot has mastered this. Car dealers are not far behind in their progress.

Mistake #4: Reducing Price Rather Than Adding Value

Giving the customer a price discount may result in a sale. It can also encourage the customer either to expect further discounts in the future or to ask, "If you can afford to reduce the price now, does that mean that you were gouging me in the past?"

Your objective is to create a loyal market, not merely to make a sale. Pressures to reduce the price are lessened when you add value to the sale. Value-added features could include:

- Faster delivery
- Higher quality
- Educating customers on product applications
- User conferences
- Focus groups for product improvement
- Improved customer service

These activities enhance your competitive position.

Remember: Getting a new customer is very difficult. Keeping an existing customer happy is a great challenge. Getting back a customer that you have already lost is almost impossible.

Mistake #5: Ignoring the 80/20 Rule

You need to realize that 20 percent of your customers provide 80 percent of your revenue, and 20 percent of your products result in 80 percent of your shipments. Less positively, 20 percent of your employees account for 80 percent of your absenteeism, and 20 percent of your customers are responsible for 80 percent of your overdue accounts receivable.

Companies confuse activity with productivity and productivity with effectiveness. They try to be all things to all people. Every order receives fanatical attention from exhausted, overworked people who hope and believe that if they can just work harder, things will improve. Focus your energies on the activities that are most important. The least important 80 percent of all corporate activity results in only 20 percent of the achievement. Do not dilute the effort and compromise the performance of the most important tasks by expending too much energy on that least important 80 percent. Intelligent corporate prioritizing and time management ensures that the most important work gets done.

Achievement = Productivity = Effectiveness = Profitability

Mistake #6: Holding Onto Sacred Cows

The entire business should be evaluated periodically, perhaps at budget time. Is each of the product lines and markets still providing its expected contribution? Is any product line or market consuming an inordinate share of corporate resources, beyond what is justified by present and expected future performance? What other, more profitable ventures can be implemented with underproductive resources? Should we really be in this business?

Target is a company that held on to a "sacred cow" for too

many years at a cost of billions. It entered the Canadian retail market by opening many stores, almost at once, and by buying an unsuccessful retail chain with over 100 locations. These decisions left it with a very high fixed-cost obligation and forced huge capital outlays before it knew whether Canadian shoppers needed Target at all. To cut their losses and close these stores required that the CEO acknowledge the mistakes, which he refused to do. His initial decision was his sacred cow. The company even forecast that they would need five more years of massive losses just to break even— and it was clear that a successful, profitable future beyond those years was not assured.

A new CEO was brought into Target in 2014; he closed all of the Canadian stores and got rid of the management team that had cost them billions of dollars with this terrible strategy. Understand that there is nothing inherently wrong with Target having contemplated a Canadian market entry. Nordstrom, for example, entered the Canadian retail market with two stores and is doing quite well with minimal capital outlay. The problem with Target was the execution, not the goal—compounded by refusing to rethink their proposition even after it was clear that it was a disaster.

A company that had no sacred cows, GE Capital was the seventh largest financial institution in the country when the 2008 financial crisis hit. It represented 40 percent of GE's business at that time. GE will essentially be a pure industrial company by 2018, selling off almost all of its financial businesses by that time.

Mistake #7: Relying on a Dominant Customer

Sometimes a highly valued customer becomes too big a part of our business portfolio. This is exciting but also very dangerous. A dominant customer can disappear on no notice. They can become arrogant and dictate onerous terms including lower price and shortened delivery terms. Qualcomm lost Apple as its largest customer and is taking a long time to recover.

Never let a customer represent more than 10 percent of your business, unless you have long-term contracts with provisions for lengthy cancellation notice. In the 1980s Sears was notorious for imposing itself on its smaller vendors, extracting severe price and other concessions until the vendors became financially distressed—and worse. Sears has been among the worst financial performers of all retail chains in the 10-year time frame ending in 2016. Home Depot and Lowe's now own the business.

Financial Statement Practice

Middlesex Manufacturing Company

The following list gives all the financial categories of Middlesex Manufacturing Company, Inc. For each item in the list, identify whether it belongs on the balance sheet or the income statement and write the number in the correct places. Correctly placing the numbers will provide you with an excellent review of the structure and content of the financial statements.

Corporate Income Tax Expense	$ 2,000
Accounts Receivable	3,000
Telephone Expense	7,000
Cost of Goods Sold	140,000
Wages Expense	29,000
Total Current Assets	12,000
Advertising Expense	10,000
Inventory, End of Year	7,000

Net Other Income (Expense)	(1,000)
Beginning Balance, Retained Earnings	5,000
Dividends	2,000
Accounts Payable	6,000
Gross Profit	30%
Accumulated Depreciation	14,000
Buildings	50,000
Cash	2,000
Depreciation Expense	5,000
Total Operating Expenses	51,000
Common Stock	26,000
Purchases, Net	138,000
Inventory, Beginning of Year	9,000
Total Stockholders' Equity	35,000
Machinery & Equipment	12,000
Ending Balance, Retained Earnings	9,000
Mortgage Payable	19,000
Revenue	200,000

Middlesex Manufacturing Company, Inc.
Balance Sheet

Assets

Current Assets

* ....
* ....
* ....
Total Current Assets $ _____

Fixed Assets
* ....
* ....
* ....(.................)... _____
Net Fixed Assets $ _____

Total Assets .... $ _____

Liabilities & Stockholders' Equity

Current Liabilities
* ....
* ....
Total Current Liabilities .... $ _____

Long-Term Debt .... _____

Total Liabilities .... $ _____

Stockholders' Equity
* ....
* ....
* ....
Total Stockholders' Equity .... _____

Total Liabilities & Stockholders' Equity ...... $ _____

Middlesex Manufacturing Company, Inc.
Income Statement

Revenue .... $ _____   100%

Cost of Goods Sold Calculation
      Beginning Inventory ....
      + Purchases ....
      = Goods Available for Sale ....
      − Ending Inventory ....

= Cost of Goods Sold .... $ _____

Gross Profit .... $

Operating Expenses
* ....
* ....
* ....
* ....

Total Operating Expenses .... $ _____

Income From Operations .... $

Net Other Income (Expense) .... $ _____

Net Income Before Tax .... $

Corporate Income Tax Expense .... $ _____

Net Income (Loss) .... $ _____

Statement of Retained Earnings

Beginning Balance, Retained Earnings .... $

+ Net Income (Loss) ....

− Dividends .... _____

= Ending Balance, Retained Earnings .... $

Appendix A Answer Key

Middlesex Manufacturing Company, Inc.
Balance Sheet

Assets

Current Assets

*..........Cash	$ 2,000...	
*..........Accounts Receivable	3,000...	
*..........Inventory	7,000...	
Total Current Assets		$12,000

Fixed Assets

*..........Machinery and Equipment	12,000...	
*..........Buildings	50,000...	
*..........Accumulated Depreciation	(14,000)...	
Net Fixed Assets		$48,000
Total Assets		$60,000

Liabilities & Stockholders' Equity

Current Liabilities

*..........Accounts Payable	$ 6,000...	
*		
Total Current Liabilities		$ 6,000
Long-Term Debt		
*..........Mortgage Payable		$19,000
Total Liabilities		$25,000

Stockholders' Equity

*..........Common Stock	26,000...	
*..........Retained Earnings	$ 9,000...	
....		
Total Stockholders' Equity		$35,000
Total Liabilities and Stockholders' Equity ...		$60,000

Middlesex Manufacturing Company, Inc.
Income Statement

Revenue		$200,000
Cost of Goods Sold Calculation		
Beginning Inventory	$ 9,000...	
+ Purchases	+ 138,000...	
= Goods Available for Sale	= 147,000...	
− Ending Inventory	− 7,000...	
= Cost of Goods Sold		140,000
Gross Profit		$ 60,000
Operating Expenses		
*.....Telephone	$ 7,000...	
*.....Wages	29,000...	
*.....Advertising	10,000...	
*.....Depreciation	5,000...	
Total Operating Expenses		51,000
Income From Operations		$ 9,000
Net Other Income (Expense)		(1,000)
Net Income Before Tax		$ 8,000
Corporate Income Tax Expense		2,000
Net Income (Loss)		$ 6,000

Statement of Retained Earnings

Beginning Balance, Retained Earnings	$	5,000
+ Net Income (Loss)	+	6,000
− Dividends	−	2,000
= Ending Balance, Retained Earnings	$	9,000

Finance and Accounting Terms

Match the definitions at the right with the terms they best describe.

Select 70 of these.

Assets _____	1. Borrow with collateral
Accounting _____	2. What the company owns
Accounts payable _____	3. The value of an asset at disposal
Accrual accounting _____	4. A measure of receivable collection
AICPA _____	5. Costs that do not change with production volume
Balance sheet _____	6. Debt due within a year
Breakeven _____	7. An option to buy
Budget _____	8. A vehicle for investing
Cash flow _____	9. Laws that protect investors
CPA _____	10. Reporting the past in dollars

CFO _____	11. Important
Collateral _____	12. A ratio that measures efficiency
Corporation _____	13. Where stocks are traded
Bond _____	14. An option to buy commodities
Current liabilities _____	15. What the company owes its vendors
Debentures _____	16. Expenses paid before the time period that will benefit
Depreciation _____	17. A company owned by another company
Dividend _____	18. The corporate executive who manages cash
Stockholders' equity _____	19. A bond contract
Fiscal year _____	20. A review of a company's books
Fixed costs _____	21. An independent market maker
Goodwill _____	22. The price a buyer is willing to pay
Interest _____	23. Trading securities by computer
Inventory _____	24. Recording revenues when they are earned
Expense _____	25. Accounting year
Leverage _____	26. Profits kept within the company
LIFO _____	27. A representative of a lending organization
Liquid _____	28. The percentage of profits paid to the federal government
Material _____	29. An option to sell
Mortgage _____	30. Accountants' professional association
Prepaid expenses _____	31. Statement of financial position
Retained earnings _____	32. The point at which revenues = expenses

Sinking fund _____

Variable costs _____

Revenue _____

Ratio _____

IRS _____

Controller _____

Direct _____

Subsidiary _____

Salvage value _____

Profitability ratios _____

FIFO _____

EBIT _____

Benchmarking _____

Quick ratio _____

13D _____

Turnover _____

Days' sales outstanding _____

Treasurer _____

Banker _____

Stockbroker _____

Mutual fund _____

Stock exchange _____

33. The premium over fair market value paid for an acquisition

34. A documentation of the financial planning process

35. The fee paid to a lender for a loan

36. Funds set aside to pay debt

37. Costs that fluctuate with production volume

38. A person who helps you buy stock

39. A liquidity ratio

40. Comparing one's performance of competitors

41. Borrowing money to buy securities

42. Selling stock that one does not currently own

43. A company's chief accountant

44. Ratios to measure performance

45. An agent who helps buyers and sellers

46. The price at which a seller will sell

47. A security offering announcement

48. A group of investors

49. Net income + depreciation

50. Certified public accountant

51. Chief financial officer

52. A company's annual report to the SEC

53. Assets pledged as security for a loan

54. Labor and material are costs of this type

Indenture _____

Audit _____

Taxes _____

Stockholders _____

Investors _____

10-K _____

Greenmail _____

Tender _____

Proxy _____

Liquidator _____

Prospectus _____

IPO _____

Syndicate _____

Tombstone _____

Blue sky laws _____

Specialist _____

Bid _____

Asked _____

Broker _____

Short sale _____

Margin _____

Program trading _____

55. First-in, first-out; an inventory accounting method
56. Easily convertible to cash
57. A company's initial sale of stock to the public
58. An offer to buy stock
59. The owners of the corporation
60. Larry is one of these
61. A way of voting stock
62. An accounting entity
63. Allocation that reduces an asset's book value
64. Earnings before interest and taxes
65. A distribution of net income to the owners of a corporation
66. A mathematical comparison of two or more numbers; used to evaluate performance
67. The entity you pay taxes to
68. The dollar amount of products or services a company provides to customers
69. Last-in, first-out; an inventory accounting method
70. Document describing the terms of a stock offering
71. The use of borrowed money to expand a business
72. Products being manufactured or available for sale
73. Cost of operating the business
74. Buying out an undesirable investor
75. SEC takeover filing
76. People who buy stocks and bonds

Future _____ 77. Shareholders' ownership position

Call _____ 78. A form of corporate debt

Put _____ 79. Bonds that are not secured by specific collateral

Appendix B Answer Key

Assets	2	Liquid	56
Accounting	10	Material	11
Accounts payable	15	Mortgage	1
Accrual accounting	24	Prepaid expenses	16
AICPA	30	Retained earnings	26
Balance sheet	31	Sinking fund	36
Breakeven	32	Variable costs	37
Budget	34	Revenue	68
Cash flow	49	Ratio	66
CPA	50	IRS	67
CFO	51	Controller	43
Collateral	53	Direct	54
Corporation	62	Subsidiary	17
Bond	78	Salvage value	3
Current liabilities	6	Profitability ratios	44
Debentures	79	FIFO	55
Depreciation	63	EBIT	64
Dividend	65	Benchmarking	40
Stockholders' equity	77	Quick ratio	39
Fiscal year	25	13D	75
Fixed costs	5	Turnover	12
Goodwill	33	Days' sales outstanding	4
Interest	35	Treasurer	18
Inventory	72	Banker	27
Expense	73	Stockbroker	38
Leverage	71	Mutual fund	8
LIFO	69	Stock exchange	13

Indenture	19	Tombstone	47
Audit	20	Blue sky laws	9
Taxes	28	Specialist	21
Stockholders	59	Bid	22
Investors	76	Asked	46
10-K	52	Broker	45
Greenmail	74	Short sale	42
Tender	58	Margin	41
Proxy	61	Program trading	23
Liquidator	60	Future	14
Prospectus	70	Call	7
IPO	57	Put	29
Syndicate	48		

Comprehensive Case Study: Paley Products, Inc.

Phase 1

Robert Eng, vice president and loan officer of the First National Bank of Chicago, Illinois, was recently alerted by the bank's newly installed state-of-the-art computerized loan analysis program to the deteriorating financial position of one of the bank's clients, Paley Products. The bank requires quarterly financial statements (balance sheet, income statement, and sources and uses of funds) from each of its loan customers. The data from the financial statements are entered into a spreadsheet program that calculates the key ratios, charts trends, and compares a firm's ratios and trends with those of other firms in the same industry. If any of the company's ratios is significantly inferior to the industry average, the computer produces an exception report and highlights the problem. If the terms of the loan agreement require either that certain levels of assets be maintained or that a minimum of certain ratios be achieved, the output report will identify deficiencies.

Paley Products is a manufacturer of a full line of computer components. In addition to its regular products, Paley markets special lines of products for both the home and school markets, some of which are also appropriate for seasonal gift items. Its working capital needs have been financed primarily through loans from First National Bank, which has provided Paley Products with a line of credit amounting to $300,000. In accordance with common banking practices, the line of credit agreement provides that the loan shall be paid in full each July.

Earlier analyses of Paley Products had indicated a downward trend in certain performance ratios to levels below what was deemed acceptable in the component manufacturing industry, as reflected by the industry averages,. Mr. Eng had previously discussed his concern with Frank Paley, President of Paley Products, but no corrective action appeared to be taken.

Subsequent analyses continued to reflect this downward trend, and the latest analysis put the current ratio below the required 2.0 specified in the loan agreement. This conclusion was based on the financial information contained in Exhibits C-1, C-2, and C-3. According to provisions in the loan agreement, First National Bank could call the loan at any time after the ratio requirements had been violated. The company would then have 10 days to correct the problem, pay off the loan, or face foreclosure proceedings. The day of reckoning had arrived. While Mr. Eng had no intention of actually enforcing the contract to its fullest at this time, he did intend to use the provisions of the loan agreement to get Mr. Paley to take some decisive actions over the coming months to improve his company's financial picture.

Higher costs, especially increases in the costs of certain outsourced materials and in the wages of highly skilled technicians, have led to a decline in Paley Products' margins over the years. Sales increased during this time period because of aggressive mar-

Exhibit C-1. Paley Products, Inc. Income Statements for the Years Ending December 31,

	2014	2015	2016
Revenue	$2,652,000	$2,754,000	$2,856,000
Cost of Goods Sold	2,121,600	2,203,200	2,284,800
Gross Profit	$ 530,400	$ 550,800	$ 571,200
General and Adminstrative			
Expenses	$ 204,000	$ 224,400	$ 244,800
Depreciation	81,600	102,000	122,400
Miscellaneous	40,800	85,700	122,400
Net Income Before Taxes	$ 204,000	$ 138,700	$ 81,600
Income Taxes @ 35%	71,400	48,545	28,560
Net Income	$ 132,600	$ 90,155	$ 53,040

Exhibit C-2. Computer Component Manufacturing Industry Financial Ratios, 2016

Quick Ratio	1.0
Current Ratio	2.7
Inventory Turnover	7.0
Average Collection Period	32 days
Total Asset Turnover	2.6×
Fixed Asset Turnover	13.0×
Return on Assets	11.7%
Return on Net Worth	23.4%
Debt Ratio	50.0%
Profit Margin on Sales	4.5%

Industry averages have been constant during this time period. These numbers are based on year-end amounts.

keting programs. Competition within various segments of the computer industry is continuing to grow more intense, both technologically and financially.

Mr. Paley received a copy of the latest analysis from the bank, along with a blunt statement that the bank would insist on complete retirement of the loan unless corrective actions were imple-

Exhibit C-3. Paley Products, Inc. Comparative Balance Sheets, December 31,

	2014	2015	2016
Cash	$ 61,000	$ 28,600	$ 20,400
Accounts Receivable	245,000	277,400	388,000
Inventory	306,000	510,000	826,200
Current Assets	$612,000	$ 816,000	$1,234,600
Gross Book Value	$600,000	$ 730,500	$ 826,300
Accumulated Depreciation	(371,400)	(473,400)	(595,800)
Net Book Values:			
Land and Building	49,000	130,600	122,400
Machinery	151,000	118,300	102,000
Other Fixed Assets	28,600	8,200	6,100
Total Assets	$840,600	$1,073,100	$1,465,100
Bank Notes Payable	$ —	$ 102,000	$ 286,000
Accounts Payable	98,000	155,000	306,000
Accruals	49,000	57,000	77,500
Current Liabilities	$147,000	$ 314,000	$ 669,500
Mortgage	45,000	40,800	36,700
Common Stock	365,000	365,000	365,000
Retained Earnings	283,600	353,300	393,900
Liabilities + Equity	$840,600	$1,073,100	$1,465,100

mented. Although he was not in complete agreement with the bank's assessment of his company's financial condition and was not fully certain of what his future course of action should be, Mr. Paley began to develop a "recovery" plan. He immediately concluded that sales growth could not continue without an increase in the bank line of credit from the current $300,000 to $400,000. Also, progress payments of $100,000 for construction in progress were due the following year. There was a sense of urgency to Mr. Paley's state of mind at this time, despite the fact that the relationship between Paley Products and First National Bank of Chicago had begun many years earlier.

Industry averages have been constant during this time period. These numbers are based on year-end amounts.

For phase 1, calculate the key ratios for 2014–2016 using the formulas available in Exhibit C-4. How is Paley doing? What are the issues?

Exhibit C-4. Formulas for Ratio Calculations

$$\text{Current Ratio} = \frac{\text{Current Assets}}{\text{Current Liabilities}}$$

$$\text{Quick Ratio} = \frac{\text{Current Assets} - \text{Inventory}}{\text{Current Liabilities}}$$

$$\text{Inventory Turnover} = \frac{\text{Cost of Goods Sold}}{\text{Inventory}}$$

$$\text{Collection Period} = \frac{\text{Accounts Receivable}}{\text{Annual Revenue}/365 = \text{Average Revenue per Day}}$$

$$\text{Asset Turnover} = \frac{\text{Annual Revenue}}{\text{Total Assets}}$$

$$\text{Fixed Asset Turnover} = \frac{\text{Annual Revenue}}{\text{Fixed Assets}}$$

$$\text{Return on Assets} = \frac{\text{Net Income}}{\text{Total Assets}}$$

$$\text{Return on Net Worth} = \frac{\text{Net Income}}{\text{Net Worth (Equity)}}$$

$$\text{Debt Ratio} = \frac{\text{Total Debt}}{\text{Total Assets}}$$

$$\text{Profit Margin on Sales} = \frac{\text{Net Income}}{\text{Annual Revenue}}$$

Phase 2

Here is Mr. Paley's proposed improvement program:

PALEY PRODUCTS, INC.
PROFIT IMPROVEMENT PROGRAM, 2017

Revenue: +3% growth
Gross margin: 20%
Expenses: Same amounts as prior year
Days' sales outstanding: Improve to 40 days
Inventory turnover: Improve to 4×
Capital expenditures: $100,000
Dividends: None until bank debt is retired
Accruals/mortgage/accounts payable: Same amounts; no
    changes

He was not sure what bank debt payments he could make or how much debt he could retire, nor was he sure what his cash position would be.

Forecast the income statement, balance sheet, and sources and uses of funds statement for Paley Products. Will the company be able to pay off any of its debt?

Appendix C Answer Key

Phase 1

Paley Products, Inc.
Calculation of Ratios

	Industry Average	Paley Products 2016	2015	2014
Quick Ratio	1.0	0.61	1.0	2.1
Current Ratio	2.7	1.8	2.6	4.2
Inventory Turnover	7.0×	2.8×	4.3×	6.9×
Average Collection Period (Days)	32	50	37	34
Total Asset Turnover	2.6×	1.9×	2.6×	3.2×
Fixed Asset Turnover	13.0×	12.4×	10.7×	11.6×
Return on Assets	11.7%	3.6%	8.4%	15.8%
Debt Ratio	50%	48%	33%	22%
Return on Sales	4.5%	1.8%	3.3%	5.1%
Return on Net Worth (Equity)	23.4%	7.0%	12.0%	20.0%

What issues are faced by Paley Products, as evidenced by these answers. Are they problems of the company? Of the industry? Both?

A Sources and Uses of Funds Statement for the past year is provided as reference.

Paley Products, Inc.
Sources and Uses of Funds
2016

Sources of Funds		Uses of Funds	
Net Income	$ 53,040	Increase in Accounts Receivable	$110,600
Depreciation	122,400	Increase in Inventory	316,200
Increase in Bank Notes	184,000	Capital Expenditures	95,800
Increase in Accounts Payable	151,000	Decrease in Mortgage	4,100
Increase in Accruals	20,500	Dividends	12,440
Total Sources	$530,940	Total Uses	$539,140
Decrease in Cash Balance 2016			$ 8,200

Notice that each of these numbers ties exactly to the changes in the Paley balance sheets between 2015 and 2016, including the decline of $8,200 in the cash balance.

Phase 2

Paley Products, Inc.
Forecast Income Statement, 2017

	Actual 2016	Forecast 2017	
Revenue	$2,856,000	$2,941,680	+3%
Cost of Goods Sold	2,284,800	2,353,344	
Gross Profit	$ 571,200	$ 588,336	20%
General and Administrative Expenses	$ 244,800	$ 244,800	Same
Depreciation	122,400	122,400	Same
Miscellaneous	122,400	122,400	Same
Net Income Before Taxes	$ 81,600	$ 98,736	
Income Taxes @ 35%	28,560	34,558	
Net Income	$ 53,040	$ 64,178	

Paley Products, Inc.
Forecast Balance Sheet

	Actual 2016	Forecast 2017
Cash	$ 20,400	$ 124,466
Accounts Receivable	388,000	322,376
Inventory	826,200	588,336
Current Assets	$1,234,600	$1,035,178
Gross Book Value	$826,300	$926,300
Accumulated Depreciation	(595,800)	(718,200)
Net Book Value	230,500	208,100
Total Assets	$1,465,100	$1,243,278
Bank Notes	$ 286,000	$ —
Accounts Payable	306,000	306,000
Accruals	77,500	77,500
Current Liabilities	$ 669,500	$ 383,500
Mortgage	36,700	36,700
Common Stock	365,000	365,000
Retained Earnings	393,900	458,078
Liabilities + Equity	$1,465,100	$1,243,278

Paley Products, Inc.
Cash Flow Forecast 2017

Sources of Funds

Net Income	$ 64,178
Depreciation	122,400
Decrease in Inventory	237,864
Decrease in Accounts Receivable	65,624
Total Sources of Funds	$490,066

Uses of Funds

Pay Off Bank Debt	$286,000
Capital Expenditures	100,000
Total Uses of Funds	$386,000

Net Increase in Cash	$104,066
Plus Beginning Cash	20,400
Ending Cash Balance	$124,466

If the improvements forecast for 2017 are achieved, cash flow will grow significantly. Working capital performance (DSO and Inventory turnover) can never recover past "glories" after years of neglect. Improving inventory by one "turn" and DSO by 10 days is more than adequate to pay off the bank and finance Paley's future growth. These are not easy, but are possible achievements.

Ratio Matching Challenge

Exhibit D-1 gives 10 sets of ratios and other financial information. The names of 10 companies, representing different industries, are given below. Match each set of financial information with the company that produced it.

1. Con Edison: A major power utility based in New York City

2. eBay: This includes the Internet marketplace and also PayPal before the spinoff.

3. Ford Motor: A global manufacturer of cars and trucks. The only U.S.-based automobile company that did not file for bankruptcy in 2008.

4. Johnson & Johnson: A very successful global manufacturer of pharmaceuticals, medical products, and health-related consumer products.

5. Home Depot: A very successful nationwide retail chain of home improvement and garden centers.

6. Activis: A multibillion dollar global pharmaceutical company. Assembled mostly by acquisitions and focusing largely on generic products.

7. Walt Disney: Movies, theme parks, ESPN, TV stations, and a wide variety of entertainment products.

8. Hess: An oil and gas exploration and refinery company.

9. Hain Celestial: A manufacturer of healthy foods sold through most retail food stores but also Target and WalMart.

10. Accenture: A global management consulting firm.

Exhibit D-1.

Company:	A	B	C	D	E	F	G	H	I	J
Cash and Equivalents	4.3%	1.0%	4.2%	4.2%	1.4%	14.4%	1.1%	25.2%	34.0%	0.2%
Accounts Receivable	3.7%	6.2%	8.2%	9.7%	6.2%	38.9%	24.5%	8.4%	19.8%	3.0%
Inventory	27.7%	1.8%	2.2%	10.8%	7.9%	3.2%	0.2%	6.2%	—	0.1%
Current Assets	4.8%	18.0%	20.4%	27.1%	19.5%	59.4%	56.1%	45.2%	70.2%	9.5%
Net Fixed Assets	56.9%	22.2%	67.3%	1.0%	7.1%	14.4%	0.7%	12.2%	29.3%	65.0%
Other Assets and Goodwill	4.8%	44.4%	12.0%	71.9%	73.4%	26.2%	43.2%	42.1%	0.5%	25.5%
Total Assets	100.0%	100.0%	100.0%	100.0%	100.0%	100.0%	100.0%	100.0%	100.0%	100.0%
Short-Term Debt	1.0%	2.5%	—	—	2.3%	—	—	2.8%	—	1.1%
Accounts Payable	14.5%	9.0%	5.0%	8.0%	10.3%	9.6%	23.1%	5.8%	13.0%	26.3%
Current Liabilities	28.2%	15.8%	15.3%	14.1%	14.5%	30.5%	30.5%	19.3%	48.4%	11.6%
Long-Term Debt	42.2%	15.0%	12.7%	25.8%	37.5%	57.1%	10.0%	11.5%	.12%	5.8%
Other Liabilities	6.3%	11.6%	14.0%	5.2%	6.1%	2.8%	12.5%	16.0%	22.4%	57.5%
Stockholders' Equity	23.3%	57.2%	58.9%	54.1%	41.9%	11.9%	57.0%	53.2%	29.4%	30.1%
Total Liabilities + Equity	100.0%	100.0%	100.0%	100.0%	100.0%	100.0%	100.0%	100.0%	100.0%	100.0%
Selected Ratios:										
Current Ratio	1.36	1.14	1.3	1.9	1.3	1.9	1.8	2.4	1.45	.82
Gross Profit %	34.8%	45.8%	53.4%	26.3%	46.0%	14.2%	68.6%	69.4%	30.9%	41.3%
Days' Sales Outstanding	2	58	52	49	90	20.5	21	54.0	40.1	37
Inventory Turnover	4.7×	3.2×	12×	4.9×	2.6×	15.7×	—	2.7×	—	20×
Debt/Equity	180%	.30%	.21%	47%	.89%	48.0%	0.18%	21%	86%	86%
Return on Equity	68.0%	16.1%	2.1%	8.6%	3.1%	2.8%	12.1%	23.4%	71.7%	8.7%
Return on Assets	15.9%	10.8%	12.2%	4.7%	1.3%	1.5%	6.9%	12.4%	21.1%	2.6%
Return on Sales	7.67%	15.8%	21.4%	6.5%	3.4%	2.7%	17.8%	22.2%	11.7%	8.6%
Revenue/Assets	2.1	0.58	0.58	0.73	0.38	0.7	0.39	0.57	0.8	0.31
Revenue/Employee ($000)	$224	$271	$1,990	$489	$501	$770	$440	$589	$110	$850

Appendix D Answer Key

Here are the companies that match the sets of financial statements. For each company, a few of the ratios and other financial information that should have led you to match the company to the correct set of financial statements are mentioned.

A. Home Depot

Home Depot is the country's largest and most successful home improvement chain. They turn over inventory about 4.5 times per year, which corresponds to the seasons. Most sales are by credit card, which explains the low accounts receivable. Most stores are stand-alone rather than in malls, which explains the high fixed assets. Because customer service is so critical to their success, revenue per employee is relatively low.

B. Walt Disney Company

Intellectual property is a very critical feature of this company's success, and the numbers include recent acquisitions of Marvel Comics, Lucas Films (Star Wars), and Pixar (originally owned by Steve Jobs, whose family is among Disney's largest shareholders). It is made up of very high-margin, fixed-cost businesses—think theme parks, cruise ships, and movies. Some receivables are low because some entertainment is paid in advance but the remainder is longer term financing.

C. Hess Oil

Hess is a very profitable oil exploration and refinery business and no longer focuses on retail operations. Its facilities are mostly in the Western hemisphere. When oil is either drilled or goes through a refinery, it flows through quite rapidly. This explains high inventory turnover experience (approximately one month). This is an extremely capital-intensive, fixed-cost business.

D. Hain Celestial (Foods)

This company sells healthy versions of regular food products. It has really good margins and is growing rapidly as more outlets adapt healthy food strategies. Receivables are quite good given that sales are to retail chains which usually don't pay too fast.

E. Activis (Pharmaceuticals)

This is a roll-up of many acquisitions. Most of its products are generic versions of successful drugs that are off-patent. Its margins are quite good even though they are lower than biotech and traditional pharmaceutical manufacturing companies. They probably do much less R&D than proprietary pharmaceutical manufacturers. The high goodwill is characteristic of a serial acquisition strategy.

F. Ford Motor

This a global manufacturer with a vertically integrated business with fixed costs. It does well in North America but is having difficulties in Europe and Latin America (as are most global auto companies).

G. eBay (before PayPal spinoff)

This is really two distinct businesses that do not belong together and will be separated by 2016. eBay is an online marketplace; Pay-

Pal is a high-tech, point-of-sale payment company that processes payments from smartphones through the banks back to the accounts of the buyer and seller of products and services. One of its key competitors is ApplePay.

H. Johnson & Johnson

This tremendously successful manufacturer of pharmaceuticals, medical products and health-related consumer products sells primarily to hospitals and other healthcare providers. In this context, receivables are not terrible. Margins are very high. Inventory turnover is low because most products are manufactured internally and often require lengthy processing.

I. Accenture

This is a global management consulting firm serving large businesses and governments. There is no inventory, no debt, and its fixed assets are primarily buildings and computer equipment. Revenue per employee is surprisingly low given that they provide high-value-added services.

J. Con Edison

This is a very asset-intensive business. Its utility marketplace is very geographically concentrated in and around New York City, which contributes to a low days' sales outstanding. It achieves high margins because it is a fixed-cost business in an expanding residential and business marketplace.

Comprehensive Case Study: Woodbridge Manufacturing

This case study provides an overview of the entire process of analyzing an investment opportunity using the discounted cash flow technique. In addition to this overall review, a number of issues will surface that the analyst should consider. These include working capital investment and the impact that product introductions may have on other parts of the business.

Woodbridge Manufacturing Company is considering the introduction of a new product, an especially ergonomically correct computer pad. Sales of one of the company's existing products will definitely be affected. The bad news is that Woodbridge's existing product will lose some sales, although not customers. The good news is that the sales will be "lost" to Woodbridge itself rather than to a competitor. The best defense is a strong offense. Someone, whether Woodbridge or a competitor, is going to modernize the product line.

Exhibit E-1 provides sales and cost information for both the

Exhibit E-1. Sales Forecast and Other Information

New Product:

Annual Sales	50,000 units
Product Selling Price	$2.00 per unit
Direct Manufacturing Cost (Without Depreciation)	$0.50 per unit
Marketing Support	$0.25 per unit

Existing Product:

Lost Sales Annually	5,000 units
Selling Price	$1.80 per unit
Direct Manufacturing Cost	$0.60 per unit
Marketing Support	$0.25 per unit

Other Important Information:

Fixed Asset Investment	$100,000
Forecast Life	5 years
Accounts Receivable	30 days' sales outstanding
Inventory Turnover	4 times per year
Income Tax Rate	50%
Corporate Hurdle Rate	10%
Depreciation	Straight-line, 5 years

new product and the product that will lose some sales. All the events that are incremental to this decision, and only those events, are included in the forecast.

Exhibit E-2 is a forecast income statement for the decision, assuming that the decision is to go ahead with the new product. In this exhibit, the incremental revenue and gross profit resulting from the introduction of the new product are calculated. The gross profit associated with the lost sales of the old product is also reflected. It is subtracted from the forecast gross profit achieved by the project. Because this is an incremental analysis, the forecast does not include any costs or expenses that are not affected by this decision. In line 9, depreciation expense (a noncash expense) is calculated on a straight-line basis, based upon the capital expenditure of $100,000. In line 13, depreciation expense is added back to net income to forecast the after-tax cash flow resulting from the introduction of the new product.

Exhibit E-2. Forecast Income Statement

	Year				
	1	2	3	4	5
New Product:					
1. Revenue	$100,000	$100,000	$100,000	$100,000	$100,000
2. Direct Cost	25,000	25,000	25,000	25,000	25,000
3. Marketing	12,500	12,500	12,500	12,500	12,500
4. Gross Profit	$ 62,500	$ 62,500	$ 62,500	$ 62,500	$ 62,500
Existing Product:					
5. Revenue	$ 9,000	$ 9,000	$ 9,000	$ 9,000	$ 9,000
6. Costs	4,250	4,250	4,250	4,250	4,250
7. Gross Profit	$ 4,750	$ 4,750	$ 4,750	$ 4,750	$ 4,750
Incremental:					
8. Gross Profit (4–7)	$ 57,750	$ 57,750	$ 57,750	$ 57,750	$ 57,750
9. Depreciation	20,000	20,000	20,000	20,000	20,000
10. Net Income Before Tax	$ 37,750	$ 37,750	$ 37,750	$ 37,750	$ 37,750
11. Income Tax	18,875	18,875	18,875	18,875	18,875
12. Net Income	$ 18,875	$ 18,875	$ 18,875	$ 18,875	$ 18,875
13. + Depreciation	20,000	20,000	20,000	20,000	20,000
14. Cash Flow	$ 38,875	$ 38,875	$ 38,875	$ 38,875	$ 38,875

Line 1. 50,000 units × $2.00 per unit = $100,000
Line 2. 50,000 units × $0.50 per unit = $25,000
Line 5. 5,000 units × $1.80 per unit = $9,000
Line 6. 5,000 units × $0.85 per unit = $4,250
Line 9. Depreciation = $100,000/5 years = $20,000 per year
Line 11. Tax rate is 50%
Line 14. Line 12 + Line 13

Exhibit E-3 is a calculation of working capital requirements. This consists of the working capital necessary to support the new product minus the working capital that will no longer be required because of reduced sales of the existing product. Inventory calculations are based upon direct costs, while accounts receivable is based on revenue forecasts.

Exhibit E-3. *Working Capital Investment*

Inventory Calculation:

$$\frac{\text{Cost of Goods Sold}}{\text{Inventory Turnover}} = \text{Inventory}$$

Accounts Receivable Calculations:

$$\frac{\text{Annual Revenue}}{365} = \text{Average Revenue per Day}$$

Average Revenue per Day × Days' Sales Outstanding = Accounts Receivable

New Product:

Inventory
$0.50 × 50,000 units = $25,000/4 = $6,250
Accounts Receivable

$$\frac{\$\,100,000}{365} = \$273.98 \times 30 =$$ $8,219

Working Capital Investment for New Product $14,469

Existing Product:

Inventory
$0.60 × 5,000 = $3,000/4 = $ 750
Accounts Receivable

$$\frac{\$9,000}{365} = \$24.66 \times 30 =$$ $ 740

Working Capital for Existing Product $ 1,490

Incremental Working Capital Investment $12,979

Comprehensive Cash Flow Forecast

Exhibit E-4 is the comprehensive cash flow forecast. It combines the investment of $100,000 plus the incremental working capital required to support the new product with the improved cash flows that are forecast to result from implementing the new product, thus combining all the elements of the forecast into a comprehensive analysis. The capital expenditure is placed as an up-front investment because it is required before the production of revenue can begin. Working capital investment is placed in period 1 on the

Exhibit E-4. Comprehensive Cash Flow Forecast

Investment		After-Tax Cash Flows	Present Value Factors @ 10%	Present Value Amounts	
				Investment	Cash Inflows
0.	$ 100,000			$ 100,000	
1.	12,979	$38,875	0.909	11,798	$ 35,337
2.		38,875	0.826		32,111
3.		38,875	0.751		29,195
4.		38,875	0.683		26,551
5.	($14,469)	38,875	0.622	(8,999)	24,180
Present Value Amounts				$102,799	$147,374

Profitability Index:

$$\frac{\$147,374}{\$102,799} = 1.43$$

Net Present Value:

$147,374
− 102,799
$ 44,575

premise that it will become necessary as operations begin. The analytical life of this opportunity is five years. This is the lesser of the physical life of the equipment to be purchased and the expected marketing life of the product. Notice that the working capital investment is recovered in the fifth year of this forecast. Conceptually, as the company phases out this product, its inventory will be consumed and the accounts receivable will be collected.

Since the proposal has a profitability index of 1.43 and a net present value of $44,575, the ROI is clearly above the target of 10 percent. At 24 percent, the present value of the cash inflows is $106,712 and the present value of the cash outflows (the capital expenditure and the working capital investment less the working capital recovery) is $105,747. Therefore, the actual ROI is just above 24 percent.

Additional Issues

There are many simplifying assumptions that go into a forecast. The first is that the forecast will be achieved. Notice that the working capital investment is placed in Year 1. It could be argued that the inventory will be needed before the project starts (in period 0), whereas the accounts receivable will begin in Year 1. The statement that the working capital investment will be fully recovered in Year 5 is also speculative. Some analysts use Year 6 for this recovery, after the project is over. The idea that all of the inventory can be sold at full price in Year 5 is also questionable. The solution is to prepare the investment and cash flow forecast with as much objectivity and thought as possible, but to never forget that this is a forecast.

The return on investment on this opportunity would have been affected had the accountants chosen to use accelerated depreciation, rather than the straight-line method used in this analysis. The method used in the analysis should reflect what the company will actually use in its tax reporting. Had the analysis reflected the double-declining-balance method of calculating depreciation, the after-tax cash inflows would have been affected as follows:

Depreciation	1	2	3	4	5	Total Project
Straight line	$38,875	$38,875	$38,875	$38,875	$38,875	$194,375
Accelerated	48,875	40,875	36,075	34,275	34,275	194,375
Difference	$10,000	$ 2,000	($2,800)	($4,600)	($4,600)	0

Accelerating depreciation by using the double-declining-balance method has no effect on the cumulative cash flows over the five-year period. What it does do is accelerate the achievement of those cash flows. The benefit in the first year is a very real $10,000. This reduces the payback period and the associated risk. It also provides the company with more cash that it can reinvest elsewhere. The use of the discounted cash flow technique confirms these improvements. The return on investment with double-declining-balance depreciation is 29 percent. This is only one example of why the company's accounting policies need to be considered.

Comprehensive Case Study: Bensonhurst Brewery

This case study analyses a decision that a company must make focusing on whether it is favorable to have its costs fixed or variable depending upon circumstances and expectations for the business. This issue is discussed fully in Chapter 9.

The Bensonhurst Brewing Company has some major decisions to address. You have been hired by that Company's senior management to assist them.

The company currently operates a labor-intensive business. Its costs of labor and product are volume-sensitive, and therefore quite variable. Bensonhurst has the opportunity to replace its facility with a very modern, technology-driven operation. The proposed facility would employ state-of-the-art brewing processes that have already proven successful by much larger competitors. The new production techniques would greatly reduce the labor content of the operation. Both the existing and proposed new facility would have the productive capacity to handle forecast volume increases for the next three years. Capital expenditures are not an issue in this circumstance.

The marketing director is concerned. A major brewing company is considering entering the marketplace currently served and dominated by Bensonhurst. It is possible that this competitor may absorb all of the growth projected in this market if it begins production. Of greater concern, the new competitor may severely penetrate Bensonhurst's existing market share and cause its revenue to actually decline.

	Pro Forma Unit Information	
	Current	Proposed
Labor	$11.66	$1.66
Power & Utilities	5.00	1.66
Fixed Costs	$4,000,000	$26,000,000
Unit volume	2,400,000	2,400,000
Revenue ($20 each)	$48,000,000	$48,000,000
Total Cost	43,984,000	43,968,000
Profit	$4,016,000	$4,032,000

Here is a financial presentation of the profitability of this business at current level of volume:

	Pro Forma Financial Results for 2015	
	Current	Proposed
Revenue (2,400,000 kegs @ $20/keg)	$48,000,000	$48,000,000
Variable Operating Costs:		
Labor	28,000,000	4,000,000
Power & Utilities	12,000,000	4,000,000
Fixed Operating Costs		
Plant Maintenance	2,000,000	12,000,000
Other Operating Costs	2,000,000	24,000,000
Operating Income	$ 4,000,000	$ 4,000,000

The company has the financial capability to build the new facility. However, cost and competitive issues are difficult to resolve.

Help this company to evaluate the marketing, competition, and profitability issues associated with this decision. What would you do? And why?

This is the revenue history and a forecast without and with the entrance into the business of a new company.

	Current	New Competitor
2013 Actual	$38,000,000	
2014 Actual	42,000,000	
2015 Actual	48,000,000	
2016 Forecast	51,000,000	$47,000,000
2017 Forecast	55,000,000	44,000,000

Appendix F Answer Key

For this exercise, we need to look at the fixed-costs and variable-costs alternatives. Whether you want costs to be fixed or variable depends upon what you expect future volume will be. In this particular situation you also have to decide whether you expect to have a new competitor—and if you expect that it can gain market share.

In order to advise Bensonhurst we want to look at three situations. In Exhibit F-1:

1. Column A is the profit forecast for 2017 without a new competitor at current variable-cost structure.
2. Column B is the profit forecast with the new competitor and a fixed-cost structure.
3. Column C is the profit forecast with the new competitor and a variable-cost structure.

The exhibit shows that, if volume is improving, then fixed costs are beneficial. This is called *operating leverage*. If you expect vol-

Exhibit F-1. Fixed Versus Variable Costs

	A	B	C
Units	2,750,000	2,350,000	2,350,000
Revenue	$55,000,000	$44,000,000	$44,000,000
Labor	32,065,000	3,901,000	27,401,000
Power & Utilities	13,750,000	3,901,000	11,750,000
Fixed Costs	4,000,000	36,000,000	4,000,000
Total Cost	$49,815,000	43,802,000	43,151,000
Profit	$5,185,000	$198,000	$849,000

ume to decline or if there is great uncertainty (will we have a competitor, or won't we?), you are better off with varible costs. The profit opportunity is significant if you fill up an airplane or run an oil refinery at full blast. Both airlines and oils refineries are fixed-cost businesses, where costs do not really increase with volume. On the other hand, if volume is down drastically or an oil refinery isn't too busy, the financial losses will be dramatic. You can't run half an airplane or shut down a refinery a few hours per day.

Glossary

10-K The annual report that every issuer of public securities, every company whose stock is listed on any stock exchange, and any company with 500 or more shareholders must submit to the Securities and Exchange Commission. The 10-K is similar to the annual report that every shareholder receives; it contains a complete set of financial statements and more backup detail, but no photographs or "public relations"–type information.

Accelerated Cost Recovery System (ACRS) A depreciation methodology prescribed by the Internal Revenue Service. It has been modified a number of times since it was first introduced; the version currently prescribed is known as the Modified Accelerated Cost Recovery System (MACRS). It shortens the depreciable lives of equipment but provides less than the full straight-line deduction the first year. The depreciable lives prescribed by MACRS are changed frequently as the technological lives of equipment become shorter. The use of MACRS is required by the IRS for tax reporting but is not acceptable under GAAP for financial reporting.

Accounting The reporting of the past in dollars. Accounting records business transactions after they occur. When all of these transactions are recorded, the results are compiled (added up) and summarized in what we know as financial statements.

Accounts Payable The amount the company owes to its suppliers for products and services that it has already received, but has not yet paid for. Accounts payable is a short-term liability, meaning that it is due in less than one year; it is probably due within 30 to 60 days from the date of the balance sheet.

Accounts Receivable The amount of money that the company is owed by its customers for products and/or services that it has provided but for which it has not yet been paid. It is a current asset, meaning that it is due in less than one year; it is probably due within 30 to 60 days of the balance sheet date.

Accounts Receivable Financing A form of borrowing in which the company uses accounts receivable as collateral for loans provided by banks or commercial finance companies.

Accrual Accounting The accounting methodology used by essentially all public corporations and almost all private companies. With this methodology, revenues are recorded when the money is earned and expenses are recorded when the resource is consumed, without regard to when cash is received or spent. The alternative methodology is doing the accounting on a cash basis. This means that revenue is recorded when the cash is received and expenses are recorded when the bills are actually paid.

Acid Test Ratio (Quick Ratio) See *Quick Ratio.*

Acquisition Generally, the purchase of one company by another. The transaction can be for cash, stock, debt, or any combination of these.

Administrative Expenses What the company spends on its support staff and the infrastructure that that support staff needs in order to contribute to the company's success. Included in the support staff are:

> Accounting
> Legal
> Human resources
> Management information systems

The supporting infrastructure includes such things as:

> The corporate headquarters
> Office supplies
> The computer system

Aging Schedule   A detailed listing of how long the company has been waiting for its customers to pay their bills. This is an analytical tool that helps management to gauge the effectiveness of the company's accounts receivable collection efforts. While days' sales outstanding (DSO) identifies the average age of receivables, it may mask specific problem situations. The aging schedule of a company that sells with 30-day payment requirements might be:

0–30 days	Not yet due
30–45 days	Should be received soon
45–60 days	Indicative of a problem; put on credit watch
60–75 days	Very serious; consider stopping shipments
Above 75 days	Collection in doubt

AICPA   The accountants' professional organization. The initials stand for American Institute of Certified Public Accountants.

Amortization   For investments, the accounting mechanism for apportioning an investment in an intangible asset over the years of its productive (useful) life. Intangibles that are amortized include copyrights, licenses, trademarks, and goodwill. Each year a commensurate share of the whole investment will be included as a noncash expense on the income statement. This concept is very similar to depreciation expense, except that depreciation is for fixed (tangible) assets.

For a loan, an arrangement whereby fixed monthly payments that include principal and interest are calculated. Each payment includes interest for the period and a sufficient amount of principal to retire the loan after the specified number of payments. A loan that is amortized over 20 years will have 240 equal monthly payments.

Angel Financing   A form of venture capital that finances a start-up at its earliest stages. The business is probably only an idea at this point. There may be a business plan, but not necessarily. The "angel" is probably a wealthy friend or relative, although it may be a venture capital firm if the idea involves a high-tech concept developed by someone with a track record in the field. The angel provides cash and management expertise in exchange for a portion of the equity.

Asset-Based Lending   Borrowing funds from a bank or other financial institution using the company's assets as collateral for the loan. A home mortgage is a form of asset-based lending that uses real estate as collateral. Working capital loans use accounts receivable and inventory as the collateral asset.

Using assets as collateral is often the only way a smaller business can borrow from a commercial bank. It can also result in lower interest rates and fees because it reduces the lender's risk.

Assets   Those resources owned by the company. These are classified as follows:

Very liquid:
➢ Cash and cash equivalents
➢ Short-term marketable securities

Working capital:
➢ Accounts receivable
➢ Inventory

Tangible or fixed assets:
➢ Land
➢ Buildings
➢ Machinery and equipment
➢ Vehicles, furniture, and fixtures

Intangible or financial assets:
➢ Ownership of other companies
➢ Other equity or debt investments
➢ Copyrights
➢ Patents
➢ Trademarks
➢ Goodwill

Audit   A review and critique of the company's accounting system, its control procedures, and the actual accounting process by a disinterested party. The elements reviewed include the recording of events and the preparation of the financial statements. The audit process also involves gaining assurance that the numbers presented in those financial statements are reasonably accurate.

A certified audit is performed by an outside, independent CPA firm that is hired by the stockholders. Such a firm sometimes achieves these objectives by supervising people called "internal auditors." These internal auditors are employees of the company but are supervised by the CPA firm.

Audit Letter (Certification Letter)   The letter written by the CPA firm to the stockholders that provides assurance (or creates doubt) that the audit was performed correctly and that there is a reasonable certainty that the financial statements are presented accurately.

The letter appears in the company's annual report and should be read. It alludes to the complexities and uncertainties of the accounting process. It is often the focal point of litigation because of differing views of what it does and does not promise.

Balance Sheet   A financial statement prepared by the company at the end of every fiscal period that presents the company's assets, liabilities, and stockholders' equity at a point in time. The balance sheet equation is:

$$\text{Assets} - \text{Liabilities} = \text{Equity}$$

Banker's Acceptance   A bank-originated corporate credit instrument that is often used to finance product import activities. It helps the importer to be sure that it will get what it ordered and the seller to be sure that it will be paid when the product is "accepted" by the importer.

Bankruptcy   The unhappy experience that results from a company's inability to pay its bills. It can be:

Involuntary, when creditors petition the court to declare the debtor insolvent
Voluntary, when the debtor company files the petition

Under Chapter 7 (of the bankruptcy code), the court appoints a trustee with broad powers to take actions, which usually lead to the liquidation of the firm's assets and cessation of its operations.

Chapter 11 permits the company to continue operating. The company and its creditors will work together to try to salvage the business and their relationships. Payment schedules and settlements are negotiated, and debt is restructured. Creditors will often provide new loans and credit to the company in the hope that it will survive and prosper.

Basis Point   A finance and banking term that means 1/100 of one percent. One full percentage point equals 100 basis points. When the Federal Reserve reduces interest rates by $1/2$ percent, it has reduced the rates by 50 basis points.

Bill of Lading   The documentation that supports the shipment of products.

Billing Cycle   The interval between the times that companies send out invoices. It can be as short as a day or as long as a month. Companies should examine their customers' payment practices and shorten the billing cycle if doing so will accelerate payments. This decision should also reflect the administrative costs of sending out invoices, a cost that frequently may be ignored.

Board of Directors   The governing body of a corporation. It is elected by and accountable to the stockholders. It hires the senior executives of the organization (who may also be directors) and holds them accountable for business performance and financial integrity.

Bond   A corporate debt security that is sold to the public or by private placement in order to raise funds. The maturity is usually between 5 and 30 years. The coupon rate is the stated rate of interest when the bond is issued. Corporate bonds are usually sold in units of $1,000; a bond that is selling at its face value is said to be selling at par. The price of a bond will often fluctuate in response to market conditions during the years in which the bond is outstanding. However, the corporation is obligated to refund the full par value of the bond at maturity.

Book Value   An accounting term that describes the original purchase cost of fixed assets less the accumulated depreciation charged against those assets. In this regard, *book value* and *net book value* are synonymous terms.

The term *book value* is also used to describe the stockholders' equity section of the company's balance sheet. The total amount of equity shown on the balance sheet divided by the number of common shares outstanding is referred to as the *book value per share:*

$$\frac{\text{Stockholders' Equity}}{\text{Common Shares Outstanding}} = \text{Book Value per Share}$$

In stock market analysis, the market price of a share of the common stock is then compared with the book value per share, which is used as a benchmark to establish the "premium" at which the shares are selling.

Breakeven Analysis   A financial analysis technique that involves studying the relationships among a product's selling price, variable and fixed costs, and production volume and their cumulative impact on business profitability. The specific formula is:

$$\text{Volume} = \frac{\text{Fixed Cost} + \text{Profit}}{\text{Price per Unit} - \text{Variable Cost per Unit (Contribution Margin)}}$$

See Chapter 9 for a full discussion of this procedure.

Budget   Essentially, a financial process of prioritizing the benefits resulting from business opportunities and the investments required to implement those opportunities. Each year the company undertakes what we shall call the planning process. Management thinks about and plans for the future, and makes strategic, operational, and spending decisions. It basically allocates cash to those departments, projects, markets, and endeavors that it believes will add the most value to the business. When all of these decisions have been made, they are recorded in a document called the budget. Therefore, the budget is essentially a documentation of the planning process. It serves as a record, guide, and standard of performance against which to measure and evaluate future results.

Burden   See *Cost Allocation*.

Capital   A generic term that describes the total resources available to the company. It is sometimes used to describe total assets. For example, one might say that a cash-rich company is "well capitalized." This means that the company has adequate resources to finance its future. A company that is under-capitalized is one that does not have adequate resources.

Capital Assets   Usually synonymous with fixed or tangible assets. This includes:

Land
Buildings
Machinery and equipment
Furniture and fixtures
Vehicles

Capital Budget   The portion of the budget process in which management focuses specifically on the company's fixed asset needs.

Capital Expenditure   The expenditure or disbursement of funds for the purpose of purchasing fixed assets.

Capital Gain   The delightful experience that results from selling an asset held for a period of time at a profit. Revisions in tax laws keep the exact definition of short- and long-term capital gains changing, but the concept does not change.

Capital Lease   A long-term contract in which the lessee or user of a fixed asset essentially assumes ownership, along with possession. The issues considered in deciding whether a lease is in fact a capital lease are:

➤ The life of the asset compared to the life of the lease

> Transfer of title
> Existence of an option to purchase the asset at a bargain price
> The total amount of lease payments compared with the market value of the asset

If the structure and terms of the lease meet certain criteria, the lessee or user may have to include the asset on the company's balance sheet even though the company does not technically "own" it.

Capital Stock   Common stock of the company.

Capital Structure   The proportions in which the company's assets are financed by lenders (debt) and by stockholders (equity). It addresses, conceptually, whether the company has too much risk (debt) and the degree to which the owners have invested (common stock) and reinvested (retained earnings) in the business.

Capitalization   Sometimes defined as long-term debt plus stockholders' equity.

Cash Flow   The overall amount of cash generated by the company that is available to the company to manage the business. It is sometimes also expressed as:

$$\text{Net Income}$$
$$+ \text{ Depreciation}$$
$$= \text{Cash Flow}$$

Cash Flows, Statement of   A required financial statement in every annual report and 10-K. It provides a summary of all cash flows generated and used, categorized as:

> Operative activities
> Investing activities
> Financing activities

Cash Management   A company's operation of the payment and collections functions. This can include short-term investing. The goal is to accelerate the receipt of cash, wisely disburse funds to the company's advantage, and achieve interest income while minimizing administrative expenses.

Certificate of Deposit (CD)   An investment security issued by a commercial or other bank. The denominations of these securities can be as little as $1,000 or as large as millions of dollars. Companies often buy these securities as investments because they provide quite good interest income and are relatively safe. Their maturity can be as short as one month or as long as many years.

Certified Public Accountant (CPA)   A person who is well trained in GAAP and related accounting matters and has passed state CPA exams. CPAs are licensed to provide audit, tax, and other accounting advisory services to companies as an independent, disinterested party.

Chief Financial Officer (CFO)   The top financial executive in the company. The CFO is responsible for all treasury, controllership, and regulatory compliance functions. As the chief financial analyst for the company, this person can be a valued business adviser to the entire management team.

COGS   See *Cost of Goods Sold.*

Collateral   Assets pledged as security for a loan. If payments are not made, the creditor can take possession of the assets and sell them to satisfy the debt. A house is collateral on a home mortgage. If there is specific collateral on a loan, the bank or other creditor is described as a *secured lender.*

Collection   The process of ensuring that customers who owe the company funds for products and services that the company provided pay in a timely manner. The process also includes processing payments received and depositing the funds in a bank rapidly.

Commercial Loan   Funds borrowed from a commercial bank. Commercial loans are usually short term, covering seasonal needs, large orders, and other temporary cash requirements.

Commercial Paper   Promissory notes issued by very large, high-quality corporations. Commercial banks often purchase these investment-grade securities from their client companies in lieu of making a commercial loan. Large industrial corporations sometimes purchase these securities, as do investment companies and mutual funds. Their maturity is always short term. Because the buyer has a high-quality negotiable instrument, the interest rate is often below the prime rate.

Common Stock   Shares of ownership in a corporation. Owners of the shares usually have the right to vote for members of the board of directors and on other issues, although some companies' stock does not have a one-share, one-vote relationship. The dollar amount of common stock shown on the balance sheet is the historical amount that the owners paid when they purchased the stock from the company.

Compensating Balance   A minimum balance that bank loan clients must maintain in their checking accounts at all times. Because not all of the amount borrowed is available to the borrowing company, the existence of a compensating balance results in an interest rate that is considerably higher than the stated loan rate.

Completed Contract Method   An accounting procedure used for long-term, multiperiod contracts in which the profit achieved is not recognized until the work is completed. The completed contract method is usually used in the construction industry and by defense contractors.

Consideration   Something of value that is provided by a party to a contract. Consideration is an essential part of every contract; each party must provide something of value (consideration) for the contract to be valid. A very common form of consideration is cash.

Consignment Sale   A method of selling products in which the vendor (the consignor) places its products on the premises of a customer entity (the consignee). Although the consignee possesses the product and must assure its safety, it remains the property of the consignor. When the product is sold to a third party, it becomes the property of that purchaser and is subject to whatever credit terms were agreed upon. This method is most common in a retail environment, especially when the product's marketability is unproven.

Contribution Margin   The price of the product less the variable cost to produce it. This term is sometimes used interchangeably with the terms *gross margin* and *gross profit.* It may be expressed on a per-unit basis or be given for the entire product line in dollar or percentage terms.

Convertible Securities   Bonds or preferred shares issued by a company that can be exchanged for common shares under certain terms and conditions.

Correspondent Bank   A bank that serves as a depository or provides check clearing or other services for smaller commercial banks.

Cost Accounting   The accounting practice of measuring the cost incurred to produce a unit of product by cost element—direct labor, direct materials, and supporting overhead.

Cost Allocation   An accounting methodology in which a portion of manufacturing overhead is charged to each unit of product that passes through the facility. The mathematical apportionment may be based on:

➤ Units of production
➤ Labor hours
➤ Pounds of material inputs
➤ Machine hours

Cost allocation is required by GAAP accounting and is built into the standard cost system. It is also called absorption accounting. The portion of the overhead charged to each unit is often called the *burden.*

Cost of Goods Sold (COGS)   The cost of producing the products that are delivered to customers to create revenue. In a manufacturing company, COGS would include:

➤ Direct labor: the amounts paid to the people who actually create and assemble the product
➤ Materials: the cost of all the inventory that goes into the product
➤ Manufacturing overhead: some portion of the spending that supports the assembly process

Credit Department   The department that qualifies and monitors the creditworthiness of customers, sends out invoices, and does the accounting for customer collections. It is usually part of the controller's office.

Current Assets   The assets on the balance sheet that are expected to become cash within one year from the date of that balance sheet. These assets include:

➤ Cash
➤ Marketable securities
➤ Accounts receivable
➤ Inventory
➤ Prepaid expenses

Current Liabilities   The liabilities of the company that are due within one year from the date of the balance sheet. They include:

➤ Accounts payable
➤ Bank debt
➤ Current portion of long-term debt

Current Portion of Long-Term Debt   Liabilities that had a maturity of more than one year when the funds were originally borrowed, but that now, because of the passage of time, are due in less than one year. It is similar to the principal portion of the next 12 monthly payments on your home mortgage.

Current Ratio   A measure of corporate liquidity. It is calculated as:

$$\frac{\text{Current Assets}}{\text{Current Liabilities}} = \text{Current Ratio}$$

Current Yield   The rate of interest earned on the purchase price of a bond, whether or not the bond is purchased at face value. The formula is:

$$\frac{\text{Annual Interest Income}}{\text{Purchase Price of the Bond}} = \text{Current Yield}$$

Days' Sales Outstanding   A measure of how much time, on average, is being required for the company to receive the cash it has earned from its customers. The time begins when the invoice is sent and ends when the check is received.

$$\frac{\text{Annual Revenue}}{365} = \text{Average Revenue per Day}$$

$$\frac{\text{Accounts Receivable}}{\text{Average Revenue per Day}} = \text{Days' Sales Outstanding}$$

Debenture   A type of corporate bond secured only by the full faith and credit of the debtor company, not by specific collateral. In a bankruptcy, holders of these bonds would be general creditors.

Debt Amortization   See *Amortization.*

Debt/Equity Ratio

$$\frac{\text{Long-Term Debt}}{\text{Stockholders' Equity}} = \text{Debt/Equity Ratio}$$

Debtor   A person or company that owes money to another.

Deferred Charges   An asset account, sometimes part of "other assets." This is an accumulation account into which payments for future benefits are placed. These cash outlays will be converted into expenses gradually as the operations begin. Examples are start-up costs of a new business and up-front fees associated with stock and bond offerings.

Deferred Revenue   A short- or long-term (or both) liability on a company's balance sheet. It results from the company's receiving payments in advance for services or products that have not yet been provided. The company now "owes" that amount of services or products to its customer. This "debt" will be satisfied when those services or products are provided. For example, a magazine subscription results in deferred revenue for the publisher because the payment is received in advance; it will be converted into actual revenue as issues of the magazine are delivered.

Deferred Taxes   Tax liabilities of the company. Most companies pay less in taxes in any one year than the corporate income tax rate because of differences between the accounting methodology used in the published financial statements and that used in filings with the IRS. The difference between the two amounts, deferred income taxes, appears as a current liability and/or a long-term debt on the company's balance sheet. An increase in this liability is evidence that the company actually paid less in taxes than is indicated in the income statement. Notice that on the income statement, the caption reads "Provision for income taxes" and represents 34 percent of the pretax amount. Most companies' actual tax rate is in the 20 to 25 percent range.

Demand Deposit   Funds on deposit in a bank that the owner of the funds can withdraw without notice. The owner of the funds may access these funds easily, usually by writing a check. A checking account in a commercial bank is a common example of a demand deposit.

Demand Loan   A bank loan that has no fixed maturity. The loan must be repaid "on demand," meaning that the lender can "demand" the funds from the borrower without notice or reason.

Depreciation   A noncash expense that results from the apportionment of a capital expenditure over the useful life of the asset. It is the prime example of the concept that an expense and an expenditure are not the same.

Direct Costs   Those costs of producing a product or service that are absolutely essential if the product is to be made or the service to be provided. In creating a product, the labor that makes the product and the material that becomes the product are true direct costs. Some supporting costs in the factory are also classified as direct in a company's standard cost system.

Dividend   A payment to holders of preferred and common shares. Dividends are usually a distribution of net income.

Dividend Payout Ratio   The portion of net income that is paid to shareholders as a dividend.

$$\frac{\text{Dividend Payment}}{\text{Net Income}} = \text{Payout Ratio}$$

Due Diligence   Conceptually, ensuring that the information that was presented is true. Before making a loan, a bank does "due diligence" to make certain that the collateral (receivables, inventory, or real estate) is actually worth the stated value. In the acquisition of another company, the buyer does due diligence to make certain that the seller's representations are accurate and that the buyer's company is getting what it paid for. This is very similar to a home inspection before the closing.

Earnings per Share (EPS)   The portion of the company's net income that is attributable to each share of outstanding common stock. It is calculated as follows:

$$\frac{\text{Net Income} - \text{Preferred Dividends}}{\text{Common Shares Outstanding}} = \text{Earnings per Share}$$

Earnings per Share (EPS) Fully Diluted   A calculation of earnings per share that includes the following in the number of common shares outstanding:

Earned or vested stock options that have not yet been exercised
Shares that would result from conversion of any convertible securities

Primary earnings per share is the EPS calculated without including the effects of potential dilution.

EBIT   Earnings before interest and taxes.

EBITDA   Earnings before interest, taxes, and depreciation and amortization. This is the equivalent of operating income on a cash basis.

Economic Order Quantity (EOQ)   The amount of product that the company should buy each time it makes a purchase. Buying in massive quantities will probably reduce purchase cost per unit but will increase inventory, inventory risk, warehouse expense, and financial carrying costs. Buying only the minimum amount needed will reduce those inventory-related costs and the related risk. It will, however, result in increased purchase cost per unit and make the company more vulnerable to stock-outs. EOQ techniques assist management in balancing these issues to identify the most efficient amount to purchase at one time and how frequently to make these purchases.

The way this quantity is calculated is changing because of the technological connection between customer and supplier. But the concept still has validity.

Electronic Data Interchange (EDI) A computerized connection between customer and supplier that permits more economic control of inventory and more efficient supply-chain management.

Electronic Payments Transfers of cash between banks that are accomplished without the actual writing of checks. Float is essentially eliminated because checks need not clear. Direct deposit of your payroll check is an excellent example of this.

Escrow Money or other property held by a disinterested party, known as an escrow agent, until the conditions of a contract are fulfilled. The closing on a house is an escrow process, especially when funds are held for a while after the meeting because one of the parties has not satisfied all of the conditions.

Factoring Selling accounts receivable to a third party, usually a bank factoring department or a finance company. The credit risk can be sold with the paper (factoring without recourse) or be kept by the company until the funds are collected (factoring with recourse). This is a very expensive form of financing. It is often used by clothing manufacturers and distributors.

FASB Financial Accounting Standards Board. A professional accounting organization that researches accounting and reporting issues and recommends revisions to accounting and reporting rules. The products of the FASB's efforts are called *FASB Bulletins.*

Federal Funds Rate Interest rate charged by banks when they lend to each other.

Federal Reserve System An independent agency of the executive branch of the U.S. government that is responsible, among other things, for regulating many activities of commercial banks. Through its monitoring of the money supply, it has vast influence on interest rates and on overall economic and business activity. The Federal Reserve System has a board of governors in Washington, D.C., and 12 regional banks that focus on issues relating to the economies of their respective regions.

Finance Charge Interest payments on borrowed funds and the related fees for arranging the loans.

Finance Company A private, for-profit organization that lends money to companies. It may originate those loans on behalf of banks or actually make the loans itself. These loans can then be sold to banks or other finance companies. Finance companies often function as factors.

Fiscal Year An accounting year. It may or may not coincide with the calendar year.

Fixed Assets Assets owned by the company and used in the operation of its business that are expected to last more than one year; also called tangible assets. They include:

> ➢ Land and buildings
> ➢ Machinery and equipment
> ➢ Furniture and fixtures
> ➢ Vehicles

All of these assets except land are subject to depreciation.

Fixed Costs   Costs that a company incurs that are not directly sensitive to volume changes.

Float   Funds in transit between banks. From the time a check is written and sent until the receiver deposits the check and the check clears, neither the sender nor the receiver has the use of the money. The depository bank has free use of the money until the check clears. No corporation can write a check on funds that have not yet cleared.

Footnotes   That section of the annual report (or any financial statement package) that provides greater detail than the financial statements themselves. The notes describe various accounting procedures and policies, and provide considerable critical backup information necessary for understanding the financial statements.

Foreign Currency Translation   Gains and losses that the company experiences on investments and debts that are denominated in foreign currency as a result of changes in the value of that foreign currency relative to the dollar.

Freight on Board (FOB)   The concept that determines exactly when title to goods that have been shipped transfers to the recipient. FOB Origin means that the receiver owns and is responsible for the product from the time it leaves the seller's premises. FOB Destination means that the shipper remains responsible until the product reaches the customer.

General and Administrative Expense   All the staff expenses and other supporting expenses necessary to operate the business. Among the many expenses included might be:

> ➢ Building rent
> ➢ Staff salaries
> ➢ Costs of operating the accounting and legal departments

General Ledger   The summary set of accounting books that contains consolidated information on each account. The general ledger serves as the basis for the preparation of financial statements.

Generally Accepted Accounting Principles (GAAP)   The general principles and rules that govern the efforts of the accounting profession. Their focus is on the way in which accounting information is prepared and reported.

Goodwill   The amount of money that the company paid to acquire other companies in excess of the value of the tangible assets acquired as part of the transaction. This accounting definition of goodwill is not at all related to the more common use of the term to describe the market value of the company's reputation. Goodwill appears as a long-term asset on the company's balance sheet.

Gross Margin

Revenue
− Cost of Goods Sold
= Gross Margin

Gross margin is sometimes called, but is not necessarily always the same as, gross profit.

Hurdle Rate The minimum ROI that companies require before they will approve a capital expenditure proposal.

Income Statement A report of revenues, expenses, and profit that describes a company's performance during a fiscal period.

Indirect Costs Costs that are not attributable to a single area but support the entirety of the business.

Industrial Revenue Bond A long-term bond issued by a municipal government on the behalf of a company. The proceeds are loaned to the company for the purpose of facilities expansion and, more importantly (from the government's point of view), job creation. The government agency usually sells the bond to a bank. The use of these bonds provides tax advantages for the investor, interest rate benefits for the company, and job creation opportunities for the municipality.

Initial Public Offering (IPO) The first offering of a company's common stock to the public. It requires registration with the Securities and Exchange Commission and is usually underwritten by investment bankers.

Insolvency A serious financial condition resulting from a company's inability to pay its bills. It often results in bankruptcy.

Installment Credit Loans that are repaid through fixed periodic payments of principal and interest.

Institute of Management Accountants A professional and educational association whose membership includes accountants and financial analysts.

Intangible Assets Assets that cannot be seen or touched but may have considerable value. Evidence of these assets may literally be only a piece of paper. Examples are investments in other companies, licenses, copyrights, and trademarks.

Interest The fee paid to a lender for funds borrowed.

Internal Rate of Return The actual return on investment (ROI) based upon the discounted cash flow method of investment analysis. Using time value of money concepts, it is calculated by equalizing the present value of the cash inflows (PVCI) and the present value of the cash outflows (PVCO). The formula, which appears in all computer software that calculates ROI, is:

$$PVCO = PVCI \times F \, (\%, yrs)$$

where F is the present value factor corresponding to the ROI percentage (%) and the number of years in the project forecast (yrs).

Internal Revenue Service (IRS) The part of the Treasury Department of the U.S. government that is responsible for the administration and collection of taxes and the enforcement of the tax laws as prescribed by Congress.

Inventory The financial investment that the company has made in the manufacture or production (or, in the case of a retail store, the purchase) of products that will be sold to customers. There are two primary methods of accounting for Inventory:

LIFO, or last-in, first-out

FIFO, or first-in, first-out

Invoice A notification to a customer that the customer owes the company money for products and services provided. It may contain some details of the sale and certainly should communicate a due date.

Lease A contract to obtain the use of an asset over an extended period of time. This often results in the lessee (user) owning the asset after the lease ends.

Lender A provider of loans.

Lessee The party that leases an asset from the owner, who is the lessor.

Letter of Credit A bank document issued on behalf of the buyer of a product that guarantees that the seller will be paid upon delivery of the product. This eliminates the seller's credit risk. Letters of credit are often used in international transactions. They are a form of banker's acceptance.

Letter of Intent A document, bordering on a contractual promise, that specifies certain actions that will be taken by the writer if certain conditions are met. Banks write letters of intent before they make loans, and buyers of businesses may write such a letter before entering the due diligence process.

Leverage (Financial) The use of borrowed funds to expand the business and increase its profitability.

Leveraged Buyout The use of the assets being purchased as collateral for the loan that will finance that purchase. The term is usually applied to the purchase of a company; however, conceptually, the purchase of a house is also a leveraged buyout, as the collateral for the loan is the house being purchased. The collateral must be of high quality, and the borrower's ability to repay the loan needs to be demonstrated.

Lien An attachment of an asset, often used as collateral for a loan. The lien can be involuntary, resulting from a borrower's inability to pay bills.

Line of Credit Arranging for a loan in advance of the time the funds are required. This ensures that they will be available if and when they are needed. It saves interest expense because the funds are not actually borrowed until they are required.

The existence of a line of credit demonstrates the company's borrowing power and financial strength. Information about the company's lines of credit is often found in the footnotes of a public company's annual report.

Liquidity The ability of the company to pay its bills on a regular basis and maintain the working capital levels necessary to support the business.

Lockbox A payment mechanism. Customers send their payments to a post office box located near the company's bank. The bank collects the payments from the box and deposits them in the company's checking account. The company is then immediately notified of the deposit by the bank. This accelerates the clearing process, reduces float, and increases the company's interest income.

London Interbank Offered Rate (LIBOR) A benchmark interest rate that is used in many contracts and variable-rate loans. It is the interest rate that European banks charge each other for interbank loans. It is very similar to the American federal funds rate.

Long-Term Debt Borrowed funds that are not due until more than one year from the date of the balance sheet.

Lower of Cost or Market An accounting principle that governs the reporting of assets on the company's balance sheet. Assets are presented at their historical cost or their current market value, whichever is lower. GAAP rules do not permit reflection of improved market value of assets on certified financial statements.

Management Discussion and Analysis A critical, required section of a company's annual report to shareholders. It is a letter from management, usually the CEO, that identifies, describes, and comments on all of the critical events of the past year that had a material effect on the past performance or anticipated future performance of the company.

Maturity Date The date on which loans are required to be repaid.

Mezzanine Financing Financing that companies use on an interim basis pending a stock issue or refinancing. Since it is often subordinated to other debt, it will usually have a higher interest rate.

Milestone Accounting A method of recognizing revenue and billing the customer during a multiperiod contract. When the product is delivered, its value, and therefore the amount of the invoice, is readily determinable. In a long-term contract such as a construction contract, however, identifying when money is earned is not as clear. In milestone accounting, the company and the customer establish a predetermined series of events, the achievement of which permits the company to bill. These milestones might occur monthly or be based upon some other measure of completion.

Minority Shareholders Shareholders who own too few shares to have any control over or influence on the activities of management or the future of the company.

Mortgage Bonds Long-term debt of the company that is secured by specific assets, usually real estate.

Net Book Value See *Book Value.*

Net Income Bottom-line profit, recorded after all costs, expenses, and taxes have been subtracted from revenue.

Net Present Value The present value of the cash inflows from an investment minus the present value of the cash outflows; a discounted cash flow measure for evaluating an investment. A positive net present value indicates that the investment opportunity being measured is more profitable than the company's minimum ROI requirement.

Note, Promissory A written agreement to repay a debt plus interest at a certain date or on demand.

Operating Income A company's profit before one-time events, other income and expenses, and corporate taxes. It is usually defined as:

> Revenue
> − Cost of Goods Sold
> = Gross Profit
> − Selling, General, and Administrative Expenses
> − Depreciation and Amortization
> = Operating Income

Operating Lease   A contract giving the lessee the use of a fixed asset for a relatively short period of time. The lessee or user assumes little or no responsibility for the asset and has no intention of buying it. Renting a car at the airport for two days is an operating lease.

Operating Margin   A company's operating income as a percentage of revenue:

$$\frac{\text{Operating Income}}{\text{Revenue}} = \text{Operating Margin \%}$$

This is a measure of a company's operating performance. It is widely used and is an excellent measure of profit center performance.

Outsourcing   Hiring outside people or another company to accomplish work or produce product. Buying components from a supplier for in-house assembly is "outsourcing" the production of those components. Hiring a law firm, an insurance consultant, or computer software developers for specific projects are all forms of outsourcing. The company usually gets better expertise than what it can afford internally and does not end up with unneeded employees after the project is completed.

Overdraft Account   An account at a commercial bank that gives the company the privilege of writing checks for more than its balance. It is essentially a line of credit attached to the account that gives the company some cash flexibility and ensures that its checks will not bounce.

Overhead   Costs of doing business that are not directly related to the actual manufacturing process. This includes all costs for the corporate staff. Conceptually, there is considerable overlap between overhead and general and administrative expenses.

Paid-In Capital   The total amount that the shareholders have invested in the company in either common or preferred stock in excess of the par value of the shares. Many companies' stock does not have a par value. Therefore, these companies do not have any paid-in capital. The par value of common or preferred stock has no operational or stock market significance, with the exception that it might become important if the company should become bankrupt.

Par Value   A nominal or face value given to a bond or share of stock. Par for a bond is usually $1,000. Par value for a common share is a purely arbitrary amount. It has no relation to what the price was when the shares were originally sold or to their current market value.

Performance Bond   A form of insurance purchased by the party to a contract who is undertaking to do some work; it provides a guarantee to the other party that the work will be done. It offers financial assurance and protection if terms of the contract are not fulfilled.

Preferred Dividend   Distribution of a portion of net income to the holders of preferred shares. Like all dividends, these dividends are not tax-deductible for the company.

Preferred Stock   A hybrid class of stockholders' equity. Owners of these shares receive a dividend that, unless the company is in financial distress, is essentially fixed. They do not normally have the right to vote (for the board of directors), but they have priority in receiving dividends in that their dividends must be paid before anything can be paid to the holders of common shares.

Prepaid Expenses   Expenses that are paid before the time period that will benefit. For example, insurance premiums might be paid in advance at six-month intervals. The payment is a current asset on the balance sheet. The amount paid is then amortized, with one-sixth of the amount being charged to each of the monthly periods as an expense.

Price/Earnings Ratio   The relationship between the price of a company's stock and the company's earnings per share:

$$\frac{\text{Common Stock Price}}{\text{Earnings per Share}} = \text{Price/Earnings Ratio}$$

To the extent that the stock market is a rational business, the price/earnings ratio reflects the market's perception of the company's future prospects for earnings growth. The higher the ratio, the more positive is the market's outlook for the stock.

Prime Rate   The interest rate that commercial banks charge on loans to their largest, most creditworthy customers.

Principal   The face amount of any debt, without inclusion of future interest payments.

Profit Center   An independent organization within a company that has a readily identifiable market and core competencies. Its performance is usually measured by its revenues, expenses, and profitability. The profit center is often responsible for the assets that are available for its use.

Pro Forma Statement   A financial statement that incorporates information other than actual accounting information. A budget is a pro forma statement, as is a forecast.

Property, Plant, and Equipment   A term that is usually synonymous with fixed assets. It is sometimes used to refer to the gross book value, and at other times to the net book value.

Quick Assets   Cash and near-cash assets, including short-term marketable securities and accounts receivable.

Quick Ratio   A ratio that assists management in assessing the company's liquidity position. The formula is:

$$\frac{\text{Cash} + \text{Marketable Securities} + \text{Accounts Receivable}}{\text{Accounts Payable} + \text{Bank Debt}}$$

$$= \text{Acid Test/Quick Ratio}$$

This ratio basically compares near-cash assets with current liabilities (those that are due within the next year). The ratio differs from the current ratio in that inventory is excluded. Finished goods inventory still has to be sold and delivered. Raw materials and work in process inventory require additional effort and expenditure just to be completed. So in terms of their ability to be turned into cash, there is a wide gap between accounts receivable and inventory.

Because service businesses have little or no inventory, their quick and current ratios will be the same.

Ratio   A mathematical comparison of two or more numbers. It assists management in evaluating some area of company performance. A ratio can be fully financial, such as return on equity (ROE), or statistical, such as capacity utilization or order backlog.

Reserves   Allowances for future negative events. Accounting requires recognition of bad news as soon as the possibility arises, but permits recognition of good news only after it actually occurs.

One example of a reserve is the allowance for bad debts. A company knows that its accounts receivable are sometimes not 100 percent collectible. It statistically determines that, over time, 1 percent of its funds have not been fully collected. Therefore, the company creates a reserve in the amount of 1 percent of accounts receivable, the allowance for bad debts, which is subtracted from accounts receivable on the balance sheet. Another type of reserve would be set up by a retail store that has Christmas products left over in January. Knowing that the product will have to be sold at below normal prices, it will create a reserve for the estimated losses that it will experience on this sale.

Retained Earnings   The cumulative amount of the company's net income that the owners have reinvested in the business during its entire corporate history. It is part of stockholders' equity on the balance sheet. Corporate net income can either be retained or be paid out as dividends to holders of preferred and common shares. The cumulative total of the amounts not paid out as dividends is the Retained Earnings account on the balance sheet.

Return on Equity   A ratio that measures the overall performance of the company. It reflects profitability, efficiency, and the effective use of debt. The ratio is traditionally:

$$\frac{\text{Net Income}}{\text{Stockholders' Equity}} = \text{Return on Equity (ROE)}$$

Rollover   A delay in making principal payments on a loan. It could be a positive action to extend the duration of existing loans for a longer period, or it could take place because the debtor does not have the cash to make the payments. The bank will dictate the terms of the rollover if it is necessitated by debtor weakness. Alternatively, a strong company may make a rollover a condition of a future client relationship with the bank. The connotation of the term *rescheduling* is almost always debtor weakness.

Sales   A very vague, often misinterpreted term. *Revenue* is a precise concept; it is the amount recorded on the income statement when the company earns money by providing products and services to the customer. Sales sometimes means revenue. It can also mean customer orders, which are not yet revenue. If the production operation is busy, some might say that "sales are going well." "Business is excellent" might mean that there are many customer inquiries. This is not sales (orders), deliveries (revenue), or cash (collections).

Secured Loan   Borrowing funds using specific assets as collateral for the loan. A mortgage is a secured loan because real estate is pledged as collateral. Accounts receivable financing is another form of secured loan. In a bankruptcy, a secured lender has first priority on the pledged asset to satisfy the debt before the remainder of the proceeds become available to the general (unsecured) creditors.

Securities and Exchange Commission (SEC)   A U.S. government agency with oversight responsibility for the securities industry. Among its many responsibilities, it specifies the substance of a public company's annual report and 10-K, oversees the fairness of stock trading, and monitors insiders' buying and selling of their company's shares.

Standard Cost System   An accounting mechanism that provides information necessary to determine how much it costs the company to produce its products. It requires definite assumptions concerning volumes, efficiency, and product mix. In a manufacturing environment, it is the basis for the accounting system.

Stock Option   A contract that gives the owner the right to purchase a predetermined number of shares of a company's stock at a specified price. It is a very common form of executive compensation at public companies. Earned options are part of the dilution effect in the company's earnings per share calculation.

Stockholders' Equity   This is a measure of risk for both the company and its current and future creditors.

Subordinated Debenture   A corporate bond on which, should the company issuing it have financial difficulties and become bankrupt, the payment of interest and repayment of principal will have a lower priority than the payment of interest and repayment of principal on senior debentures.

Supply-Chain Management   The strategies associated with sourcing and receiving purchased products and the related management of raw material and components inventory. Technological advances have drastically improved information and communication, leading to lower inventories and improved efficiency at all phases of the process.

Term Loan   A long-term debt; traditionally, one that has a maturity of one to five years.

Three Cs of Credit: Capacity, Collateral, Character   The traditional criteria that bankers use when evaluating a loan application.

Treasury Management   The entire range of responsibilities for cash within a company. Among the treasurer's many responsibilities are cash collections, the mobilization of the funds into usable form, investment of funds, and also future planning.

Treasury Stock   Company stock that was issued to the public and subsequently repurchased by the company on the open market. In the equity section of the balance sheet, the stock appears as negative shares outstanding at the cost of the repurchase rather than the current market value. Once treasury stock has been purchased, it can be retired to improve earnings per share or held for resale later.

Variable Costs   Costs that a company incurs that will be significantly affected by changes in production volume. For example, the number of workers necessary to produce the product will certainly be affected by how much product needs to be produced. The amount of material, components, and parts needed will fluctuate with volume on a direct cause-and-effect basis. Therefore, these are variable costs.

Venture Capital   A form of financing used in the early stages of a company's life. At best, the company being financed probably has little or no track record and products that are not yet market-proven. Or the company may be at a still earlier stage; it may have developed a business plan and product prototype, or it may be only an idea. This is a highly speculative and risky form of investing.

Warrant   A security giving the holder the right to buy stock in the company. Stock options are given to employees, whereas warrants are often given to lenders or investors as an inducement to do a transaction. Options are nontransferable, whereas warrants may have an independent value and may also be marketable securities.

Working Capital   A term usually used to refer to cash and other current assets such as marketable securities, accounts receivable, and inventory. Sometimes working capital is defined as being synonymous with current assets. Other times, it is defined as:

Current Assets − Current Liabilities = Working Capital

The term is sometimes used as a generalized reference to a company's overall liquidity condition. For example, someone might say, "The company has adequate working capital," meaning that it has adequate cash-related assets to run the business.

Zero-Based Budgeting   Budgeting philosophy and technique that requires a company to regularly rethink and reevaluate all aspects of how it conducts its business. It was first promulgated in a *Harvard Business Review* article and was made famous by then Governor Jimmy Carter of Georgia.

Technology has made it possible to include this concept in our regular annual budget process. Having become comfortable with change, companies do rethink their ways of doing business. They outsource less important, resource-consuming activities and focus on their core competencies. This was the basis of zero-based budgeting: It deemphasized last year's spending in developing the current year's budget requirements.

Zero-Coupon Bond   A corporate bond that pays no annual cash interest but is sold at a discount from face value such that, if the bond is held to maturity, it will yield the indicated, competitively priced interest rate. During its life, the price of this bond will fluctuate in accordance with market conditions. As it gets closer to maturity, the bond price will gravitate toward its face amount. A U.S. savings bond is a form of zero-coupon bond.

Index